The Recipe Girl

cookbook

dishing out the best recipes for entertaining and every day

Lori Lange

Photography by Matt Armendariz

Houghton Mifflin Harcourt

Boston New York

This book is printed on acid-free paper. ∞

Copyright © 2013 by Lori Lange. All rights reserved.

Cover and interior photography copyright © 2013 by Matt Armendariz

Food Styling by Adam Pearson

Prop Styling by Dani Fisher

Cover Design by Suzanne Sunwoo

Interior Design by Waterbury Publications, Inc., Des Moines, IA

Published by Houghton Mifflin Harcourt Publishing Company

For information about permission to reproduce selections from this book, write to Permissions, Houghton Mifflin Harcourt Publishing Company, 215 Park Avenue South, New York, New York 10003.

www.hmhbooks.com

Library of Congress Cataloging-in-Publication Data:

Lange, Lori.
The Recipe girl cookbook : dishing out the best recipes for entertaining and every day / Lori Lange ; photography by Matt Armendariz.
    pages cm
Includes index.
ISBN 978-1-118-28239-7 (pbk.); 978-1-118-44803-8 (ebk); 978-1-118-44804-5 (ebk); 978-1-118-44806-9 (ebk)
 1. Cooking, American. I. Title.
 TX715.L2773 2013
 641.5973--dc23

2012017213

Printed in the United States of America

DOC 10 9 8 7 6 5 4 3 2
4500439315

The Recipe Girl

cookbook

Dedication

For the two most supportive and wonderful taste testers and loves of my life: my husband Brian and my son Brooks. I couldn't have done this without you.

And for my Mom, who introduced me to the joys of being in the kitchen without even realizing it.

Contents

acknowledgments

First of all, a major thank you needs to go to all of my food blog friends out there on the Internet. Without bloggers and blog readers, I wouldn't have a blog, and I thank my lucky stars on a daily basis that I've become connected with you in such a wonderful way!

To Ree Drummond and Elise Bauer—I have so much respect for what you've been able to accomplish with your blogs, and I consider you both to be my greatest mentors and sources of inspiration. XOXO

Thanks to Steve Krengel of Kitchens.com for putting the idea of a Web site into my head in the first place. Your guidance and mentoring helped turn RecipeGirl.com into what it is today!

This book is a whole lot better because of the numerous friends and family who tested recipes for me and gave me honest and helpful feedback. I'm so appreciative of the time you took to help a Recipe Girl out!

Big thanks to my agent Stacey Glick for seeking me out and encouraging me to take the big leap and write a cookbook, and to my editor Justin Schwartz for his brilliant guidance and patience throughout the project.

A huge thank you to the photography and styling team of Matt Armendariz, Adam Pearson and Dani Fisher for taking on the project and making my recipes look so delicious!

David Wiesley, thanks for lending us your photography skills and capturing some great family photos for the book.

To my fabulous group of gourmet dinner friends in "The Luz": You girls and guys have been such a fun part of my life for so many years now, and I appreciate how you've always cheered me on. It means a lot.

Thanks to Mom and my in-laws Ann and Roy for being my biggest cheerleaders from the start. Your encouragement and love mean the world to me.

Sister Susie—you have always been there for me. Thank you for letting me bounce recipe ideas off of you and for always listening to my crazy food blog rambling. I love that we're sisters who are best friends too.

Brother Bruce—I wish you lived closer so you could sample my creations. Be sure to bookmark what I know will be your favorite Mom's Tacos and make them often for your family. Love you!

And finally, I couldn't have written this book without the love and support of my husband Brian and my Recipe Boy Brooks. You are the loves of my life, and you are the reason I want to be in the kitchen.

the story of recipe girl

I'd love to be able to divulge a glamorous, Hollywood-like romantic story of how I became Recipe Girl. I'm afraid I don't have anything like that to dish out. Instead, I'll share the story of how a girl like me discovered passion and joy in the kitchen, and how I turned that into a career that I so dearly love.

I suppose it all began with my mother. She made the basics for us kids back in the 70s—tacos, spaghetti and boxed spice cake. We didn't go out to eat a whole lot, so I had the experience of watching Mom in the kitchen doing her thing. Every Christmas we baked our traditional batches of cookies together, and by high school I assisted with getting roasts and Sloppy Joe's ready for dinner before Mom got home from work. Even then, I was obsessed with a tidy kitchen, stacking dishes neatly, organizing the plastic bowls and alphabetizing spices. In college I cooked pasta with roommates and baked chocolate chip cookies for boyfriends. I started to amass a ridiculously large collection of recipes from magazines and cookbooks, always testing out those new recipes on friends and family. Grad-school catering work really got me interested in entertaining and in styling the food to make it look beautiful. I married Brian (the man of my dreams), and together we traveled, enjoyed discovering new foods, hosted parties and had a baby.

In my professional life, I was an elementary school teacher and taught the little ones for 12 years before

I made the decision to stay home with our son, Brooks. At home I continued to collect recipes and cook for my family. I started a Gourmet Dinner Club in our neighborhood, sharing my love for cooking and entertaining with like-minded friends. People began calling me for recipes and asking for advice on what to serve for various occasions, and neighborhood kids seemed to find their way into my kitchen to see what Mrs. Lange was cooking on any given day. A dear friend of ours with an Internet business of his own weighed in with a recommendation that I start a website to share my passion. I listened to that wonderful friend, and RecipeGirl.com was up and running by mid-2006. It was a place for me to share recipes and menus for entertaining, and I eventually added a food blog, too. I taught myself the basics

"I love spending time in the kitchen with my son Brooks."

of html and food photography, and included big (eventually), beautiful photos of the recipes I shared online. Companies started contacting me and asking me to create recipes for their brands. The online food community and home cooks all over the world began visiting RecipeGirl.com, and its following and readership has been steadily increasing ever since. With roughly 2 million page views a month currently,

entertaining. There are some website favorites included in the book, but more than 80 percent of the recipes are brand-new.

I like to think of *The Recipe Girl Cookbook* as a cookbook for home cooks—at all levels—who might like to entertain once in a while. There are easy recipes in the book such as Perfect, Fluffy Pancakes, Chicken with Sweet Apricot and Balsamic Vinegar Glaze, Slow Cooker Italian Pot Roast, and Snickerdoodle Blondies, and then there are recipes in the book that are more appropriate for times when you don't mind whipping up something a little more involved—such as Grandma Billie's Cinnamon Rolls, Chopped Chicken and Couscous Salad with Sweet Basil Dressing, Spinach and Cheese–Stuffed Manicotti, and Red Velvet–Cheesecake Cake.

Icons indicate recipes that are **GF** gluten-free (or adaptable), **DF** dairy-free (or adaptable), **V** vegetarian (or adaptable), or **W** a web favorite. There are also several tips listed for each recipe to make your preparation of the recipe that much easier. Change It Up! is a feature that will show you how to change the recipe to create something new by following simple suggestions.

I like to think of *The Recipe Girl Cookbook* as a cookbook for home cooks— at all levels— who might like to entertain once in a while.

readers now come to RecipeGirl.com to browse over 2,600 recipes for dinner ideas, sweet treats, holiday inspiration and themed party menus.

And what do I get out of this? I get to live my dream every day . . . absorbed in the world of food and recipes and communicating with home cooks and food professionals via email, blog comments and social media. Writing a cookbook just seemed like the next step in this lifelong love for what I do!

What's in this cookbook?

The Recipe Girl Cookbook covers all meals of the day—from breakfast to brunch, then lunch and Happy Hour, dinner with salads and side dishes, and then desserts. My love for entertaining is evident in the final chapter, where I include complete menus for themed

"My best taste testers: husband Brian and son Brooks."

olive oil

penne

spaghetti

fennel seed

orecchiette

cracked black pepper

lasagna

cherry tomatoes

stocking your kitchen: the basics

The key to a well-stocked pantry is an organized pantry. How do you know what's lurking in the pantry if it's not well organized? Arrange your most-used ingredients in spots that are most easily accessible. Label containers, as needed. Alphabetize your spices so they're easy to find, and if your pantry is packed, compile a list of everything you have and hang it on the wall. Cross out items on the list as they are used up. Keep a running list of things you need at the grocery store too. Maintaining an organized, well-stocked pantry will help you in making meal decisions, and it will save you from purchasing duplicate ingredients at the market.

pantry basics

General

Baking powder
Baking soda
Bread crumbs (Italian and panko)
Chocolate (unsweetened and white)
Chocolate chips (semisweet, bittersweet, milk, miniature)
Cocoa powder (unsweetened)
Cornmeal
Cornstarch
Couscous
Dried fruits (raisins, cranberries, apricots, figs)
Flour (all-purpose and whole wheat)
Graham crackers
Nuts (pine nuts, walnuts, pecans, almonds)
Oats
Pasta (spaghetti, orzo, penne, elbows, egg noodles)
Polenta (not quick-cooking)
Rice (white, brown, Arborio)
Sugar (white, brown, powdered)
Yeast (active dry)

Cans, Jars and Bottles

Applesauce (unsweetened)
Barbecue sauce
Beans (kidney, black, white, garbanzo, refried, chili)
Broth (vegetable, chicken, beef)
Capers
Chipotles in adobo sauce
Coconut milk
Corn syrup (light)
Honey
Horseradish
Jam (strawberry and apricot)
Ketchup
Marinara sauce
Mayonnaise
Milk (evaporated and sweetened-condensed)
Molasses (dark)
Mustard (yellow, whole grain, Dijon)
Nutella
Oils (canola, olive, nonstick spray)
Olives (black and Kalamata)
Oreo cookies
Peanut butter
Pumpkin puree
Roasted red peppers
Salsa
Shortening
Soy sauce
Sun-dried tomatoes packed in oil
Syrup (maple)
Tabasco sauce
Tomatoes (paste, sauce, crushed, chopped, Ro-Tel)
Vanilla extract
Vinegar (white, white wine, red wine, cider, balsamic, rice)
Worcestershire sauce

herbs and spices

When you purchase a new spice or herb, stick a round label on the bottom of the jar with the current date. Ground spices are good for 2 to 3 years, herbs like oregano and basil will be okay for 1 to 3 years, and whole spices/seeds are good for 4 years. Adding a labeled date will help you remember when it's time to replace that spice.

Allspice
Basil
Bay leaves
Celery salt
Chili powder
Cinnamon
Cloves
Cumin
Curry powder
Garlic powder
Ginger
Italian seasoning
Mustard powder
Nutmeg
Onion powder
Oregano
Paprika (regular and smoked)
Pepper (ground black pepper, peppercorns for freshly ground, white, cayenne)
Red pepper flakes
Salt (Kosher, sea, table, garlic, onion)

fresh herbs

Purchasing fresh herbs every time a recipe calls for them can be downright expensive (and unnecessary!). If you have a little space in your yard (or even an outdoor spot where you can tend to containers), head to your local nursery to purchase some potting soil and small herb plant starters so you can grow your own fresh herb garden. Plant herbs that you use most in your cooking, and cut off sprigs as you need them. You'll save a boatload of money in the end.

Grow Your Own
Basil
Chives
Cilantro
Dill
Italian parsley
Mint
Oregano
Rosemary
Sage
Thyme

the refrigerator

Having an organized refrigerator is just as important as having an organized pantry. There are just a few key ingredients that I always keep in my refrigerator and freezer. These are all things that are utilized often in recipes and last-minute meal ideas.

Refrigerated Basics
Bacon
Bread
Butter (salted and unsalted)
Buttermilk
Cheese (Parmesan, cheddar, Monterey Jack, mozzarella, feta)
Cream cheese
Eggs (large)
Milk
Orange juice
Ravioli
Sour cream
Tortillas (flour and corn)
Yogurt (plain)

Must-Have Produce
Carrots
Celery
Garlic
Ginger
Lemons
Limes
Onions (red and white)
Salad greens
Shallots
Tomatoes (pear and/or vine-ripened)

Always in the Freezer
Chicken (breasts and thighs)
Chopped spinach
Corn
Frozen fruits
Ground beef
Ground turkey
Peas
Pie crust
Puff pastry
Sweet Italian sausage

Plant herbs that you use most in your cooking, and cut off sprigs as you need them. You'll save a boatload of money in the end.

dried chiles

thyme

peppercorn blend

italian seasoning

the liquor cabinet

If you keep a liquor cabinet, you're likely to have some of the basics already. Here's a bare minimum of what I like to keep on hand, always making sure I have dry white and red wines since those are both used frequently in my cooking.

Beer
Club soda
Dry sherry
Grand Marnier
Grenadine
Kahlúa
Rum (light and dark)
Sparkling water
Tequila
Triple Sec or Cointreau
Vodka
Wine (red and white)

must-have kitchen tools and appliances

I'm guilty of owning a special tool that cuts an avocado into slices, another that promises to scrub a potato better than I can do it myself, and also a tool to help me get started on peeling an orange. I don't use any of these gadgets, however. There are plenty of kitchen tools and appliances in my kitchen that I do use, though. These are special things that every kitchen should be equipped with since they make being in the kitchen that much easier.

Blender
Bowls (big for mixing and small for prep)
Cake pans (round 8- or 9-inch)
Can opener
Casserole dishes (2- and 3-quart)
Cheese shredder
Cutting boards

Food processor
Hand mixer
Knives (a good set)
Loaf pan (4 x 8- or 5 x 9-inch)
Measuring cups and spoons (metal are the most accurate)
Meat thermometer
Microplane (for zesting)
Pots and pans (a good set—some nonstick and some metal)
Pyrex measuring cup (for ounces)
Rectangular dish (Pyrex 9 x 13-inch)
Rimmed cookie sheets
Roasting pan with a rack
Rubber spatulas
Slotted spoon
Spatulas (big for cooking and small for cookies)
Square pan (8 x 8- or 9 x 9-inch)
Strainer (fine-mesh and pasta drainer)
Toaster or toaster oven
Tongs
Vegetable peeler
Whisk
Wooden spoons (round and square-edged)

optional kitchen tools
(for your wish list)

If you happen to enjoy cooking and you plan to do it often, the following items should be added to your kitchen, too. These are the tools and appliances that you don't absolutely have to have in your kitchen, but you'll be better equipped to be more of a rock star in the kitchen if you do.

Candy thermometer (for accurate temperatures)
Cast-iron skillet (searing steaks, skillet baking)
Citrus press or juicer (easy juicing)
Cookie dough scoopers (so easy for baking cookies)

Decorator tips (for decorating cupcakes and cakes)
Dutch oven (slow cooking on the stove)
Ice cream scoop (for ice cream, but also to scoop pancake and muffin batter)
Immersion blender (for pureeing soups)
Kitchen scale (for accuracy and easy measuring)
Mandoline (for thin slicing)
Mini chopper or food processor (for the small jobs)
Muffin pans (if you like to bake muffins and cupcakes)
Offset spatula (for frosting cakes)
Pastry brush (for brushing . . . everything)
Piping bags (cloth or disposable—for decorating cupcakes and cakes)
Silicone (Silpat) baking mats (for baking)
Slow cooker (easy dinners)
Springform pan (9-inch for cheesecakes)
Stand mixer (easy mixing and kneading)
Waffle iron (if you like to make waffles)

Hungry Mornings

Some mornings are hurried, and breakfast is almost an afterthought. Those are the mornings where nobody in my house eats anything better than a bowl of cereal or a bagel-to-go. There's certainly nothing wrong with that, but it's nice to be able to have some freshly baked muffins on hand or a homemade granola with yogurt. I savor the mornings that are more relaxed . . . the Hungry Mornings, as I call them. My family usually asks me to make something special for them on those more relaxed mornings, and I eagerly oblige. Those mornings are filled with pancakes and oven-baked bacon or homemade scones, fresh fruit and hot chocolate. Hungry, relaxed mornings are times to share food as a family and enjoy time eating together. Here are my Hungry Morning favorites with a few grab-and-go type recipes included too.

Recipes

W WEB FAVORITE   V VEGETARIAN *(or adaptable)*   GF GLUTEN-FREE *(or adaptable)*   DF DAIRY-FREE *(or adaptable)*

pumpkin spice latte

Makes: 1 drink   Prep Time: 10 minutes   Cook Time: 4 minutes

On fall mornings, my husband often gathers a few dollars and trudges off to the local coffee shop for his fancy drink fix. It turns out that those dollars eventually add up to a whole lotta cashola that he doles out for his specialty drink. In an effort to keep him home and keep more dollars in the bank, I worked out a pumpkin spice latte recipe that he enjoys just as much as the real deal.

½   **cup whole milk**
1   **tablespoon unsweetened canned pumpkin puree**
1   **teaspoon packed light brown sugar**
1   **teaspoon vanilla extract**
¼   **teaspoon pumpkin pie spice**
1   **cup hot, brewed strong coffee**
2   **tablespoons half-and-half**
1   **teaspoon granulated white sugar + more to taste**
    Whipped cream, optional
    Ground nutmeg

In a glass measuring cup or microwave-safe bowl, whisk together the milk, pumpkin, brown sugar, vanilla and spice. Microwave for 1 to 2 minutes, watching closely, and remove the cup from the microwave when the milk is hot and frothy.

Pour the pumpkin milk into a tall mug or glass. Add the hot coffee. Pour in the half-and-half. Add the 1 teaspoon sugar. Stir, taste and add more sugar if desired.

Optional, but oh-so-good, add whipped cream on top and a sprinkle of nutmeg. Serve immediately.

TIP If you don't have pumpkin pie spice in your spice collection, make your own! Mix equal amounts of cinnamon, ginger, allspice and nutmeg and then measure from there.

CHANGE IT UP!

Lighten up this recipe by using nonfat milk and fat-free half-and-half. The drink won't be quite as rich, but you'll still get that delicious pumpkin spice latte flavor.

cheesecake hot chocolate

Makes: 4 servings   Prep Time: 25 minutes   Cook Time: 5 minutes

Picture a cold and windy day, snow falling, fire in the fireplace, and cozying up on your couch with a good book and a warm beverage. Now picture that warm beverage as a rich and wonderful mug full of chocolate, one that will no-doubt take care of that chocolate-craving you've been having, and now picture the whipped cream on top. Only this whipped cream is a sweetened cream cheese whipped cream, much like what you'd find in a cheesecake. This Cheesecake Hot Chocolate makes an awfully pretty picture, don't you think?

WHIPPED CREAM

¾ cup cold heavy whipping cream

3 tablespoons granulated white sugar

3 tablespoons whipped cream cheese

HOT CHOCOLATE

4 cups 2% low-fat milk (see Tips)

8 ounces milk chocolate, chopped (or milk chocolate chips)

To prepare the whipped cream, in a medium mixing bowl, use an electric mixer to blend together the cream, sugar and cream cheese. Mix until the cream has almost thickened into stiff peaks when the beaters are lifted from the mixture, 2 to 3 minutes. Set aside.

To prepare the hot chocolate, in a medium pan, heat the milk over medium heat until it is hot to touch, 3 to 5 minutes. Whisk in the chocolate and stir until it is melted and incorporated into the milk. Remove from the heat and divide the hot chocolate among 4 mugs. Top each mug with a generous spoonful of whipped cream.

GF GLUTEN-FREE ADAPTABLE Use a brand of chocolate that is known to be gluten-free.

TIP Any milk will work just fine for this recipe, with whole milk making it nice and rich and skim milk making it lighter. I use 2% to create something right in the middle of that.

CHANGE IT UP!

Change this into a white hot chocolate by substituting white chocolate for the milk chocolate, and then make this a fun holiday drink by adding a few drops of red, green or pink food coloring to the hot chocolate for Christmas, Valentine's Day or St. Patrick's Day.

peach and mango breakfast smoothies

Makes: 2 servings   Prep Time: 10 minutes

On weekday mornings, it's sometimes a little crazy trying to get everyone fed and out the door in a timely manner. These smoothies are packed full of fruit and yogurt, and they're easy to take and go. Tummies won't be rumbling for at least a couple of hours when there's a smoothie sitting inside them.

1   cup frozen sliced peaches
1   cup frozen sliced mangoes
1   6-ounce container vanilla
     yogurt
⅔   cup orange or tangerine
     juice + more as needed
1   tablespoon honey

Place all of the ingredients in a blender and blend until smooth. If the smoothie appears to be too thick to blend, just add a little more juice. Divide between two glasses and serve.

TIP You can certainly use fresh peaches and mangoes, but you'll need to add in ½ cup or so of ice cubes to obtain a frozen consistency.

CHANGE IT UP!

Substitute 1 cup frozen strawberries or blueberries plus 1 banana for the peaches and mangoes.

---

brunch punch

Makes: 20 servings   Prep Time: 15 minutes

When you have a bunch of people together for a big brunch, this fruit juice–based punch is the one to whip together. Served up in a large bowl with a ladle, your guests can help themselves. That leaves you time to prep the rest of the meal and frees you from the headache of getting drinks for everyone. This kid-friendly recipe makes enough punch for a large gathering.

64 ounces chilled pineapple juice
2 cups chilled orange juice
2 cups chilled cranberry juice
1 12-ounce can frozen limeade concentrate
1 2-liter bottle chilled club soda
   Lime and orange slices for garnish
   Ice

In a large punch bowl combine the juices and limeade. Just before serving, stir in the club soda and add the lime and orange slices. Place the ice in a bucket and let guests serve themselves—a cup of ice with a ladleful of punch.

TIP If you don't wish to bother with serving ice with this punch, consider making an ice-ring for the punch bowl instead. In a small Jello ring mold, mix equal amounts of pineapple juice, orange juice and cranberry juice. Freeze until solid. To remove the ring from the pan, turn it upside down and run it under warm water until it loosens from the pan. Float the ring in the punch bowl to keep the punch cold, and it won't water down the punch like a regular ice ring would.

CHANGE IT UP!

Experiment with mixing different juices into the punch. Substitute black cherry or pomegranate juice for the cranberry. Substitute tangerine juice for the orange.

pomegranate mimosas

Makes: 6 servings   Prep Time: 15 minutes

On Christmas morning, we use brunch as an excuse to take a break from opening gifts under the tree. During brunch we follow a family tradition of sharing what each of us has done for charities during the past year. It's a feel-good tradition and it keeps us on top of thinking about those who are less fortunate than us. Mimosas are another tradition. They're festive, they go well with brunch, and they travel along quite nicely to "Part Two" of the sharing of gifts.

3	cups ice
2	cups pomegranate juice
2	cups orange juice
1	750-milliliter bottle Champagne
	Pomegranate seeds

Fill six 12-ounce glasses with ½ cup ice each. Add ⅓ cup pomegranate juice, ⅓ cup orange juice and ½ cup Champagne to each glass. Garnish each glass with a few pomegranate seeds. Serve immediately.

TIPS Fresh orange juice will be best in this recipe.

If you do not wish to use alcohol in this recipe, it's easy to leave it out. Just substitute club soda for the champagne.

CHANGE IT UP!

Make cranberry mimosas instead by substituting cranberry juice for the pomegranate juice.

Garnish the glasses with orange wedges instead of pomegranate seeds.

apricot bellinis

Makes: 8 servings   Prep Time: 15 minutes + chill time   Cook Time: 2 minutes

Apricots make me think of bright and shiny, sunny days. Their obvious, golden color is bound to cheer up even the crabbiest of people, so I like to serve this sweet apricot sparkling cocktail at a spring or summer brunch. The bonus: when you tell your guests that you're serving up fancy-schmancy "bellinis," you'll impress them without having to go to much trouble at all to prepare them.

SIMPLE SYRUP
- ⅓ cup water
- ⅓ cup sugar

REMAINING INGREDIENTS
- ¾ cup canned apricot halves in syrup, drained
- 1 750-milliliter bottle Prosecco or Champagne, chilled
- 4 tablespoons Grand Marnier (or other orange-flavored liqueur)
- 8 fresh raspberries

To prepare the simple syrup, in a small saucepan, combine the water and sugar. Bring it to a boil and cook until the sugar dissolves, about 2 minutes. Remove the syrup from the heat, pour it into a small bowl and refrigerate until it is well chilled (about 2 hours).

To prepare the apricot puree, place the simple syrup and the apricots in a blender. Blend until smooth.

To assemble the bellinis, spoon 2 tablespoons of apricot puree into each of 8 champagne glasses. Top each with ⅓ cup Prosecco and ½ tablespoon Grand Marnier. Give each glass a gentle stir. Add a raspberry to each drink and serve.

GF GLUTEN-FREE ADAPTABLE Use a brand of apricots that is gluten-free.

QUICK AND EASY TIP Purchase apricot nectar and use 2 tablespoons per cocktail instead of making your own apricot puree.

CHANGE IT UP!

Change the flavor of your bellini! Use the same instructions using peaches or mangoes in place of the apricots, or purchase canned peach or mango nectar to use instead.

---

sugar and spice drop doughnuts

Makes: 24 drop doughnuts   Prep Time: 30 minutes   Cook Time: 12 minutes

My doughnut pan is one of those pans lurking in the back of my kitchen cupboard, collecting crumbs and wishing it had a more active lifestyle. This Portuguese-style doughnut recipe doesn't need a specialty pan at all. The batter is simply dropped into heated oil and these doughnuts puff up like magic. A quick roll in some spiced sugar and they're gobbled up in just a bite or two. Anyone want a doughnut pan?

DOUGHNUTS

4	to 5 cups canola or vegetable oil
1	cup water
4	tablespoons (½ stick) salted butter
1	tablespoon granulated white sugar
	Pinch of salt
1	cup all-purpose flour
4	large eggs
1	teaspoon vanilla extract

SPICED SUGAR

½	cup granulated white sugar
1	teaspoon ground cinnamon
½	teaspoon ground nutmeg
½	teaspoon ground cloves

Pour the oil into a medium saucepan. You'll need 2 to 3 inches of oil. Heat the oil over medium-high heat until it reaches 360°F (see Tips).

In a medium saucepan, combine the water, butter, sugar and salt over medium-high heat. Bring to a boil, whisking constantly. When the mixture comes to a boil, remove the pan from the heat and whisk in the flour until the dough comes together. Transfer the dough to a large bowl and let it cool for 5 minutes.

Use an electric mixer to beat the eggs, one at a time, into the dough. Continue beating until the eggs are well incorporated into the dough and the batter is thick, 3 to 4 minutes. Mix in the vanilla.

In a low-rimmed, wide bowl, combine the spiced sugar ingredients.

Drop the dough by the heaping tablespoonful into the hot oil, frying about 6 at a time. The dough balls will puff up into rounds and roll around in the oil as they cook. Help them along with a slotted metal spoon, turning them over occasionally until golden brown on all sides, 3 to 4 minutes. Scoop the doughnuts out of the oil and onto a paper towel–lined plate briefly, then transfer them to the bowl of spiced sugar. Spoon the sugar over and around the doughnuts until they are well coated. Serve immediately, or place them on a platter until ready to serve. Repeat with the remaining batter and sugar.

TIPS For this recipe, you'll need to have a thermometer for measuring the temperature of the oil. I like to use a candy thermometer that can clip to the side of the pan.

These doughnuts are best when served the day that they're made, but they'll also keep in a covered container for a day or two.

CHANGE IT UP!

Roll the doughnuts in powdered sugar instead.

banana scones with cinnamon glaze

Makes: 6 scones   Prep Time: 20 minutes   Cook Time: 15 minutes

I think you either love scones or you don't. At the coffee shops, it's pretty standard fare to find scones that are dry and cardboard-like. Add icing to those and they're somewhat manageable but never completely satisfying. These scones I have for you here will make a scones-lover out of you yet. They're tender as can be and are topped with a light cinnamon glaze, and they don't taste a thing like cardboard.

SCONES

2	cups all-purpose flour
½	cup granulated white sugar
1	tablespoon baking powder
½	teaspoon salt
½	teaspoon ground cinnamon
6	tablespoons salted cold butter, cut into pieces
½	cup mashed ripe banana
1	large egg
3	tablespoons whipping cream
	Additional flour, for dusting

ICING

1	cup powdered sugar, sifted
2	to 3 tablespoons milk
¼	teaspoon ground cinnamon

CHANGE IT UP!

Turn these into pumpkin scones by substituting unsweetened pumpkin puree for the banana and adding in ½ teaspoon ground nutmeg, ¼ teaspoon ground cloves and ¼ teaspoon ground ginger.

Preheat the oven to 425°F. Spray a baking sheet with nonstick spray.

To prepare the scones, in a medium bowl, whisk together the flour, sugar, baking powder, salt and cinnamon. Cut in the butter with a pastry cutter or two knives until the mixture resembles fine crumbs (alternatively, this step can be done easily by pulsing the dry ingredients and butter in the food processor).

In a separate medium bowl, whisk together the banana, egg and cream. Add the dry ingredients and gently fold them together using a rubber spatula. Scoop the mixture onto a floured surface and sprinkle with a tablespoon of flour. The dough will be a bit wet, so move it around on the floured surface until it is lightly covered with flour. Shape the dough into a rounded mound (adding more flour, as needed, to keep it from sticking to the surface).

Move the scone dough onto the prepared baking sheet and pat it into a 9-inch round, about 1½ inches thick. Use a pizza cutter or a sharp knife to cut the round in half, then cut through the center twice more to create 6 wedges. Gently pull each wedge away from the center to create about ¼-inch space between each wedge.

Bake for 15 to 18 minutes, or until the top is lightly browned and feels quite firm all the way through (no squishy center). Remove the scones from the oven and let cool at least 20 minutes.

Use a sharp knife to cut through the partially cooled, precut slices and gently pull the scones apart. Place them on a wire rack to cool completely.

To prepare the icing, in a medium bowl, whisk together the icing ingredients using 2 tablespoons of milk until smooth. Add more milk if the icing is still too thick; you want it to be a drizzling consistency. Spoon the icing over the tops of the scones. Give the icing at least 15 minutes to set and then serve.

TIP These are best eaten the day they're made, but when they're stored in a sealed container they're good the next day too. Wrap and freeze if you'd like, defrosting when the mood for a scone strikes.

grandma billie's cinnamon rolls

Makes: 24 rolls   Prep Time: 45 minutes + cooling and rising times   Cook Time: 25 minutes

My Grandma Billie used to make these cinnamon rolls whenever my family came to visit, but I especially remember eating them on Christmas morning. We'd wake up and wander into the kitchen where we'd see the counters covered with rising cinnamon rolls. Grandma liked to use a simple sweet vanilla icing to top the rolls. Perfect!

DOUGH

1   cup whole milk
½   cup shortening
1   0.25-ounce package active dry yeast
½   cup warm water (105°F to 110°F)
3   large eggs
½   cup granulated white sugar
1   teaspoon salt
5   to 6 cups all-purpose flour

FILLING

¾   cup (1½ sticks) salted butter, at room temperature
1   cup granulated white sugar
1   cup packed light brown sugar
2   tablespoons ground cinnamon

GLAZE

1   cup powdered sugar, sifted
1   to 2 tablespoons whole milk
½   teaspoon vanilla extract

To prepare the dough, in a small saucepan, heat the milk and shortening until the shortening is melted. Remove the pan from the heat and let it sit at room temperature until it has cooled to lukewarm, about 30 minutes.

In a small bowl, dissolve the yeast in the warm water and set aside until the yeast bubbles (see Tips).

In the bowl of a stand mixer, beat the eggs, sugar and salt until the mixture is foamy, 1 to 2 minutes. Mix in the milk mixture and yeast mixture. (See Tips if you do not have a stand mixer.)

Change the beaters of the mixer to a dough hook and add the 5 cups flour 1 cup at a time until the flour is incorporated, stopping to scrape down the sides of the bowl as needed. The dough should come together in a ball and begin to lift from the bottom of the mixing bowl. Add more flour a little as a time, as needed, until a ball of dough is formed and the dough is no longer sticky. Let the dough hook do its thing and knead the dough for about 5 minutes.

Spray a medium bowl with nonstick spray. Scrape the dough into the bowl and turn it over to coat all sides with the oil. Cover the bowl with a clean dish towel and set it in a warm place to rise until the dough is nearly doubled, for 1 to 2 hours. Spray two 9 x 13-inch pans with nonstick spray. Set aside.

To add the filling to the dough, punch down the risen dough and transfer it to a well-floured surface. Roll out the dough into a large rectangle, ¼ to ½ inch thick, with the long side facing you (adding more flour, as needed, to prevent the dough from sticking to the surface). Spread the dough with softened butter. Sprinkle the white sugar evenly, then sprinkle the brown sugar evenly and finally sprinkle the cinnamon evenly.

Beginning with the long side closest to you, roll the dough over the filling until you've created one big log of rolled dough. Trim the ends off and discard. Use a sharp knife to slice 1-inch-wide cinnamon rolls. Carefully remove the cut rolls to the two 9 x 13-inch oiled pans. Place 12 rolls in each pan.

Instructions for baking these now: Cover the pans loosely with clean dish towels and put them in a warm place to rise (1 to 2 hours), until they're about doubled in size.

Instructions for baking these later: Cover the pans with plastic wrap and keep them in the refrigerator for up to 1 day. When you're ready to bake, take them out of the fridge, remove the plastic wrap and cover them loosely with clean dish towels. Place the pans in a warm place to rise, until they're about doubled in size. If you'd like to have these first thing in the morning, you can place them in a cold oven (turn on the light, but not the heat) and leave them overnight. They should be risen and ready to bake in the morning. Then continue to the baking instructions below.

To bake, preheat the oven to 350°F. Remove the dish towels and bake the cinnamon rolls for 15 to 20 minutes, just until golden. Remove from the oven and let the rolls cool for a few minutes.

In a medium bowl, whisk together the glaze ingredients, adding just enough milk to create a drizzling consistency. Drizzle the glaze over the warm rolls and serve immediately.

TIPS The temperature of the water to mix with the yeast is important. If it's too hot, it might kill the yeast. Watch for the yeast to bubble; if it doesn't bubble, your yeast is likely no longer active and you should try again with a new packet.

If you don't have a stand mixer, use a regular hand mixer to beat the eggs, sugar and salt. Mix in the milk mixture and the yeast mixture. Then stir in the flour 1 cup at a time (5 cups total) until it's incorporated. Transfer the dough to a floured surface and work the dough, kneading it for 5 to 8 minutes, continuing to add flour, as needed, until the dough comes together to form a ball and is no longer sticky. Continue with the instructions for rising.

streuseled eggnog-cranberry muffins

Makes: 14 to 16 muffins   Prep Time: 15 minutes   Cook Time: 20 minutes

When the fall holidays roll around, I become completely enamored with all things eggnog. Rather than guzzle the stuff from the carton—which unfortunately goes directly to my hips—I prefer to enjoy the flavor of eggnog by baking with it instead. These eggnog-flavored muffins are certainly a treat for the eggnog-loving crowd, and they're topped with a simple sugar-and-nut streusel.

MUFFIN BATTER

2¼	cups all-purpose flour
1	tablespoon baking powder
1	cup + 2 tablespoons granulated white sugar, divided
¾	cup eggnog, low-fat or regular
⅓	cup salted butter, melted
2	large eggs
1	teaspoon almond, vanilla or eggnog extract
1	cup frozen cranberries, coarsely chopped (see Tips)

STREUSEL TOPPING

½	cup granulated white sugar
½	cup all-purpose flour
4	tablespoons (½ stick) salted butter, slightly softened
½	cup chopped pecans, optional

Preheat the oven to 400°F. Spray 16 muffin cups with nonstick spray.

To prepare the muffin batter, in a medium bowl, whisk together the flour and baking powder. Set aside.

In a large bowl, whisk together 1 cup of the sugar, the eggnog, butter, eggs and extract. Add the dry ingredients and stir just until combined. In a separate bowl, toss the cranberries with the remaining 2 tablespoons sugar. Fold into the muffin batter.

To prepare the streusel topping, in a medium bowl, combine the streusel ingredients using a pastry cutter or a fork, until the mixture is crumbly.

Fill the prepared muffin cups two-thirds full. Top each muffin cup with 1 tablespoon of the streusel topping. Bake for 18 to 22 minutes, or until a toothpick inserted into the center of a muffin comes out clean. Let the muffins cool on a wire rack for 10 minutes before removing them from the pan.

TIP Only have fresh cranberries? Spread them on a rimmed pan and pop them in the freezer until they are firm. Frozen cranberries are much easier to chop.

CHANGE IT UP!

Leave off the streusel topping and give these muffins an eggnog glaze instead! Mix ¼ cup sifted powdered sugar, 1 tablespoon eggnog and a dash of nutmeg. Drizzle over the tops of the muffins.

peanut butter and jelly muffins

Makes: 12 muffins   Prep Time: 20 minutes   Cook Time: 20 minutes

The best thing about having a kid in the house is that you always have peanut butter and jelly in the house. Well, okay . . . maybe that's not the "best" thing, but it sure is a bonus of having kids around. I've turned everyone's favorite sandwich into muffins for breakfast. A generous dollop of your favorite jam is plopped right into the middle of peanut buttery cake.

1⅔ cups all-purpose flour
½   cup packed light brown
     sugar
1   tablespoon baking powder
¼   teaspoon salt
¾   cup milk
½   cup creamy peanut butter
     (see Tips)
⅓   cup canola or vegetable oil
1   large egg
1½ teaspoons vanilla extract
½   cup strawberry jam (see
     Change It Up!)

Preheat the oven to 350°F. Spray 12 muffin cups with nonstick spray.

In a medium bowl, whisk together the flour, sugar, baking powder and salt. Set aside.

In a separate medium bowl, whisk together the milk, peanut butter, oil, egg and vanilla. Stir the wet ingredients into the dry ingredients and mix just until combined.

Scoop about 2 tablespoons of batter into each muffin cup. Spoon a heaping teaspoonful of jam on top of each cupful of batter. Then spoon about 2 tablespoons of batter over the jam. Divide any remaining batter equally among the muffin cups.

Bake for 20 to 25 minutes, or until the muffins have risen in the middle and are firm to touch.

TIP If you use a natural-style peanut butter for this recipe, just be sure to use one that is a creamy, nonstir type. You need the oils that are present in the peanut butter to create nice, moist and tender muffins.

CHANGE IT UP!

Use your favorite variety of jam for this recipe. Blackberry happens to be an especially good substitute for strawberry.

Create almond butter muffins by substituting a creamy, nonstir variety of almond butter for the peanut butter.

nutella-swirled pumpkin bread

Makes: 1 loaf   Prep Time: 20 minutes   Cook Time: 1 hour and 15 minutes

I've been making a basic pumpkin bread recipe for many years, and I give away dozens of loaves to family and friends during the fall holidays. It's anything but ordinary. It's moist and spicy and hearty and perfect. Swirl Nutella into this bread, though, and it transforms into something even more wonderful. I like to think of it as the hip and cool version of my classic pumpkin bread.

1½ cups all-purpose flour
1   teaspoon baking soda
¼   teaspoon baking powder
1   teaspoon ground cinnamon
½   teaspoon ground nutmeg
½   teaspoon ground cloves
½   teaspoon ground allspice
½   teaspoon salt
1½ cups granulated white sugar
½   cup canola or vegetable oil
2   large eggs
1   cup unsweetened pumpkin
     puree
⅓   cup water
¼   cup Nutella (or another
     chocolate hazelnut spread)

Preheat the oven to 350°F. Spray a 9 x 5-inch loaf pan with nonstick spray (see Tips).

In a medium bowl, whisk together the flour, baking soda, baking powder, spices and salt. Set aside.

In a large bowl, use an electric mixer to combine the sugar, oil and eggs. Add the dry ingredients and beat until the flour is completely incorporated. Add the pumpkin puree and the water and beat just until all of the ingredients are well combined.

Spoon the Nutella into a medium dish and soften in the microwave for about 20 seconds. Add ⅓ cup of the pumpkin batter to the Nutella and stir until they are well blended.

Pour half of the pumpkin batter into the prepared pan. Spoon half of the Nutella batter on top of the pumpkin batter (little spoonfuls about 1 inch apart). Pour the remaining pumpkin batter over the Nutella, then spoon the rest of the Nutella batter on top. Swirl the batters together a few times gently with a knife.

Bake for 1 hour and 15 minutes, or until a toothpick inserted into the center comes out clean. Cool in the pan for at least 15 minutes and then turn the loaf out onto a wire rack to cool completely.

TIPS This recipe makes a nice, large loaf of bread. Don't be tempted to use a loaf pan that is smaller than 9 x 5 inches, or if you do then you'll want to use some of the excess batter to make a few muffins too.

This bread freezes well. When cooled, cover with plastic wrap and then foil. Freeze until you're ready to eat. It keeps well in the freezer for several weeks.

CHANGE IT UP!

Leave out the Nutella completely to make the classic version of my pumpkin bread.

Turn this into Chocolate Chip Pumpkin Bread instead by leaving out the Nutella and mixing in 1 cup miniature chocolate chips instead.

apple cider bread

Makes: 1 loaf (12 servings)   Prep Time: 15 minutes   Cook Time: 50 minutes

I hope that you're lucky enough to live in a place that has apple trees. Autumn apple-picking time is just about the best family activity there is. Kids pull apples from trees and proudly place them in their collection bags. It's quite the fun experience for all. The best part is coming home with loads of apples and figuring out what you'd like to make with them. Applesauce is the obvious choice, but apple cider bread should run a close second.

2 cups all-purpose flour
1 teaspoon baking powder
1 teaspoon baking soda
1 teaspoon salt
1 teaspoon ground cinnamon
½ teaspoon ground cloves
⅔ cup granulated white sugar
⅓ cup packed light brown sugar
4 tablespoons (½ stick) unsalted butter, at room temperature
2 large eggs
½ cup apple cider (or apple juice)
2¼ cups peeled and cored chopped apples (about 3 large)
1 tablespoon freshly squeezed lemon juice

Preheat the oven to 350°F. Grease and flour an 8 x 5-inch loaf pan.

Into a medium bowl, sift the flour, baking powder, baking soda, salt, cinnamon and cloves.

In a large bowl, use an electric mixer to beat the sugars and butter until light and creamy, 1 to 2 minutes. Beat in the eggs until incorporated. Add the flour mixture half at a time, alternating with the cider, and mix just until combined.

In a small bowl, toss the apples with the lemon juice. Stir the apples into the batter.

Scoop the batter into the prepared pan. Bake 50 to 60 minutes, or until a toothpick inserted into the center comes out clean. Cool in the pan for at least 20 minutes and turn the loaf out onto a wire rack to cool completely.

TIPS I like to use a combination of apples in this bread. I recommend Gala, Granny Smith, Braeburn and Jonathon varieties.

This bread is actually one of those that tastes better the next day. It will keep for several days—just store it in a covered container or wrap it well.

CHANGE IT UP!
Turn this into dessert by plating warm slices drizzled with hot caramel sauce.

grandma amelia's french plum coffee cake

Makes: 18 servings   Prep Time: 25 minutes   Cook Time: 25 minutes

My sister Susie has a friend named Dana (are you still with me?) who brings plum coffee cake into the office to share every fall. It's her grandmother's recipe. I drooled over my sister's description of the cake . . . how it looked, how it tasted and how all of the staff at her middle school devoured the cake in nothing flat. She was nice enough to ask Dana to share the recipe. Dana asked Grandma, and Grandma gave the okay, and now we all get the benefit of sharing the delight of Grandma Amelia's French Plum Coffee Cake. It sounds fancy and all with the French plums, but you can just use regular plums in the cake and all will be fine.

CAKE
- 1 cup granulated white sugar
- 8 tablespoons (1 stick) salted butter, at room temperature
- Grated zest of 1 lemon
- 1 large egg
- Pinch of salt
- 2 cups all-purpose flour
- 2 teaspoons baking soda
- ¾ cup whole milk
- 4 small plums, cut in half, pit removed and sliced into thin wedges

STREUSEL
- ¾ cup all-purpose flour
- ⅔ cup granulated white sugar
- 4 tablespoons (½ stick) salted butter, melted
- ½ teaspoon ground cinnamon

Preheat the oven to 350°F. Spray a 13 x 18-inch jelly-roll pan with nonstick spray (see Tips).

To prepare the cake, in a large bowl, use an electric mixer to combine the sugar, butter and lemon zest. Beat in the egg and salt.

Into a separate bowl, sift the flour and baking soda. Stir the dry ingredients into the wet ingredients, a little at a time, alternating with the milk. Spread the batter into the prepared pan. Place the plum wedges on top of the batter, spacing them out decoratively in rows.

To prepare the streusel, in a medium bowl, combine the streusel ingredients and mix until crumbly. Crumble the streusel mixture evenly on top of the plums.

Bake the cake for 25 to 35 minutes, or until it is lightly browned and a toothpick inserted into the center comes out clean. Let the cake cool for at least 20 minutes before cutting and serving.

TIP A 13 x 18-inch jelly-roll pan is a standard-size, rimmed baking sheet (otherwise known as a half sheet pan). This pan will work best for baking this cake.

CHANGE IT UP!

Change this into another variety of fruit cake. Try substituting sliced nectarines or peaches for the plums.

upside-down brown butter–banana coffee cake

Makes: 6 servings   Prep Time: 25 minutes   Cook Time: 35 minutes

One Sunday morning, many moons ago, I took my creativity out on this cake recipe. My family was eagerly awaiting something special for a weekend breakfast, and I was determined to make something with brown butter . . . and bananas. . . and turn it upside down. This recipe was the result and was a big hit with my two boys. Dare I say that the three of us ate the entire cake in one sitting?

TOPPING

4	tablespoons (½ stick) salted butter
2	tablespoons packed light brown sugar
2	tablespoons granulated white sugar
¾	teaspoon ground cinnamon
1	medium ripe banana, sliced (see Tips)

CAKE

4	tablespoons (½ stick) salted butter, at room temperature
¼	cup granulated white sugar
1	cup mashed ripe banana
⅓	cup sour cream
1	large egg
½	teaspoon vanilla extract
1	cup all-purpose flour
½	teaspoon baking powder
½	teaspoon baking soda
½	teaspoon ground cinnamon
⅛	teaspoon ground ginger
⅛	teaspoon salt

Preheat the oven to 350°F. Spray an 8-inch round or 8-inch square cake pan with cooking spray.

To prepare the topping, melt the butter in a small saucepan over medium-low heat. Stir until the butter begins to brown, 5 to 6 minutes. Remove from heat and pour the browned butter into the round cake pan, swirling it around to coat the bottom of the pan.

In a small bowl, stir together the sugars and cinnamon. Sprinkle evenly over the browned butter in the pan. Evenly place the banana slices on top of the sugars.

To prepare the cake, in a medium bowl, use an electric mixer to combine the butter and sugar. Beat in the banana, sour cream, egg and vanilla.

In a separate bowl, whisk together the flour, baking powder, baking soda, cinnamon, ginger and salt. Stir the dry ingredients into the banana mixture. Spoon the batter into the pan, spreading evenly over the bananas.

Bake for 30 to 35 minutes, or until a toothpick inserted into the center comes out clean. Remove the cake from the oven, run a sharp knife along the side of the pan to loosen. Place a serving plate on top of the pan and gently flip it over. The cake should come out of the pan and onto the plate easily. Tap the bottom of the pan if the cake needs coaxing. Drizzle any remaining juices in the pan over the top of the cake. Serve immediately.

TIP Use bananas that are ripe and soft with many brown spots—not the dead black variety.

CHANGE IT UP!

Turn this cake into an Upside-Down Brown Butter–Banana-Blueberry Coffee Cake. Rather than placing banana slices on the bottom of the pan, sprinkle blueberries on there instead.

Add almond slices or toasted walnuts to the topping.

creamy greek scramble

Makes: 4 servings   Prep Time: 20 minutes   Cook Time: 4 to 6 minutes

There are no omelettes in this cookbook and that is for good reason. I simply don't like them and I've never been very skilled at making them either. Most of the time an omelette is all egg and not enough "stuff." I start in the center and eat my way through all of the good stuff, but soon I'm left with a plate full of overcooked egg leftovers. The solution? A scramble. I figure if you scramble all of that good omelette stuff into your eggs, there's little chance you'll have any unadorned egg left over.

8   large eggs
2   teaspoons water
1   teaspoon freshly squeezed
       lemon juice
1   tablespoon cream cheese
1½ cups chopped spinach
       leaves
½   cup diced cherry tomatoes
½   cup crumbled feta or goat
       cheese
1   teaspoon chopped fresh
       chives, optional
       Salt and freshly ground
       black pepper, to taste

In a medium bowl, whisk together the eggs, water and lemon juice. Whisk them well as you really want to get the water and lemon juice incorporated into the eggs. Set aside.

Heat a medium skillet to medium and spray with nonstick spray. Add the cream cheese and let it melt in the pan for 1 minute, swirling it around to soften. Give the eggs one more generous whisking, and then add them to the heated pan. Use a rubber spatula to move them around while they cook, allowing a chance for the raw egg to move around the pan. When the eggs are almost completely cooked, add in the spinach, tomatoes and cheese, continuing to stir the eggs until the spinach has wilted and the eggs are completely cooked through. Remove the pan from heat and sprinkle with chives, if desired. Serve immediately with salt and pepper, to taste.

TIP Don't try to chop your vegetables while you're cooking your eggs. Having everything chopped and ready to go ahead of time makes this recipe easy.

CHANGE IT UP!

Add in ½ teaspoon of freshly chopped dill with the veggies for a different spin on the flavor.

Switch out the feta or goat cheese for cheddar or Swiss.

Change up the vegetable additions —for example, lightly steamed broccoli, or sautéed mushrooms, zucchini and shallots.

make-ahead overnight breakfast casserole

Makes: 10 servings   Prep Time: 30 minutes + overnight in the refrigerator
Cook Time: 1 hour and 10 minutes

My family has been making different versions of this "feeds-a-large-crowd" breakfast casserole for many years now. It's the perfect, low-stress choice for company and family get-togethers since the whole thing is assembled the night before, and it's so delicious that there is rarely much left over. Leftovers of this casserole, however, are a very good thing indeed.

8   cups day-old French bread or focaccia cubes (half of a 1-pound loaf)
2   tablespoons salted butter, melted
8   ounces kielbasa sausage, sliced and cut into bite-size pieces
8   ounces (2 cups) shredded sharp cheddar cheese
4   ounces (1 cup) shredded Swiss cheese
8   large eggs
1½ cups 2% low-fat milk
¼   cup dry white wine
2   whole green onions thinly sliced, white and light green parts
2   teaspoons Dijon mustard
⅛   teaspoon cayenne pepper
¾   cup sour cream
½   cup freshly grated Parmesan cheese

Spray a 9 x 13-inch dish with nonstick spray.

Spread the bread cubes evenly in the prepared dish and drizzle them with the butter. Sprinkle with the sausage and cheeses. In a medium bowl, whisk together the eggs, milk, wine, green onions, mustard and cayenne. Pour the egg mixture over the casserole, cover with plastic wrap and refrigerate overnight.

Remove the casserole from the refrigerator at least 30 minutes before baking. Preheat the oven to 350°F.

Remove the plastic wrap from the casserole. Spray a piece of foil with nonstick spray and cover the casserole, sprayed side down. Bake for 1 hour. Remove the casserole from the oven, take off the foil, spread the sour cream on top and sprinkle with the Parmesan. Bake, uncovered, for an additional 10 minutes, or until the casserole has turned golden brown and it is cooked through. Let cool for 15 minutes before slicing and serving.

TIP I like the flavor that the wine gives to the casserole, but if you do not wish to use alcohol in this dish, just use an extra ¼ cup of milk instead.

CHANGE IT UP!

Substitute 8 ounces of cooked and crumbled sausage for the kielbasa, if desired.

Use egg bread/challah in place of the French bread.

This recipe is also good using a blend of Mexican shredded cheese in place of the cheddar-Swiss combination.

ham and swiss quiche

Makes: One 9-inch quiche   Prep Time: 35 minutes   Cook Time: 45 minutes

I can eat quiche for breakfast, lunch and dinner, and I devour it as leftovers late at night too. It's one of those things that always seems like a good meal to me. The best thing about a quiche, though, is that it feels like dessert too. A flaky crust with a creamy egg custard filling . . . baked in a pie pan. How can that not feel like you're eating dessert, even if there is broccoli and ham and Swiss cheese in it? Dessert for breakfast works for me.

CRUST

1½	cups all-purpose flour
⅓	cup cold, unsalted butter, cut into pieces
⅛	teaspoon ground nutmeg
⅛	teaspoon salt
⅛	teaspoon cayenne pepper
2	tablespoons ice water + more as needed
1	teaspoon white vinegar

FILLING

1	tablespoon olive oil
1	cup chopped onion (about 1 medium)
1	cup diced ham
1	teaspoon minced garlic (1 large clove)
2	cups small-cut broccoli florets
6	large eggs
1	cup heavy whipping cream
2	teaspoons spicy brown mustard
¼	teaspoon salt
⅛	teaspoon ground white pepper
6	ounces (1½ cups) shredded Swiss cheese

Preheat the oven to 350°F and spray a 9-inch deep-dish pie pan with nonstick spray.

To prepare the crust, in a food processor, pulse together the flour, butter, nutmeg, salt and cayenne a few times, until thick crumbs form. Mix the 2 tablespoons water and the vinegar and drizzle the mixture into the processor slowly while it is processing. The dough should come together in clumps. If necessary, add more ice water, ½ tablespoon at a time, until the dough comes together. Remove the dough from the processor, place it onto a piece of plastic wrap and pat it into a round. Wrap the round with plastic wrap and place it in the refrigerator for at least 15 minutes, while you prepare the filling.

To prepare the filling, in a large skillet, heat the oil over medium heat. Add the onion and cook until softened and lightly browned, 3 to 4 minutes. Stir in the ham and garlic and cook for an additional 2 minutes. Add the broccoli, stir to combine and cook an additional 2 minutes. Remove the pan from heat.

In a medium bowl, whisk together the eggs, cream, mustard, salt and pepper. Set aside.

continued on page 44

continued from page 43

Between two pieces of plastic wrap, roll out the crust into a round roughly 12 inches in diameter. Peel off the top layer of plastic wrap and turn the crust over the prepared pie plate. Peel off the remaining piece of plastic wrap and gently move the crust into the pan, crimping the edges around the pan as desired.

Spoon the cooked vegetables into the crust. Sprinkle the cheese on top. Pour the egg custard over.

Bake for 40 to 45 minutes, or until the filling is set and the top of the quiche starts to turn golden brown. Let cool for 15 minutes before slicing.

Ⓥ VEGETARIAN ADAPTABLE Leave out the ham and substitute another cup of vegetables in its place.

QUICK AND EASY Purchase a premade crust and then proceed with the recipe as directed.

TIP Quiche makes great leftovers for 2 to 3 days. Cover it with plastic wrap and keep in the refrigerator.

CHANGE IT UP!

Switch out the ham for cooked bacon or cooked, crumbled sausage instead.

Use your favorite cheese or a combination of cheeses in place of the Swiss cheese.

Sautéed mushrooms are very good in quiche. Add them in or use them in place of the broccoli.

---

fried egg, avocado and bacon sandwich

Makes: 1 sandwich   Prep Time: 15 minutes   Cook Time: 10 minutes

Avocados were definitely not part of the meal plan in my growing-up years. I don't know if they weren't readily available in the 70s, or if they just weren't trendy, or perhaps the average housewife had no idea what to do with one of them. In college, I was introduced to avocados by way of guacamole. Nowadays, avocados make it into my grocery cart every single time I'm at the market, and they're not just for guacamole anymore. Avocados also happen to fit in quite nicely on a sandwich cozied up next to egg, bacon, tomato and pepper Jack cheese.

2   slices bacon
2   slices bread
1   large egg
1   slice pepper Monterey Jack cheese
2   slices tomato
½   avocado, sliced
⅛   teaspoon lemon pepper
     Pinch of sea salt

In a medium skillet, fry the bacon over medium heat until crisp, 6 to 8 minutes. Remove the bacon to paper towels to drain. Wipe out the skillet.

Toast the bread in your toaster while you prepare the egg.

Heat the skillet to medium and spray with nonstick spray. Add the egg and cook until the egg white begins to turn an opaque white, 2 to 3 minutes. Use a rubber spatula to gently flip the egg over. Cook the egg until it is no longer raw, an additional 1 to 2 minutes (see Tips).

Place one slice of bread on a plate. Top it with the cheese. Slide the fried egg onto the cheese. Add the bacon, tomato and avocado. Sprinkle with lemon pepper and salt. Top with the second slice of bread. Use a sharp knife to cut the sandwich in half and serve immediately.

GF GLUTEN-FREE ADAPTABLE Use a brand of bacon that is known to be gluten-free and substitute gluten-free bread for regular bread.

DF DAIRY-FREE ADAPTABLE Leave off the cheese.

V VEGETARIAN ADAPTABLE Leave out the bacon.

TIP Cook the egg so that some of the yolk still remains a little bit runny inside. When you cut into it, some of that yolk will drizzle onto your plate and create a good dipping sauce for the sandwich!

CHANGE IT UP!

Try a different flavor of cheese or sprinkle hot sauce in there too.

sausage and scrambled egg breakfast pizza

Makes: 8 slices   Prep Time: 20 minutes   Cook Time: 20 minutes

There's a deli near my house that specializes in pizza. Their best business move was when they began selling breakfast pizza. It has been such a big hit that I thought I'd better try to re-create that recipe at home. This recipe here is pretty darn similar to what we take away in the pizza box. It's a sausage, egg and cheese pizza topped with sour cream and salsa. I love to make it on lazy Sunday mornings when my boys are lounging around watching football.

1   pound spicy ground pork sausage
6   large eggs, lightly beaten
½   teaspoon freshly ground black pepper
    All-purpose flour for rolling the pizza dough
1   pound pizza dough (see Tips)
2   tablespoons cornmeal
1   16-ounce jar salsa
8   ounces (2 cups) shredded Mexican blend cheese
¾   cup sour cream, optional

Preheat the oven to 425°F. Place a pizza stone on the bottom rack of the oven and heat for 30 minutes. (See Tips if you do not have a pizza stone.)

In a large nonstick skillet, brown the sausage over medium heat, stirring until it crumbles and is no longer pink, 5 to 7 minutes. Spoon the sausage onto a paper towel–lined plate. Set aside to drain. Wipe the skillet clean. In a medium bowl, whisk together the eggs and pepper. Set aside. On a floured surface, roll out the dough into a 12- to 14-inch circle. Sprinkle the pizza stone with cornmeal and slide the dough onto the stone. Bake the crust for 4 minutes, or until lightly browned and bubbling.

While the crust is baking, cook the eggs in a lightly greased skillet over medium heat, without stirring, until the eggs begin to set on the bottom. Draw a rubber spatula across the bottom of the skillet, creating large curds. Continue cooking until the eggs are thickened but still moist (do not stir constantly). Remove the skillet from heat and set aside.

When the crust is lightly browned and bubbling, carefully open the oven and slide out the rack. Spoon and spread the salsa over the partially baked crust and then top it evenly with sausage, scrambled eggs and cheese. Bake for 8 to 12 more minutes, or until the cheese is melted and the crust is a deep, golden brown.

Remove the pizza from the oven and let cool for at least 10 minutes before slicing. Serve slices with sour cream, if desired.

TIPS Make your own Pizza Dough (page 248), purchase premade pizza dough from your market, or ask a pizza shop to sell you a 1-pound ball of dough.

If you do not have a pizza stone, use a pizza pan or a cookie sheet instead. Just be sure to sprinkle the pan with cornmeal before placing the dough on the pan and don't preheat the pan in the oven as you would the stone.

To lighten up this recipe, use reduced-fat sausage, egg whites, reduced-fat cheese and low-fat sour cream.

CHANGE IT UP!

Add some of your favorite pizza toppings to this breakfast pizza! Try cooked bacon, tomato, caramelized onions, different cheeses and ham.

swiss breakfast egg bake

Makes: 6 servings   Prep Time: 25 minutes   Cook Time: 30 minutes

When the weekend rolls around, my family wants a little something special for breakfast. I'm more than happy to make that something special for them. If we eat breakfast out, we're likely to spend a boatload of money and eat far more than one should ever eat in the first meal of the day. One of my favorite weekend breakfasts is this baked egg casserole. It has veggies packed inside of it, and it gives you a whole lot more energy than sluggishness on a relaxing weekend day.

1	tablespoon salted butter
1	medium leek, sliced (about ¾ cup)
2	cups thinly sliced Swiss chard (3 to 4 big leaves, ribs removed)
1	cup halved pear tomatoes
8	large eggs
¾	cup ricotta cheese
½	cup whole milk
⅔	cup shredded Swiss cheese, divided
1	tablespoon Dijon mustard
½	teaspoon salt
¼	teaspoon cayenne pepper

Preheat the oven to 350°F. Spray a 9-inch square pan with nonstick spray.

In a medium skillet, melt the butter over medium heat. Add the leek and cook until it begins to soften, 2 to 3 minutes. Add the Swiss chard and tomatoes. Cover the pan and cook until the chard has wilted, an additional 2 to 3 minutes. Remove the pan from heat and set aside to cool.

In a large bowl, whisk together the eggs, ricotta, milk, ⅓ cup of the Swiss cheese, the mustard, salt and cayenne.

Spread the cooled vegetables into the bottom of the prepared pan. Pour the egg mixture on top.

Bake for 20 minutes. Sprinkle the remaining ⅓ cup Swiss cheese on top of the egg. Bake an additional 10 minutes, or until a knife inserted into the center of the egg bake comes out clean.

GF GLUTEN-FREE ADAPTABLE Use a brand of Dijon mustard that is known to be gluten-free.

TIP For ease of making this quickly in the morning, do all of your chopping the night before. It'll be a snap to prepare the next day.

CHANGE IT UP!

This egg dish recipe is vegetarian, but you can certainly change things up by adding in cooked bacon, ham or sausage. Feel free to switch up your choice of cheese too.

o'brien egg frittata for two

Makes: 2 servings   Prep Time: 30 minutes   Cook Time: 30 minutes

Once in a while, after I've scooted my son off to school, I like to whip up a little breakfast for just the husband and me. Heck, sometimes this one even shows up as lunch or dinner. Here's an egg and potato dish with plenty of cheese, onions, bell peppers and bacon mixed in. The best part is that it serves just two, so if there are, in fact, only two of you, then overeating is not an option!

2	medium red potatoes, halved
4	large eggs, lightly beaten
¾	cup shredded cheddar cheese, divided
1	tablespoon unsalted butter
½	cup diced red bell pepper
½	cup diced Canadian bacon or prosciutto
⅓	cup thinly sliced green onion, white and green parts
2	garlic cloves, minced
¼	cup sour cream

Preheat the oven to 450°F.

Place the potatoes in a small saucepan and cover with water. Bring the water to a boil. Cook until the potatoes are just tender, 10 to 15 minutes. Drain, then chop, leaving the peel on.

In a bowl, combine the eggs and ¼ cup of the cheese, stirring well. Set aside.

In a 10-inch oven-safe skillet, melt the butter over medium heat. Add the bell pepper, bacon, onion and garlic and cook, stirring, until the onion is softened, about 5 minutes. Add the potatoes into the pan and pour the egg mixture over and around the potatoes, spreading evenly in the skillet. Cook over medium-low heat until almost set, about 5 minutes. Sprinkle with the remaining ½ cup cheese.

Bake for 5 minutes, or until set. If your skillet has a plastic handle, cover the handle tightly with foil before placing it in the oven. Divide the frittata in half and top each serving with sour cream.

GF GLUTEN-FREE ADAPTABLE Use a brand of prosciutto or Canadian bacon that is known to be gluten-free.

V VEGETARIAN ADAPTABLE Leave out the bacon/prosciutto.

TIP Don't add salt to the dish, at least until after you taste it. The bacon/prosciutto will provide a good dose of sodium all on its own.

CHANGE IT UP!

Experiment with different flavors of cheese and vegetable additions, such as Swiss cheese, zucchini and sun-dried tomato.

cinnamon roll pancakes

Makes: Eight 5-inch pancakes   Prep Time: 25 minutes   Cook Time: 10 minutes

There is little on this earth that is more satisfying than a freshly baked cinnamon roll with cream cheese oozing down the sides. One Sunday morning, it came to me. . . pancakes deserve to have that cinnamon–cream cheese goodness too. The result was pancakes with crusty cinnamon craters held within. A hefty drizzle of cream cheese icing makes them a lot like those beloved cinnamon rolls.

CINNAMON FILLING

4   tablespoons (½ stick) unsalted butter, melted
¼   cup + 2 tablespoons packed light brown sugar
½   tablespoon ground cinnamon

CREAM CHEESE GLAZE

4   tablespoons (½ stick) unsalted butter
2   ounces cream cheese, at room temperature
¾   cup powdered sugar, sifted
½   teaspoon vanilla extract

PANCAKES

1   cup all-purpose flour
2   teaspoons baking powder
½   teaspoon salt
1   cup milk
1   large egg, lightly beaten
1   tablespoon canola oil

To prepare the cinnamon filling, in a medium bowl, stir together the butter, brown sugar and cinnamon. Scoop the filling into a quart-size heavy zip baggie. Set aside (see Tips).

To prepare the glaze, in a small pan, melt the butter over low heat. Whisk in the cream cheese until smooth. Remove the pan from heat. Whisk in the powdered sugar and vanilla and set aside.

To prepare the pancake batter, in a medium bowl, whisk together the flour, baking powder and salt. Whisk in the milk, egg and oil just until the batter is moistened (a few small lumps are fine).

To cook the pancakes, heat a large skillet or griddle over medium heat. Spray with nonstick spray. Use an ice cream scoop or ⅓ cup measuring cup to add the batter to the skillet. Use the bottom of the scoop or cup to spread the batter into a nice, even circle (about 5 inches in diameter). Reduce the heat to medium-low. Snip the corner of the baggie with the cinnamon filling and squeeze the filling into the open corner. Starting at the center of the pancake, squeeze the cinnamon filling on top of the pancake batter in a swirl (just as you see in a regular cinnamon roll; see Tips). Cook the pancake until bubbles begin to appear and burst on top of the pancake and it is golden brown on the bottom, 3 to 4 minutes. Slide a thin spatula underneath the pancake and gently but quickly flip it over. Cook until the other side is golden as well, an additional 2 to 3 minutes. When you flip the pancake onto a plate, you will see that the cinnamon filling has created

continued on page 52

continued from page 51

a crater-swirl of cinnamon. Wipe out the pan with a paper towel and repeat with the nonstick spray and the remaining pancake batter and cinnamon filling. Serve pancakes topped with a drizzle of warm cream cheese glaze.

TIPS Before swirling the cinnamon filling, open up the baggie again and give it a good stir to reincorporate any butter that may have separated. You want the mixture to thicken a bit—it's best when it's similar to the squeezing texture of toothpaste, which will happen if you leave it at room temperature for several minutes (refrigerate it for a few minutes if you need to). Don't try to use the filling for the pancake swirl unless it has thickened as it will be too runny to make a solid swirl.

It's best if you pour the batter into your skillet, wait a minute or so and then swirl the cinnamon onto the batter. That'll give the batter a chance to set a little before you add the swirl.

QUICK AND EASY TIP Use a boxed pancake mix as the base for this recipe.

CHANGE IT UP!

If you're trying to justify your intake of decadent cinnamon rolls, you can make this a tad bit healthier by using half whole wheat flour and low-fat cream cheese, or enjoy the pancakes without the glaze.

pumpkin spice pancakes

Makes: 4 to 6 servings   Prep Time: 15 minutes   Cook Time: 6 to 8 minutes per pancake

It's such a simple concept, really. Add pumpkin puree and spices to pancake batter and you'll end up with tender, moist and fluffy pancakes that need little adornment for serving. When fall rolls around, I recommend that you stock up on canned pumpkin puree. Sometimes it's tough to find in the middle of July and you'll likely be craving these pumpkin pancakes all year long.

2½ cups all-purpose flour
¼   cup packed light brown
     sugar
1   tablespoon + 1 teaspoon
     baking powder
2   teaspoons ground cinnamon
1   teaspoon ground allspice
1   teaspoon salt
2   cups milk
⅔   cup unsweetened pumpkin
     puree
4   tablespoons (½ stick)
     unsalted butter, melted
2   large eggs
1   teaspoon vanilla extract
     Butter and powdered sugar
     and/or warmed maple
     syrup, for serving

In a medium bowl, whisk together the flour, sugar, baking powder, cinnamon, allspice and salt.

In a separate large bowl, whisk together the milk, pumpkin, butter, eggs and vanilla. Add the dry ingredients and stir just until combined.

Preheat a large skillet or griddle over medium heat. Spray with nonstick spray. Use an ice cream scoop (2 scoops) or ½ cup measuring cup to add the batter to the center of the skillet. Use the bottom of the scoop or cup to spread the batter into a nice, even circle. Reduce the heat to medium-low and let the pancake cook until bubbles begin to appear and burst on top of the pancake and it's turning golden brown on the bottom, 3 to 4 minutes. Flip the pancake and cook until the other side is golden brown as well, an additional 2 to 3 minutes. Repeat with the nonstick spray and the remaining pancake batter. Serve the pancakes with butter and powdered sugar and/or warm maple syrup.

TIP I like to warm up the skillet to medium heat and then reduce it to medium-low once the pancakes get going. It gives the pancakes a little head start with cooking, but you don't want to keep the heat that aggressively hot throughout the whole cooking process or you'll end up with a tough crust.

CHANGE IT UP!

Add in toasted pecans to create pumpkin-pecan pancakes.

Turn these into Pumpkin–Cinnamon Roll Pancakes by adding a cinnamon swirl filling and a cream cheese glaze. See the Cinnamon Roll Pancakes recipe (page 51) and follow the same instructions for swirling and topping for this variation.

bacon and corn griddle cakes

Makes: Eight 4-inch griddle cakes   Prep Time: 25 minutes   Cook Time: 25 minutes

Truth be told, we are normally a banana-pancake kind of family. Rarely does a regular-old pancake grace a plate in the Recipe Girl house. Bananas are pretty much always sliced up and cooked right on in there with the batter. It's the way we do our pancakes around here, plain and simple. I was feeling a little wild and crazy one weekend morning when I created this pancake recipe though, and I surprised my family with a savory sort of pancake. It's a pancake where corn and bacon and melted cheese are lurking, and bananas are nowhere to be found. With extra bacon sprinkled on top and a generous drizzle of maple syrup, these have become a popular favorite on the website.

8	slices bacon, cut into ½-inch pieces
⅓	cup finely chopped sweet onion
1	cup all-purpose flour
2	tablespoons chopped fresh chives
1	teaspoon baking powder
½	teaspoon salt
⅛	teaspoon cayenne pepper
⅔	cup milk
1	large egg, beaten
1	tablespoon canola or vegetable oil
1	cup frozen, canned or fresh corn kernels
½	cup shredded Monterey Jack cheese
	Warmed maple syrup, for serving

In a medium skillet, cook the bacon pieces over medium-high heat until they begin to brown. Add the onion and continue to cook until the bacon is crisp and the onion is softened. Scoop out a heaping tablespoon of the bacon mixture to garnish the griddle cakes and set aside.

While the bacon is cooking, in a medium bowl, combine the flour, chives, baking powder, salt and cayenne. Stir in the milk, egg and oil just until moistened. Stir in the remaining bacon mixture, corn and cheese. The mixture will be thick. If you'd like the griddle cakes to be thinner, just add a little bit more milk to thin out the batter.

Preheat a griddle or large skillet over medium heat. Spray with nonstick spray. Scoop a heaping ¼ cup of the batter onto the griddle, using the bottom of the cup to spread it into an even circle. Cook the griddle cake until it is golden brown, 3 to 4 minutes per side. Repeat with the nonstick spray and the remaining batter.

Serve stacks of griddle cakes topped with a sprinkle of the reserved bacon mixture and the warm maple syrup.

(V) VEGETARIAN ADAPTABLE Substitute vegetarian sausage for the bacon.

TIP For a more decadent option, use the skillet in which you fried the bacon and cook your pancakes in the bacon grease.

> **CHANGE IT UP!**
>
> Other add-ins that would be great in this savory pancake: chopped ham, green and red bell peppers, hot sauce, jalapeño cheese and sausage.

perfect, fluffy pancakes

Makes: 4 servings   Prep Time: 10 minutes + resting time   Cook Time: 4 minutes per pancake

I have always, always been on the hunt for the perfect pancake. Good pancakes are fluffy pancakes. The batter should be thick and bubbly. The pancakes should puff up substantially on the griddle, and they should hold their shape when stacked with maple syrup drizzling down their sides. I believe that I've perfected the fluffy pancake in this recipe.

2   cups all-purpose flour
2   tablespoons granulated
        white sugar
2   teaspoons baking powder
1   teaspoon baking soda
½   teaspoon salt
1½   cups buttermilk
½   cup milk
2   large eggs
4   tablespoons (½ stick) salted
        butter, melted
1   teaspoon vanilla extract
        Warmed maple syrup, for
        serving

In a medium bowl, sift the flour, sugar, baking powder, baking soda and salt.

In a separate medium bowl, whisk together the buttermilk, milk and eggs. Slowly whisk in the melted butter and vanilla.

Add the wet ingredients to the dry ingredients and stir gently with a fork. Stir only until the batter is mostly combined. It will be a thick and lumpy batter—that's what you want. Place the batter into the refrigerator and let it rest for 15 minutes.

Preheat a large skillet or griddle over medium heat. Spray it with nonstick spray. Use an ice cream scoop (2 scoops) or ½ cup measuring cup to add the batter to the center of the skillet. Use the bottom of the scoop or cup to spread the batter into a nice, even circle. The batter will be thick. Cook the pancakes until bubbles begin to appear and burst on top of the pancakes and they are golden brown on the bottom, 2 to 3 minutes. Flip the pancakes and cook until the other sides turn golden brown as well, an additional 1 to 2 more minutes. Repeat with the nonstick spray and the remaining batter. Serve with the warm maple syrup.

TIP Don't skip the step of letting the batter rest in the refrigerator. "Resting" gives the glutens in the flour a chance to relax, which will result in more tender and fluffy pancakes, and keeping the batter chilled will keep your baking powder and soda from activating too early.

CHANGE IT UP!

Add in some goodies to make these pancakes extra special! Suggested add-ins: sliced banana, blueberries, raspberries, or chocolate chips. After you've scooped the batter onto the pan and formed it into a round shape, just drop your add-ins on top of the batter. Flip the pancakes carefully so you don't lose your add-ins!

french toast with crunchy cinnamon crust

Makes: 6 slices   Prep Time: 15 minutes   Cook Time: 8 minutes

I think my Mom made French toast every weekend when I was growing up. At least that's the way I like to remember it. I'm sure she made it simple. . . with just milk, eggs and cinnamon, but that's what made it so good. Mine is made simple like that too but with the addition of a cinnamon graham cracker crumb crust clinging to the custard-soaked bread.

¾ cup whole milk (see Tips)

3 large eggs

2 teaspoons ground cinnamon, divided

1½ teaspoons vanilla extract

12 whole cinnamon graham crackers, crushed into fine crumbs

3 tablespoons salted butter, divided

6 slices sandwich bread (or thin-cut French bread)
Warmed maple syrup, for serving

In a medium, low, wide bowl, whisk together the milk, eggs, 1 teaspoon of the cinnamon and the vanilla. Pour the graham cracker crumbs into a separate low wide bowl and stir in the remaining 1 teaspoon cinnamon.

Heat a large skillet or griddle over medium heat. Add 1 tablespoon of butter, melt and swirl around to cover the bottom of the skillet. Dip 1 slice of bread into the milk mixture to cover both sides and then dip it into the crumbs to coat both sides. Place the bread in the skillet. Repeat with as many slices as you can fit in the skillet. Cook until the bread is golden and toasted on the bottom, 3 to 4 minutes. Flip the slices and cook until the other sides turn golden as well, an additional 2 to 3 more minutes. Repeat with the remaining butter, slices of bread and dipping mixtures. Serve warm with maple syrup.

TIPS Substitute half-and-half for the whole milk if you like. It will just make your French toast that much more decadent. On the flip side, avoid using nonfat milk—which makes for a soggy French toast.

If you only have regular graham crackers in your pantry, use those and add an additional ½ teaspoon cinnamon to the crushed crumbs.

Our family loves this recipe made with Hawaiian egg bread or challah. You should be able to find both varieties of bread in your market's bread aisle or bakery.

CHANGE IT UP!

Turn this recipe into Pumpkin French Toast by adding in ¼ cup unsweetened pumpkin puree, 1 tablespoon granulated white sugar and ¼ teaspoon ground nutmeg to your milk mixture. You'll be able to dip 8 slices of bread into the custard with those added ingredients.

challah french toast with kahlúa–brown sugar bananas

Makes: 4 servings   Prep Time: 20 minutes   Cook Time: 25 minutes

Once upon a time, my husband and I had a romantic weekend getaway in Montecito, a darling little town near Santa Barbara. We noshed on local seafood and homemade ice cream, we searched for Oprah (a local resident) to no avail, and then we discovered the most amazing breakfast place called, "Jeannine's." It's a good thing the pastries and desserts were enclosed in a glass case or I might have helped myself. The oatmeal they served was a thing of beauty with perfectly sliced strawberries and big juicy blueberries, and then my husband ordered their Kahlúa French Toast with Sautéed Bananas, otherwise known as Heaven on a Plate. This recipe pays homage to Jeannine's and that decadent French toast.

BANANAS

8 tablespoons (1 stick) salted butter
¾ cup packed light brown sugar
3 large bananas, sliced
¼ cup Kahlúa

FRENCH TOAST

4 large eggs
½ cup whole milk
½ teaspoon vanilla extract
½ teaspoon ground cinnamon
⅛ teaspoon ground nutmeg
¾ pound loaf challah, sliced into 1-inch-thick slices (8 slices)

To prepare the bananas, in a medium skillet, melt the butter over medium heat. Stir in the brown sugar and bananas. Cook the bananas, stirring often, until the mixture begins to thicken, 4 to 5 minutes. Add the Kahlúa and continue to cook until the bananas are soft and the sauce has a thick syrup consistency, an additional 2 to 3 minutes. Remove the skillet from heat, cover and set aside.

To prepare the French toast, in a low, wide bowl, whisk together the eggs, milk, vanilla, cinnamon and nutmeg. Preheat a large skillet over medium heat. Spray it with nonstick spray. Dip 1 slice of bread into the egg mixture to cover both sides. Place the bread in the skillet. Repeat with as many slices as you can fit in the skillet. Cook until the bread is golden brown on the bottom, 3 to 4 minutes. Flip the slices and cook until the other sides are golden brown as well, an additional 2 to 3 minutes. Repeat with the nonstick spray and the remaining bread. Serve the French toast topped with a scoop of the reserved bananas.

GF GLUTEN-FREE ADAPTABLE Use your favorite gluten-free bread in place of the Challah.

TIPS There is no need to use any syrup with this French toast. The bananas make a perfectly decadent and wonderful topping.

If you don't wish to use alcohol in the dish, it's okay to leave it out of the sauce. Just add in a tablespoon of maple syrup in place of the Kahlúa.

CHANGE IT UP!

The banana sauce happens to be wonderful as a topping for ice cream too.

Serve with a peach–brown sugar topping instead. Substitute peeled and sliced peaches for the bananas and 1 tablespoon vanilla extract for the Kahlúa.

---

apple-bacon waffles with cider syrup

Makes: 6 servings   Prep Time: 25 minutes   Cook Time: 3 to 5 minutes per waffle

I'd put bacon in everything if I could. That smoky flavor and subtle crunch makes a great addition to just about everything. In these waffles you get to eliminate that step of serving bacon on the side. Here you just dump the bacon crumbles into the waffle batter and enjoy bacon in every bite, and it happens to pair nicely with apple too, the other hidden ingredient in these waffles. Top it all off with a sweet cider syrup and you've got breakfast.

CIDER SYRUP

½	cup granulated white sugar
1	tablespoon cornstarch
¼	teaspoon pumpkin pie spice
1	cup unsweetened apple cider
1	tablespoon freshly squeezed lemon juice
2	tablespoons salted butter

WAFFLES

1½	cups all-purpose flour
2	tablespoons granulated white sugar
½	teaspoon baking soda
½	teaspoon salt
¾	cup buttermilk
¾	cup milk
8	tablespoons (1 stick) salted butter, melted
3	large eggs
1	medium apple, peeled, cored and grated (see Tips)
8	slices of bacon, cooked and crumbled

To prepare the cider syrup, in a medium saucepan, combine the sugar, cornstarch and pumpkin pie spice. Whisk in the cider and lemon juice. Turn the heat to medium and bring the mixture to a boil, stirring often. Reduce the heat to low and continue to simmer until the mixture begins to thicken. Remove the pan from heat and add the butter. Stir until the butter has melted and is well combined with the syrup.

Preheat your waffle iron, according to manufacturer's instructions.

To prepare the waffles, in a medium bowl, whisk together the flour, sugar, baking soda and salt. In a separate large bowl, combine the buttermilk, milk, butter and eggs. Add the dry ingredients and stir just until combined. Stir in the apple and bacon.

Spray the preheated waffle iron with nonstick spray. Scoop the batter into your waffle iron and close the lid. The waffles should take between 3 to 5 minutes to cook, depending on the type of waffle iron you have. Repeat with the remaining batter. Serve waffles with warmed cider syrup.

TIPS Apple varieties that are best for cooking into pancakes are Granny Smith, Braeburn or Jonathon.

The cider syrup may be made 2 to 3 days before serving. Keep it covered and refrigerated and just heat it up again to serve.

Waffles may be made and frozen. Pop them into the toaster to heat them up again.

CHANGE IT UP!

Try using turkey bacon in place of regular bacon. Fry up extra bacon to crumble on top of individual servings.

oven-baked maple bacon

Makes: 12 strips of bacon   Prep Time: 10 minutes   Cook Time: 18 minutes

The first time I baked bacon in the oven, it changed my life forever. No more trying to squish long strips of bacon into a round pan. No more messing up a large skillet and splattering oil all over my stovetop, and no more burning the bacon in the pan because I'm too busy attending to other things. This bacon is timed just right, it comes out nice and crispy, and has some great flavors.

12	slices of bacon (see Tips)
2	tablespoons maple syrup
½	teaspoon Dijon mustard
	Freshly ground black pepper

Preheat the oven to 400°F. Line a rimmed baking sheet with enough foil so that it comes up and over the sides, and place a rack on top. Spray the rack with nonstick spray.

Lay the bacon slices on the rack. Bake the bacon for 15 minutes, or until it is beginning to brown.

While the bacon is in the oven, prepare the maple glaze. In a medium, shallow bowl, whisk together the syrup and mustard until smooth.

When the bacon has cooked for 15 minutes, carefully remove the pan from the oven and brush the tops of the bacon slices with the maple glaze. Sprinkle the pepper on top. Return the pan to the oven and bake for an additional 3 minutes, or until the bacon is brown and crisp. Move the bacon strips to a paper towel–lined plate to drain the fat from the bottom of the bacon and then serve immediately.

GF GLUTEN-FREE ADAPTABLE Use brands of bacon, Dijon mustard and maple syrup that are known to be gluten-free.

TIP Timing may vary slightly depending on the thickness of the bacon that you're using. The instructions given are for regular sliced bacon. Thick-sliced bacon may take a little longer to cook.

CHANGE IT UP!

Add a sprinkle of cinnamon instead of the pepper to create a spicy sweet treat.

Make honey-glazed bacon instead by substituting honey for the syrup.

susie's breakfast potatoes

Makes: 12 servings   Prep Time: 35 minutes + cooling time   Cook Time: 45 minutes

My sister Susie has always had the best recipes. When I was in college, I'd go and visit my older sister and spend hours reading through her cookbooks and recipe collections, copying down recipes I thought I'd try out someday. This recipe is inspired from one I copied down such a long time ago. It has since become our family's go-to breakfast potato recipe for large holiday brunch gatherings to serve alongside egg casseroles or baked ham. It's simple and it's delicious.

5	to 6 medium (4 to 5 pounds) russet or Yukon gold potatoes, scrubbed clean and cut in half
4	tablespoons (½ stick) salted butter
½	cup finely chopped onion
½	cup finely chopped red bell pepper
1	tablespoon all-purpose flour
½	cup chicken broth
½	cup milk
2	cups sour cream
1	cup shredded sharp cheddar cheese
¼	teaspoon salt
¼	teaspoon freshly ground pepper
1	cup crushed cornflakes

Preheat the oven to 350°F. Spray a 9 x 13-inch pan with nonstick spray.

Fill a large pot with water and bring it to a boil. Add the potatoes (skin-on) and boil for 20 minutes. Drain the water and cool the potatoes until they are comfortable enough to handle (about 20 minutes). Peel off the skin and discard. Grate the potatoes into the prepared pan.

In a medium saucepan, melt the butter over medium heat. Add the onion and bell pepper and cook until softened and lightly browned, 3 to 4 minutes. Whisk in the flour. Slowly drizzle in the chicken broth, then the milk. Bring the mixture to a boil and stir until the sauce becomes slightly thickened. Stir in the sour cream, cheese, salt and pepper, and continue to stir until the cheese is melted. Pour the sauce over the potatoes. Sprinkle the crushed cornflakes on top.

Bake for 45 to 60 minutes, or until the potatoes are hot and bubbly and beginning to turn golden brown.

GF GLUTEN-FREE ADAPTABLE Use an alternative thickener in place of the all-purpose flour, such as potato starch or cornstarch. Use brands of chicken broth and cornflakes that are known to be gluten-free.

V VEGETARIAN ADAPTABLE Use vegetable broth in place of the chicken broth.

TIP This recipe works just fine with reduced-fat sour cream. Avoid using low-fat cheese, though, since it doesn't tend to melt very well.

QUICK AND EASY TIP Use one 2-pound package of frozen hash brown potatoes (defrosted) in place of the fresh potatoes.

CHANGE IT UP!

Make this a festive Christmas brunch recipe by adding in chopped green bell peppers too.

cranberry-almond granola

Makes: 4 cups   Prep Time: 20 minutes   Cook Time: 25 minutes

When I told my husband that I was creating a granola recipe for the cookbook, he said, "Why would you make granola when you can just buy it at the store?" I'll tell you why Mr. Recipe Husband: It's super easy to make, I know what I'm putting into it, and it's outta-this-world delicious! And since I eat a sprinkle of granola on my Greek yogurt almost every day of my life, having a good stash of homemade granola around makes me happy. So there.

2	cups old-fashioned oats
1	cup whole, unsalted almonds, roughly chopped
½	cup unsweetened coconut flakes, optional
⅓	cup oat bran, ground flax or wheat germ
½	teaspoon ground cinnamon
¼	teaspoon salt
⅓	cup honey
¼	cup vegetable or canola oil
¼	cup freshly squeezed orange juice
2	tablespoons packed light brown sugar
½	teaspoon vanilla extract
½	cup dried cranberries

Preheat the oven to 325°F. Spray a rimmed baking sheet with nonstick spray.

In a large bowl, toss together the oats, almonds, coconut flakes, oat bran, cinnamon and salt.

In a medium bowl, whisk together the honey, oil, orange juice, sugar and vanilla. Add to the dry ingredients and stir to combine.

Spread the mixture onto the prepared baking sheet. Bake 15 minutes, then stir. Bake for an additional 5 to 10 minutes, or until the oats have turned golden brown (watch the granola carefully at this point, making sure it doesn't brown too much). Remove from the oven, stir in the dried cranberries and let the granola cool to room temperature.

When the granola has completely cooled, scoop it into a covered container where it will stay fresh for up to 2 weeks.

GF GLUTEN-FREE ADAPTABLE Use brands of oats and dried cranberries that are known to be gluten-free. Avoid using wheat germ; use ground flax or gluten-free oat bran instead.

TIP The oats will remain soft while baking and will transform into crispy oats after they have cooled off.

GIFT IDEA Spoon the granola into small plastic gift bags and tie on festive ribbons and labels for a fun, homemade gift.

CHANGE IT UP!

Use different combinations of fruit and nuts—raisins and walnuts, dried apricots and pecans, etc.

maple-cinnamon applesauce

Makes: 3 cups   Prep Time: 25 minutes   Cook Time: 45 minutes

The fall season is pretty much nonexistent where I live in Southern California. Unfortunately, we miss the leaves changing colors and that chill that announces a seasonal change. We continue to endure 75 degrees and sunny well into November, when the leaves decide to fall off of the trees all at once, dead instead of multicolored. To get our fill of fall, we head up into the local mountains every September where we can wear our fleece jackets and do some serious apple picking. Those apples ultimately become applesauce in my house, sweetened with a bit of maple syrup and spiced with cinnamon.

10	medium apples (see Tips)
⅓	cup water
¼	cup pure maple syrup (see Tips)
1	teaspoon freshly squeezed lemon juice
½	teaspoon ground cinnamon
⅛	teaspoon allspice

Core and peel all of the apples, chop them into 1-inch pieces and place them in a medium saucepan. Add the remaining ingredients to the pan and stir. Heat the mixture over medium-high heat until the liquid comes to a boil, peeking underneath the apples to check. Stir again and reduce the heat to the lowest heat possible. Cover the pan and simmer until the apples begin to soften and break apart, 45 minutes to 1 hour, stirring every 15 minutes.

Remove the pan from heat and mash the apples with a fork or potato masher until they reach the consistency you prefer for applesauce. Serve warm, or refrigerate and serve cold at a later time.

TIPS Using a couple of varieties of apples makes for good flavors in the applesauce. I recommend these: McIntosh, Golden Delicious, Cortland, Empire, Fuji, Spartan and Winesap.

Most syrup sold as pancake syrup is not real maple syrup. These syrups are made of either cane sugar or corn syrup and contain a small percentage of maple syrup for flavor. Pure maple syrup has a much more prominent maple flavor and is better for cooking and baking. Look for Grade A or B on the label.

Keep the applesauce stored in the refrigerator in a covered container for up to 2 weeks.

CHANGE IT UP!

This recipe turns out a chunky applesauce. If you prefer to have a pureed applesauce, let the apples cool and then transfer them to a food processor to puree.

oatmeal-blueberry breakfast bars

Makes: 12 bars   Prep Time: 20 minutes   Cook Time: 20 minutes

In this fast-paced world of seemingly nonstop busy family activities, the ability to hold breakfast in one's hand and walk out the door appeals to many. Breakfast-on-the-go doesn't have to be unhealthy. These lightly sweetened whole wheat bars are packed with dried blueberries, pecans and oats. They put a delicious little something in your stomach in the morning without throwing you in the midst of a sugar high. It's a nice way to start the day.

¾   cup whole wheat flour
¾   cup all-purpose flour
¾   cup old-fashioned or quick-cooking oats
1   teaspoon ground cinnamon
½   teaspoon baking soda
⅛   teaspoon sea salt
⅓   cup honey
⅓   cup unsweetened applesauce
⅓   cup nonfat milk
4   tablespoons (½ stick) salted butter, melted
1   large egg
2   tablespoons packed light brown sugar
1   teaspoon vanilla extract
1   cup dried blueberries
½   cup roughly chopped pecans

Preheat the oven to 350°F. Spray a 9-inch square pan or 7 x 11-inch pan with nonstick spray.

In a medium bowl, combine the flours, oats, cinnamon, baking soda and salt. In a separate medium bowl, whisk together the honey, applesauce, milk, butter, egg, sugar and vanilla. Add the dry ingredients and stir. Add the blueberries and pecans, stirring just until combined (see Tips).

Scrape the batter into the prepared pan and smooth the top to even it out. Bake for 20 to 22 minutes, or until a toothpick inserted in the center comes out clean. Cut into bars and serve.

TIPS Don't overmix the batter, which can result in a tougher, denser consistency.

These bars keep well for 2 to 3 days at room temperature when they are kept in a sealed container. Alternatively, freeze bars in individual zip baggies for up to 1 month, taking them out to defrost for a quick breakfast as desired.

CHANGE IT UP!

Swap out the blueberries and pecans for another dried fruit and nut combination—apricot/almond, cherry/almond or apple/walnut.

Let's Do Lunch

A midday meal should consist of something hearty and filling. It should have enough umph to give you ample energy to have a productive afternoon. When I was a young bride, I prepared large dinners so that my husband and I would each have leftovers to bring to work for our lunch the following day. Our colleagues were envious, and with our bellies full, the rest of the workday didn't seem so bad. If folks took the time to make sure they had themselves a healthy, more satisfying meal at lunch, people just might find themselves in a better mood and be better prepared to tackle whatever the day brings. Soups, salads and sandwiches are all acceptable options here.

Recipes

(W) WEB FAVORITE   (V) VEGETARIAN *(or adaptable)*   (GF) GLUTEN-FREE *(or adaptable)*   (DF) DAIRY-FREE *(or adaptable)*

tomato-basil soup with garlic-cheese croutons

Makes: 4 to 6 servings   Prep Time: 40 minutes + cooling time   Cook Time: 1 hour

Tomato soup is best when served alongside a grilled cheese sandwich for dunking. When I was little, I shortcut the whole sandwich-making process by adding cubes of bread and chunks of cheddar cheese to my tomato soup. Every bite would nab a piece of bread and strands of melted cheese. It did the trick. My grown-up version of tomato soup packs homemade garlic-cheese croutons instead, a seemingly perfect solution for satisfying the grilled cheese and tomato soup craving.

CROUTONS

4	cups cubed stale French bread
4	tablespoons (½ stick) salted butter, melted
1	teaspoon garlic powder
½	teaspoon Italian seasoning
¼	cup freshly grated Parmesan cheese

SOUP

1	tablespoon salted butter
1	small onion, chopped (about 1 cup)
1	small carrot, peeled and finely chopped
1	stalk celery, finely chopped
1	teaspoon minced garlic
1	tablespoon balsamic vinegar
2	tablespoons all-purpose flour
1	28-ounce can San Marzano tomatoes (see Tips)
1	cup vegetable broth
1	tablespoon finely chopped basil
½	teaspoon granulated white sugar
½	teaspoon kosher salt
⅛	teaspoon cayenne pepper
1½ to 2	cups 1% milk

To prepare the croutons, preheat the oven to 350°F. In a medium bowl, toss the bread cubes, butter, garlic powder and Italian seasoning. Spread the bread onto a rimmed baking sheet. Sprinkle with the cheese. Bake for 15 minutes. Let cool.

To prepare the soup, in a medium skillet, melt the butter over medium heat. Add the onion, carrot and celery. Cook, stirring, until the vegetables are softened, 4 to 5 minutes. Stir in the garlic and cook for 1 minute. Add the vinegar, stir the vegetables to incorporate and then sprinkle in the flour. Stir again. Add the tomatoes and broth. Turn the heat to high and bring the mixture to a boil. Cover the skillet and reduce the heat to low. Simmer for 30 minutes. Remove the skillet from heat and stir in the basil, sugar, salt and cayenne. Let cool for 15 minutes.

Scoop half the mixture into a food processor or blender. Process until smooth. Transfer the pureed soup to a large saucepan. Repeat with the remaining mixture. Stir in 1½ cups of the milk. Add up to ½ cup more, depending on how thin you'd prefer the soup to be. Heat the soup over medium heat until heated through. Serve warmed cups of soup topped with the croutons (see Tips).

continued on page 70

continued from page 69

GF GLUTEN-FREE ADAPTABLE Prepare the croutons using gluten-free bread. Thicken the soup with a gluten-free flour blend or potato starch in place of the all-purpose flour.

TIPS San Marzano tomatoes are a variety of plum tomato considered by many to make the best sauces. Most well-stocked grocery stores carry canned Marzanos. If you're unable to find them, an acceptable substitute would be canned Italian plum tomatoes.

Any extra croutons will keep in a covered container for up to 2 weeks. They're great tossed into salads too.

CHANGE IT UP!

Turn this soup into a creamier variety by adding whipping cream instead of milk.

If you don't wish to make the croutons, serve this soup with grilled cheese sandwich halves instead!

slow cooker beef and lentil soup

Makes: 4 servings   Prep Time: 25 minutes   Cook Time: 8 hours

The fact that I even have more than one slow cooker recipe in this book is a bit shocking. I've never been much of a fan of slow cooker recipes. I've tried so many, and there are very few that actually get placed in that "recipes to repeat" pile. Yet I need good slow cooker recipes! I'm busy, and I need a soup that will feed my husband quick lunches. Soups like this one—with beef in there and lentils and many vegetables—are filling for lunch and are even hearty enough for dinner, too, with a good hunk of Italian bread to soak up the broth. This recipe is definitely one for the "recipes to repeat" pile.

2   tablespoons olive oil, divided
1   pound boneless beef chuck,
      cut into ½-inch pieces
⅓   cup dry red wine (see Tips)
1   cup chopped celery
1   cup thinly sliced leek, white
      and light green parts only
1   cup thinly sliced, peeled carrot
1   teaspoon minced garlic
3   cups beef broth
3   cups water
1   14.5-ounce can petite diced
      tomatoes
1   cup dried lentils
1   bay leaf
3   cups fresh spinach, stems
      trimmed and discarded
1   tablespoon chopped fresh
      oregano
    Salt and freshly ground
      black pepper, to taste

Heat 1 tablespoon of the olive oil in a large skillet over medium heat. Add the beef and cook until browned on all sides, 5 to 6 minutes, stirring often. Add the wine to deglaze the skillet, scraping up any browned bits from the bottom. Scoop the meat and juices into your slow cooker.

Wipe out the skillet with a paper towel and then heat the remaining 1 tablespoon of oil over medium heat. Add the celery, leek and carrot to the skillet and cook, stirring, until the vegetables are softened, 4 to 5 minutes. Stir in the garlic and cook for 1 additional minute. Add the vegetable mixture to the slow cooker. Add the broth, water, tomatoes, lentils and bay leaf to the slow cooker. Cover and cook on low for 7 to 8 hours, or on high for 3½ to 4 hours. When you are ready to serve your soup, remove the bay leaf and stir in the spinach and oregano. Taste to see if you'd like to add any salt or freshly ground black pepper.

continued on page 72

continued from page 71

 GLUTEN-FREE ADAPTABLE Use a brand of beef broth that is known to be gluten-free.

TIPS When cooking with red wine, choose a wine that you'd enjoy drinking too. Cabernet Sauvignon works well in this recipe.

If you don't have a slow cooker, prepare the soup in a Dutch oven instead. Follow the same instructions and let it simmer over low heat until the lentils are tender, 35 to 45 minutes.

MAKE-AHEAD TIP Prepare everything and place it into the pot of your slow cooker the night before (leaving out the lentils). The next day, just add the lentils and continue the slow-cooking process as instructed.

CHANGE IT UP!

Swap out onions for the leeks.

Change the flavor of the soup by using fresh thyme or rosemary in place of the oregano. Or use a combination of herbs.

Swiss chard is another great addition to this soup. Leave out the ribs and chop the leaves. Add it to the soup in the end and leave out the spinach.

new england clam chowdah

Makes: 6 servings   Prep Time: 20 minutes   Cook Time: 20 minutes

The best clam chowder (chowdah) out there is at Haddad's Ocean Café in Brant Rock, Massachusetts. Owner Chuck Haddad tells me that the secret is lots and lots of buttah! As much as I want to use a ton of butter in my recipe, there's only so much I can add before I start thinking of how tight my jeans are going to fit the next day. This is my family's special recipe for clam chowder that we've eaten and enjoyed for many years now. I've added a twist or two to our original recipe to make it cookbook-worthy and comparable to (or dare I say, better than?) Haddad's chowder.

SOUP

1	tablespoon salted butter
1	cup diced onion
1	cup diced celery
2	cups diced unpeeled red potato
1	8-ounce bottled clam juice
2	6-ounce cans clams, juice reserved
½	teaspoon salt

WHITE SAUCE

8	tablespoons (1 stick) salted butter
½	cup all-purpose flour
2	cups half-and-half
2	cups whole milk
2	bay leaves
½	tablespoon chopped fresh thyme
¼	teaspoon salt
⅛	teaspoon freshly ground black pepper

TOPPINGS (OPTIONAL)

6	slices of bacon, cooked and crumbled (see Tips)
	Red wine vinegar

To prepare the soup, in a large saucepan, melt the butter over medium heat. Add the onion and celery and cook, stirring, until the vegetables begin to soften, 3 to 4 minutes. Add the potato, bottled clam juice and the reserved juice from the cans of clams. Add just enough water to cover the vegetables. Stir in the salt. Bring the liquid to a simmer, reduce the heat to low and continue to simmer until the potatoes are tender, 8 to 10 minutes.

While the potatoes are simmering, prepare the white sauce. In another large saucepan, melt the butter over medium heat. Whisk the flour into the butter. Slowly whisk in the half-and-half and milk. Add the bay leaves. Turn the heat up to medium-high and bring to a boil, whisking often until slightly thickened, 3 to 5 minutes.

Add the white sauce to the rest of the soup. Simmer over low heat, adding the clams, thyme, salt and pepper. Simmer until the soup is heated through, 3 to 4 minutes. Ladle the soup into bowls and top with crumbled bacon and drizzle of red wine vinegar, if desired.

continued on page 74

continued from page 73

GF GLUTEN-FREE ADAPTABLE Use ¼ cup cornstarch, tapioca starch or potato starch in place of the all-purpose flour. Mix it with a little bit of the cream before adding it to the soup. Use a brand of bacon that is known to be gluten-free.

TIPS Use 1 cup fresh clams in place of canned clams if you'd like. You'll need an additional ½ cup clam juice.

For easy clean-up, cook your bacon in the oven. Preheat the oven to 400°F. Line a large, rimmed baking sheet with foil and place a rack on top. Spray the rack with nonstick spray. Lay the bacon slices on the rack. Bake for 15 to 20 minutes, or until the bacon is crisp. Timing will vary depending on the thickness of your bacon.

CHANGE IT UP!

Lighten up this soup by using 2 cups of whole milk and 2 cups of nonfat milk (in place of the cream/whole milk combo). Your soup won't be quite as creamy and thick, but you'll still get that great flavor.

Hollow out small loaves of sourdough bread and serve the soup in the sourdough bowls. Soup-eaters can tear apart the bowl and eat up the bread too!

italian vegetable soup

Makes: 8 servings   Prep Time: 30 minutes   Cook Time: 25 minutes

I love my pasta, and I love my Mexican food, and I especially love my desserts. But every once in a while, my body needs a little time to detox. A hearty, healthy soup is just the ticket for that sort of thing. It must be a soup that is chock-full of vegetables and beans, and maybe even a little potato, all gathered together in a rich and flavorful broth. This vegetable soup does the trick. It's filling and detoxifyingly delicious. If you happen to have a good hunk of crusty bread nearby for soaking up the remnants of the broth, that makes it even better.

1	tablespoon olive oil
½	large onion, chopped
2	large leeks (white and light green parts), thinly sliced and rinsed well
4	medium garlic cloves, minced
2	cups chopped zucchini (2 medium)
2	cups chopped carrot (3 medium)
2	cups cabbage, thinly sliced (¼ head)
3	14.5-ounce cans low-sodium chicken broth
2	14.5-ounce cans petite diced tomatoes
1	15-ounce can white beans, rinsed and drained
1	large potato, peeled and chopped (about 1½ cups)
3	cups thinly sliced kale or Swiss chard (ribs removed)
1	cup fresh or frozen corn kernels
1	tablespoon finely chopped fresh oregano or basil
1	teaspoon salt
½	teaspoon freshly ground black pepper
1	cup freshly grated Parmesan cheese

In a large saucepan, heat the olive oil over medium heat. Add the onion and leeks and cook, stirring, until softened, 3 to 4 minutes. Add the garlic and cook for 1 additional minute. Add the zucchini, carrot and cabbage and cook, stirring often, until slightly softened, 3 to 4 minutes. Stir in the broth, tomatoes, beans and potato. Bring the mixture to a boil, then reduce the heat to low and simmer until the potatoes are tender, 7 to 10 minutes. Stir in the kale, corn, oregano, salt and pepper. Cook until the kale is wilted and soft, 3 to 4 minutes. Ladle the soup into bowls and sprinkle with the cheese.

GF **GLUTEN-FREE ADAPTABLE** Use brands of broth and beans that are known to be gluten-free.

TIP Chopping vegetables early in the day makes preparing dinner a snap. Just chop everything (except potatoes) and keep in covered bowls in the refrigerator until you're ready to make the soup!

CHANGE IT UP!

Add ½ cup Marsala wine to the soup to give it more depth of flavor, or add a tablespoon of Marsala to individual servings, as desired.

Red cabbage works equally well in this soup and it adds beautiful color too.

Contribute more vegetable favorites to this soup, or create your own mix. Green beans, winter squash and yellow squash are suggested.

butternut squash soup with pancetta and crispy sage

Makes: 4 servings   Prep Time: 30 minutes   Cook Time: 35 minutes

I'm pretty sure I could live on butternut squash and butternut squash alone. I'd happily mash roasted squash into my oatmeal (well not really, but for the sake of the story . . .), I'd eat roasted butternut squash with sage and garlic and goat cheese for lunch, and I'd eat butternut squash soup for dinner. Something tells me that my family wouldn't let me dump my butternut squash obsession on them, but on the rare occasion that I have a weekend to myself, it's all about butternut squash. This is my favorite soup recipe in the book. The soup is mildly sweet and the crunch of pancetta and sage is just perfect sprinkled on top.

SOUP

1	tablespoon olive oil
½	cup sliced shallot
1	teaspoon minced garlic
¼	cup dry white wine
2	14-ounce cans low-sodium chicken broth
8	cups chopped butternut squash (about 3 pounds)
1	tablespoon maple syrup
	Salt and freshly ground black pepper, to taste

TOPPINGS

4	ounces pancetta, chopped
¼	cup julienned sage (see Tips)

CHANGE IT UP!

If you prefer not to have a mildly sweet soup, leave out the maple syrup. Or better yet, taste the soup as prepared and then add a teaspoon of maple syrup at a time until you end up with the sweetness you prefer.

To prepare the soup, in a large, deep skillet, heat the olive oil over medium heat. Add the shallot and cook, stirring, until lightly browned and softened, 3 to 5 minutes. Add the garlic and cook for an additional 1 minute. Add the wine to deglaze the skillet, scraping up any browned bits from the bottom. Add the broth and then stir in the squash. Bring to a boil, then reduce the heat to low and simmer until the squash becomes tender (see Tips), 20 to 30 minutes. Remove the skillet from heat and let the mixture cool for 15 minutes.

To prepare the toppings, heat a medium skillet to medium heat. Add the pancetta and cook and stir until browned and crispy, 4 to 5 minutes. When the pancetta is crisp, add in the sage and stir until the sage is crispy, an additional 1 minute. Use a slotted spoon to remove the pancetta and sage to a paper towel–lined plate. Let it cool and drain until you are ready to serve the soup.

Scoop half of the cooked squash and broth into a food processor or blender. Process until smooth. Transfer the pureed soup to a large saucepan. Repeat with the remaining squash and broth. Stir in the maple syrup and season to taste with salt and pepper. Heat the soup over medium heat until heated through, 4 to 5 minutes Serve cups or bowls of soup with a sprinkle of pancetta and crispy sage on top.

GF GLUTEN-FREE ADAPTABLE Use brands of broth, maple syrup and pancetta that are known to be gluten-free.

V VEGETARIAN-ADAPTABLE Use vegetable broth in place of the chicken broth and leave out the pancetta.

TIPS Tender squash means that you can stick a fork in it gently and it pierces the squash without too much pressure. It should be soft but not mushy.

To julienne the sage, place several leaves on top of each other in a pile. Use a sharp knife to cut the sage lengthwise to result in long thin strips of fresh sage.

roasted carrot and sweet potato soup

Makes: 6 servings   Prep Time: 30 minutes   Cook Time: 1 hour and 10 minutes

Carrots are typically thought of as a rather boring vegetable. Kids dunk them in Ranch dressing to make them taste better, they're added to salads for color and people take them obligatorily from vegetable platters. But roast these earthy orange things in the oven with a drizzle of olive oil and they turn into sweet vegetables that are delightful and slightly addictive. The combined flavors of roasted carrots and baked sweet potato make for a satisfying and healthy soup. Even carrot naysayers would agree.

6   large carrots (about 1 pound), tops trimmed off and peeled

1½   tablespoons olive oil

1   teaspoon kosher salt + more to taste

¼   teaspoon freshly ground black pepper + more to taste

1   large orange-fleshed sweet potato (about 1 pound), cut in half, pierced with a fork and each half wrapped in foil

2   tablespoons salted butter

¾   cup chopped onion (about ½ medium)

1   teaspoon minced garlic (about 1 large clove)

3   cups vegetable broth + more as needed (see Tips)

½   tablespoon chopped fresh thyme

¼   teaspoon ground cumin
     Lemon wedges for serving, optional

Preheat the oven to 375°F. Spray a rimmed baking sheet with nonstick spray.

Cut the carrots into 3-inch chunks. Cut any larger pieces vertically so that they are mostly uniform in size. Place the carrots in the prepared pan and toss with the olive oil. Sprinkle with the 1 teaspoon salt and the ¼ teaspoon pepper. Add the wrapped potatoes to the baking sheet. Bake for 1 hour, stirring the carrots every 20 minutes (see Tips).

In a large, deep skillet, melt the butter over medium heat. Add the onion and cook, stirring, until softened and golden brown, 4 to 5 minutes. Add the garlic and cook, stirring, for an additional 1 minute. Add the broth and thyme. Remove from heat and stir to combine.

Add half of the carrots, one potato half, and half of the broth mixture to a food processor. Process until smooth. Transfer the pureed soup to a large saucepan. Repeat with the remaining carrots, potato half and broth. Stir in the cumin and add salt and pepper, to taste. Heat the soup over medium heat until heated through, 3 to 5 minutes. Serve bowls of soup with lemon wedges for squeezing, if desired.

GF GLUTEN-FREE ADAPTABLE Use a brand of broth that is known to be gluten-free.

DF DAIRY-FREE ADAPTABLE Use olive oil in place of butter to cook the onions.

TIPS Stir in additional broth if your soup appears to be too thick.

Keep an eye on your carrots. If they become tender and lightly browned before the 1 hour time given, remove the carrots from the oven and leave the potato roasting for the remaining time.

This soup may be prepared 1 to 2 days ahead and then warmed up when ready to serve. Leftovers are almost better than eating the same day since the flavors have a chance to intensify upon sitting.

CHANGE IT UP!

Turn this into a creamy soup by stirring in half-and-half or whipping cream.

Stir in a little bit of honey to give this soup more sweetness.

macaroni and cheese soup with roasted cherry tomatoes

Makes: 4 servings   Prep Time: 30 minutes   Cook Time: 35 minutes

I think we can all pretty much agree that macaroni and cheese is the ultimate in comfort food, right? It's rich and velvety and cheesy and ooey and gooey and over-the-top. Eating macaroni and cheese provides comfort in the sense that it quenches one's desire to eat something so incredibly irresistible. In this recipe, macaroni makes an appearance in a creamy cheese soup, and it's topped off with lightly roasted tomatoes. Now that qualifies as some good comfort food right there, doesn't it?

TOMATOES

12	cherry tomatoes, cut in half (see Tips)
1	tablespoon olive oil
	Salt and freshly ground black pepper

SOUP

2	tablespoons salted butter
2	teaspoons minced garlic (about 3 cloves)
2	tablespoons all-purpose flour
6	cups vegetable broth
1	bay leaf
1	cup dry macaroni elbows
1	cup whipping cream
1	tablespoon Dijon mustard
1	teaspoon Worcestershire sauce
½	teaspoon Tabasco sauce
½	teaspoon white pepper
8	ounces shredded extra-sharp cheddar cheese

To roast the tomatoes, preheat the oven to 425°F. Place the tomatoes, cut side up, on a rimmed baking sheet. Drizzle with the olive oil and sprinkle with salt and pepper. Roast the tomatoes for 12 minutes. Remove them from the oven and let them cool at room temperature while you prepare the soup.

To prepare the soup, in large saucepan, melt the butter over medium heat. Add the garlic and cook, stirring, until softened and fragrant, about 1 minute. Whisk in the flour. Slowly whisk in the vegetable broth and add the bay leaf. Increase the heat to high and bring the broth to a boil. Add the macaroni and boil until it is almost tender, about 8 minutes. Remove the bay leaf and discard. Stir in the cream, mustard, Worcestershire sauce, Tabasco sauce and pepper. Add the cheese and continue to stir until the cheese is completely melted. Bring the soup to a boil again for 2 minutes, stirring occasionally, then remove it from heat. Ladle the soup into serving bowls and top with the roasted tomatoes.

TIPS Smaller cherry tomatoes or pear tomatoes work best for this recipe. Larger cherry tomatoes may need a slightly longer roasting time or you may wish to cut them in fourths.

If you refrigerate leftovers, the pasta will have more of a chance to soak up the liquid in the soup, leaving you with a wonderfully creamy macaroni and cheese.

CHANGE IT UP!

The great thing about macaroni and cheese is that you can experiment with some other cheeses that are equally delicious and are perfect for melting. Try using Gruyère, Fontina or smoked Gouda (or a combination).

manly man chili

Makes: 8 servings   Prep Time: 25 minutes   Cook Time: 1 hour and 15 minutes

When we moved into our neighborhood, everything was new. It was a newly developed area with new houses, a new school, new strip malls and a new fire station. It was also Super Bowl weekend. Being the friendly neighbors that we were, we invited our local firefighters to stop by, watch the game with us and partake in consuming copious amounts of chili. They obliged. The firefighters ate some chili and then they asked for seconds. They remarked that my chili was so astoundingly irresistible because it was full of meat, it had a smoky flavor and it was topped with bacon. From there on out, I dubbed my meaty chili as Manly Man (firefighter-approved) Chili.

2	tablespoons olive oil
2	pounds sirloin or round steak, trimmed and chopped
1	pound hot Italian sausage
1	large onion, chopped
4	large garlic cloves, minced
2	14.5-ounce cans fire-roasted tomatoes
2	12-ounce bottles beer
2	8-ounce cans tomato sauce
⅔	cup barbecue sauce (see Tips)
2	large green bell peppers, seeded, ribs removed and finely chopped
2	large jalapeños, seeded, ribs removed and finely chopped
2	tablespoons chili powder
4	teaspoons ground cumin
2	teaspoons ground coriander
2	teaspoons smoked paprika
2	teaspoons dried oregano
½	teaspoon cayenne pepper
½	teaspoon freshly ground black pepper
¼	teaspoon salt
4	cups shredded sharp cheddar cheese
2	cups sour cream
1	pound bacon, cooked and crumbled (see Tips)

In a large, deep skillet, heat the olive oil over medium heat. Add the steak, sausage and onion and cook, stirring often to break up the meat, until it is cooked through and no longer pink, 6 to 8 minutes. Add the garlic and continue to stir and cook for 1 minute. Add the tomatoes, beer, tomato sauce, barbecue sauce, bell peppers, jalapeños, chili powder, cumin, coriander, paprika, oregano, cayenne, black pepper and salt and stir to combine. Bring the mixture to a boil and then reduce the heat to low. Cover the skillet and simmer until the chili has thickened, about 1 hour. Serve in bowls and top with the cheese, sour cream and crumbled bacon.

GF GLUTEN-FREE ADAPTABLE Use 1½ cups of (gluten-free) beef broth in place of the beer. Use brands of barbecue sauce and bacon that are known to be gluten-free.

DF DAIRY-FREE ADAPTABLE Leave out the cheese and sour cream.

TIPS The barbecue sauce that you choose to use will make an impact on the flavor of the chili. I like to choose a sauce that has a smoky flavor to it.

For easy clean-up, cook your bacon in the oven. Preheat the oven to 400°F. Line a large, rimmed baking sheet with foil and place a rack on top. Spray the rack with nonstick spray. Lay the bacon slices on the rack. Bake for 15 to 20 minutes, or until the bacon is crisp. Timing will vary depending on the thickness of your bacon.

CHANGE IT UP!

If you'd like to turn up the heat on this chili, add an additional chopped jalapeño and increase the cayenne pepper to ½ teaspoon.

Add kidney or pinto beans to the mix if you'd like to make this a beef and bean chili.

Try serving this chili over a handful of corn chips too.

grilled shrimp and vegetable salad with lemon-basil vinaigrette

Makes: 6 servings   Prep Time: 25 minutes   Cook Time: 12 minutes

Summer is the perfect time to take advantage of getting the most out of fresh vegetables and grilling. Do all of the chopping of the ingredients for this one ahead of time, and then throw it all together when you're ready to grill and serve. It's great as a main-dish salad, and it's equally delicious when served as a side-dish salad to grilled meats.

SHRIMP AND VEGGIES

- 1½ pounds large shrimp, peeled, deveined and tails removed
- 2 medium red bell peppers, seeded, ribs removed and cut into large pieces
- 2 medium zucchini, ends trimmed off and sliced lengthwise
- 2 tablespoons olive oil
- Salt and freshly ground black pepper

VINAIGRETTE

- 3 tablespoons minced fresh basil
- 2½ tablespoons freshly squeezed lemon juice
- 2 tablespoons olive oil
- 2 medium garlic cloves, minced
- 1 teaspoon granulated white sugar
- ½ teaspoon freshly grated lemon zest
- Salt and freshly ground black pepper, to taste

SALAD

- 6 cups mixed greens

Preheat the grill to medium heat.

To prepare the shrimp and vegetables, add them to a medium bowl and toss with the olive oil and a generous sprinkle of salt and pepper. Place a grill basket on top of your grill and add the shrimp and vegetables (see Tips). Grill until the shrimp is pink, curled up and cooked all the way through and until the vegetables are softened and blackened on the edges. Transfer the shrimp and vegetables to a cutting board. Chop the vegetables into bite-size pieces and transfer the shrimp and vegetables to a medium bowl.

To prepare the vinaigrette, in a small bowl, whisk together the vinaigrette ingredients. Drizzle the vinaigrette over the shrimp and vegetables and toss to coat. If you are not serving the salad right away, cover the bowl with plastic wrap and keep it refrigerated. When you're ready to serve, place the greens in a large salad bowl and scoop the shrimp and vegetables on top. Toss and serve.

TIPS If you don't have a grill basket, place the vegetables directly on the grill and string the shrimp onto skewers for easy grilling.

This is a great make-ahead salad. I prefer to serve it cold, so I grill the vegetables and shrimp in the morning and let them marinate in the vinaigrette all day long.

CHANGE IT UP!

Substitute 1½ pounds scallops or chicken (cut into bite-size pieces) for the shrimp.

broiled salmon with sweet and spicy pineapple slaw

Makes: 4 servings   Prep Time: 25 minutes   Cook Time: 10 minutes

I think it was my sister who first introduced me to the beauty of salmon. Of course, she lives in the Northwest, where they truly have the best salmon of anywhere I've ever been, and that probably prompted me to declare my love for it right then and there. To this day, salmon is my favorite go-to quick dinner. I enjoy it lightly seasoned with a little added sweetness and broiled, and it's terrific when paired with a simple sweet slaw.

SLAW

5	cups finely shredded cabbage (about ½ small head)
1½	cups finely chopped canned pineapple (reserve 2 tablespoons juice for dressing)
1	medium red bell pepper, seeded, ribs removed and cut into very thin strips
1	large carrot, peeled and shredded
½	medium red onion, very thinly sliced (about 1 cup)

DRESSING

2	tablespoons pineapple juice (from canned pineapples for slaw)
½	tablespoon canola or vegetable oil
2	teaspoons honey
1	teaspoon freshly squeezed lime juice
¼	teaspoon hot sauce
⅛	teaspoon salt
⅛	teaspoon freshly ground black pepper

SALMON

4	6-ounce skinless salmon fillets, rinsed and patted dry
¼	cup honey
1	tablespoon freshly squeezed lime juice
1	teaspoon chili powder
⅛	teaspoon cayenne pepper
⅛	teaspoon salt

To prepare the slaw, in a large bowl, toss together the slaw ingredients.

To prepare the dressing, in a small bowl, whisk together the dressing ingredients.

Pour the dressing over the slaw and toss. Set the slaw aside while you prepare the salmon.

Preheat the oven to broil. Spray a small roasting pan or Pyrex dish with nonstick spray.

To prepare the salmon, place the salmon in the pan. In a small bowl, whisk together the honey, lime juice, chili powder, cayenne and salt. Spoon the sauce over the salmon. Broil the salmon for 5 minutes and then spoon the sauce over the salmon again. Broil for an additional 5 to 7 minutes, or until the salmon flakes easily with a fork and is cooked through to the center.

To serve, toss the slaw one more time to reincorporate the dressing. Divide the slaw among 4 bowls. Top the slaw with the broiled salmon and serve immediately.

MAKE-AHEAD TIP This recipe can be quickly assembled by doing all of your chopping and shredding in advance (up to 1 day). The dressing may also be prepared the day before serving.

turkey and cranberry salad with toasted pecans and smoked gouda

Makes: 4 servings   Prep Time: 20 minutes

The day after Thanksgiving for our family has always been about eating open-faced turkey sandwiches covered with mashed potatoes, bits of stuffing, hot gravy and a glob of cranberry sauce. As much as I love the glitz and glam of that horribly delicious mess, I'm also very ready to eat a little bit lighter on the day after Turkey Day. That's where this salad recipe comes in handy. It's reminiscent of Thanksgiving with the inclusion of roasted turkey and dried cranberries, but it's jazzed up with the addition of smoked Gouda and apple. Serving it all on a bed of fresh spinach with a light vinaigrette will help you get back on track after stuffing yourself with stuffing.

DRESSING
- 2 tablespoons canola or vegetable oil
- 2 tablespoons apple cider vinegar
- 1 tablespoon finely chopped shallot
- 1 tablespoon freshly squeezed lemon juice
- 1 tablespoon maple syrup
- 1/8 teaspoon salt
- 1/8 teaspoon freshly ground black pepper

SALAD
- 8 cups baby spinach
- 1½ cups chopped roasted turkey
- 1 large Red Delicious apple, cored and chopped (unpeeled)
- ¾ cup ½-inch cubed smoked Gouda cheese
- ½ cup dried cranberries
- ½ cup chopped pecans, toasted (see Tips)

To prepare the dressing, in a small bowl, whisk together the dressing ingredients.

To prepare the salad, in a large bowl, toss together the salad ingredients.

Drizzle the dressing on top and toss. Serve immediately.

GF GLUTEN-FREE ADAPTABLE Use a brand of maple syrup that is known to be gluten-free. Make sure that your roasted turkey does not contain any gluten.

DF DAIRY-FREE ADAPTABLE Leave out the cheese.

TIP To toast the pecans, preheat the oven to 350°F. Spread the pecans on a baking sheet. Toast them in the oven just until they become lightly browned and scented, 3 to 5 minutes. Watch them closely—if they are left in the oven too long, they will go from toasted to burnt in a matter of a minute or two.

> **CHANGE IT UP!**
>
> Use roasted chicken in place of the turkey and substitute dried currants for the cranberries.
>
> Use sugared pecans instead of toasted: Add the pecans to a small skillet. Heat over medium heat and add ¼ cup granulated white sugar. Stir constantly until the sugar melts and coats the pecans. Remove the nuts from heat and spread them on a baking sheet to cool. Break the nuts apart and add them to the salad.

grilled romaine with blue cheese, tomato and bacon

Makes: 4 servings   Prep Time: 25 minutes   Cook Time: 5 minutes

My insane love-affair with all-things-bacon is almost as great as my love for blue cheese. I love to break off chunks of it and taste it all on its own, I love to pair it with fresh figs and honey and call it an appetizer and I love to toss it into risotto or nibble it with roast beef. But most of all, I adore blue cheese in salads. This salad takes the best of both worlds and combines bacon and blue cheese together.

DRESSING
¼   cup blue cheese crumbles
¼   cup mayonnaise
2   tablespoons freshly
      squeezed lemon juice
      Salt and freshly ground
      black pepper, to taste

GREENS
4   hearts of romaine (see Tips)
2   tablespoons extra-virgin olive
      oil
      Salt and freshly ground
      black pepper

TOPPINGS
6   bacon slices, cooked until
      crisp and crumbled into
      chunks (see Tips)
1   pint cherry or pear tomatoes,
      halved (about 2 cups)
      Additional blue cheese
      crumbles

To prepare the dressing, in a medium bowl, mix the blue cheese, mayonnaise, lemon juice and a sprinkle of salt and pepper, mashing the blue cheese crumbles into the mayonnaise. Cover the bowl with plastic wrap and refrigerate the dressing while you prepare the rest of the salad.

Preheat the grill to medium heat. Oil the grill grates.

To prepare the greens, drizzle the romaine hearts with olive oil and sprinkle with salt and pepper. Place the romaine on the grill and heat just until the romaine is slightly charred and slightly wilted on all sides, 3 or 4 minutes. Remove the romaine from the grill and place each heart on a serving plate.

Top each romaine heart with dressing, bacon, tomatoes and blue cheese crumbles.

GF GLUTEN-FREE ADAPTABLE Use feta or goat cheese in place of the blue cheese and use brands of mayonnaise and bacon that are known to be gluten-free.

TIPS Romaine hearts are the center leaves of romaine lettuce. Look for them sold in packages in your market's produce section.

For easy clean-up, cook your bacon in the oven. Preheat the oven to 400°F. Line a large, rimmed baking sheet with foil and place a rack on top. Spray the rack with nonstick spray. Lay the bacon slices on the rack. Bake for 15 to 20 minutes, or until the bacon is crisp. Timing will vary depending on the thickness of your bacon.

CHANGE IT UP!

If you're not a fan of blue cheese, replace it with feta or goat cheese instead.

If you don't wish to grill the romaine, chop it up instead and serve it with the same toppings.

chopped chicken and couscous salad with sweet basil dressing

Makes: 4 servings   Prep Time: 35 minutes

Chopped salads have made the rounds over the years, usually making an appearance as an Italian chopped or a chopped Cobb. I happen to prefer the "chopped" version of a salad. You see, when everything is chopped finely, the chances of all of the salad ingredients making it into a single forkful are pretty darn good. This means you get to taste the flavors of the entire salad in each and every bite. I have a favorite to-go salad that I purchase at one of my favorite markets (Trader Joe's) every chance I get. I'm obsessed with the crunch and the sweet of it all and, if it's chopped finely enough, you get the whole salad in every bite. Here's my at-home version of that favorite salad.

DRESSING
½ cup mayonnaise
2 tablespoons finely chopped fresh basil
1 tablespoon prepared pesto sauce
1 tablespoon water
2 teaspoons freshly squeezed lemon juice
1 teaspoon honey
⅛ teaspoon salt
⅛ teaspoon freshly ground black pepper

SALAD
4 cups finely chopped romaine lettuce
2 cups finely chopped roasted chicken
2 cups corn kernels (see Tips)
2 cups finely chopped red cabbage
1 cup dry Israeli couscous, cooked according to package directions, then cooled (see Tips)
1 medium red bell pepper, seeded, ribs removed and finely chopped
½ cup freshly grated Parmesan cheese
½ cup dried currants
½ cup finely chopped pecans

To prepare the dressing, in a small bowl, whisk together the dressing ingredients. If the dressing seems too thick, whisk in more water, 1 teaspoon at a time, until you get a consistency that you're happy with. It should be creamy and thick but pourable, too.

To prepare the salad, in a large bowl, toss together all of the salad ingredients.

Add the dressing and toss to coat. Divide the salad among 4 bowls and serve.

TIP Fresh corn is fabulous in this salad. Just cut it right off the cob and add raw corn kernels into the salad. Two good-size cobs should be enough to make 2 cups of corn kernels.

continued on page 90

continued from page 89

Israeli couscous (also known as pearl couscous) is twice as large as the smaller, more familiar couscous and it's toasted rather than dried. This gives it a nutty flavor and a chewy bite, which makes it more appropriate for mixing into salads where it can stand its ground among all of the other salad ingredients. You can usually find the Israeli variety where you'd normally find regular couscous.

If you prefer, you can serve the dressing on the side so that individual eaters can add their own salad dressing.

CHANGE IT UP!

Turn this into a day-after-Thanksgiving salad by using chopped turkey in place of the chicken, wild rice in place of the couscous and dried cranberries in place of the currants.

gruyère grilled cheese with arugula, white wine and whole grain mustard

Makes: 1 sandwich   Prep Time: 15 minutes   Cook Time: 8 minutes

Grilled cheese is comfort food at its best. All of that melted cheese can make anyone feel good. Even a simple, toasted sandwich of just cheese and buttered bread can send one's heart aflutter. I've created an adult version here. This sandwich sneaks in a swipe of white wine, peppery arugula and a smidgen of cream cheese too. It should give you plenty of comfort.

1   tablespoon salted butter, at room temperature
2   slices bread (see Tips)
½   tablespoon white wine (see Tips)
½   tablespoon whole grain mustard
4   thin slices Gruyère or Swiss cheese, divided
⅓   cup arugula
2   thin slices tomato
1   tablespoon softened cream cheese

Spread ½ tablespoon of the butter on each slice of bread. Set the bread slices butter side down on a cutting board. Brush one slice with the white wine and then mustard. Top with two slices of the Gruyère, breaking it apart as needed to cover the whole piece of bread. Layer the arugula and tomato on top of the Gruyère. Add the remaining slices of Gruyère on top of the tomato. Spread the second slice of bread with cream cheese and place it cream cheese side down on top of the tomato.

Heat a skillet to medium and spray with nonstick spray. Place the sandwich in the skillet and cover with a lid. Reduce the heat to medium-low. Cook for 3 to 4 minutes, then remove the lid and use a spatula to take a peek underneath the sandwich. When the bottom of the sandwich has turned golden brown, flip it over. Cover the skillet again and cook until the other side is golden too, an additional 3 to 4 minutes. Remove the pan from heat and let the sandwich sit for 2 minutes in the hot pan. Transfer the sandwich to a cutting board, cut it in half and serve immediately.

TIPS My favorite types of bread to use for this grilled cheese are a thin-sliced French or sourdough.

Leave off the wine if you don't wish to use alcohol in the sandwich.

CHANGE IT UP!

Use your favorite kinds of cheese in this sandwich. It's equally good with provolone or Jack or cheddar.

Other great grilled cheese add-ins are prosciutto, bacon and Dijon mustard.

root beer pulled pork sandwiches

Makes: 10 sandwiches   Prep Time: 25 minutes   Cook Time: 11 hours and 30 minutes

When I was pregnant with my son, there was one thing I craved beyond any other: root beer. I searched high and low for the best root beer in the land. I tried the artisan sorts as well as the generics. It all came back to Mug. Mug root beer was the one that seemed to satisfy my craving the most. No longer pregnant, I still crave the stuff, and it makes a good cooking marinade for pulled pork too. This recipe serves a large crowd or a hungry family with leftovers for days to come.

1   5- to 6-pound bone-in pork shoulder butt roast
1   1-ounce envelope dried onion soup mix
     Salt and freshly ground black pepper
1   12-ounce can root beer (I prefer Mug brand)
2   cups barbecue sauce, divided
10   regular-size hamburger buns, your favorite kind

Trim the pork roast of excess fat. It's okay to leave some on there—just get rid of the large, visible slabs. Place the roast on a work surface and sprinkle it with the onion soup mix. Use clean hands to rub the mix into the meat, reaching underneath to coat all sides. Sprinkle generously with salt and pepper. Place the seasoned roast in your slow cooker.

In a medium bowl, whisk together the root beer and ½ cup of the barbecue sauce. Pour over the roast in the slow cooker.

Cover and cook on low heat for 10 to 11 hours, or until the internal temperature is above 190°F and the meat is tender enough to pull away from the bone. Remove the roast to a cutting board and let cool for a few minutes. Pour out and discard all but about ¾ cup of the juices from the slow cooker. Use 2 forks to shred the pork, cutting around and discarding any fatty pieces. Place all of the pulled pork back into your slow cooker with the reserved juices. Add the remaining 1½ cups of barbecue sauce. Stir to combine and place the lid back on. Cook on high heat for 15 to 20 minutes, just until the pork and juices are hot and bubbly. Meanwhile preheat the oven to 200°F. Split the buns and place cut side up on a baking sheet. Warm in the oven until you are ready to serve.

Scoop the pulled pork onto the warmed buns and serve immediately.

TIPS If you don't wish to make such a large roast, use the same ingredients for a smaller roast too. Cut down a bit on the cooking time and use less barbecue sauce when adding it in at the end.

For tender pulled pork, I do not recommend trying to short-cut the recipe by cooking it on high heat. Low and slow is best!

CHANGE IT UP!

Use cola in place of root beer.

Mound some coleslaw on top of the pulled pork to create a deli-style sandwich.

lemon-scented lobster rolls

Makes: 2 lobster rolls   Prep Time: 10 minutes

The Lobster Roll is a New England specialty—a favorite that you'll see made all different ways. What business does a California girl have telling the world how to make a lobster roll? Probably none. But I spend a few weeks every summer in Massachusetts, where lobsters are boiled and torn apart into lobster rolls quite often in my kitchen. I like mine fairly simple. That wonderful lobster taste should be paired with just a few flavors to enhance it. Lobster rolls are best when served with potato chips and ice cold beer.

2   cups chopped, cooked lobster meat
2   teaspoons mayonnaise
    Sprinkle of sea salt
2   grinds freshly ground black pepper
1   teaspoon freshly squeezed lemon juice
½   teaspoon grated lemon zest
2   hot dog rolls, toasted (see Tips)

In a medium bowl, stir together the lobster, mayonnaise, salt, pepper, lemon juice and zest.

Divide the lobster mixture between the two hot dog buns and serve immediately.

TIPS I like to toast the buns by spreading a little bit of butter on them and then toasting them butter side down in a large, heated skillet.

If you live in New England, by all means use the wonderful New England style hot dog buns that are available to you. For the rest of the world, just use your favorite sort of hot dog bun.

CHANGE IT UP!

Add in chopped celery and green onions to create a little crunch in your sandwich.

avocado-topped hot dogs with creamy chipotle sauce

Makes: 8 hot dogs   Prep Time: 15 minutes   Cook Time: 10 minutes

Avocado lovers, I have the perfect hot dog for you. The very idea of adding avocado to a hot dog may sound strange to some. But if you're a lover of this green and velvety fruit, then you simply must trust me. My own husband was once a naysayer, and now he's disappointed if I just make plain old dogs. These hot dogs are topped with a mild chipotle sauce, tomato, avocado and a salty crumbled Mexican cheese called Cojita.

CHIPOTLE SAUCE

- ¾ cup mayonnaise
- 2 teaspoons chipotle adobo sauce (see Tips)

HOT DOGS

- 8 good-quality hot dogs (I like Hebrew National or Nathan's)
- 8 hot dog buns
- 4 tablespoons (½ stick) salted butter, at room temperature
- 1 cup chopped tomato
- 2 large avocados, pitted, peeled and chopped
- ½ cup crumbled Cojita cheese (see Tips)

Preheat the grill to medium heat.

To prepare the chipotle sauce, in a medium bowl whisk together the mayonnaise and chipotle sauce. Cover the bowl and keep in the refrigerator until you're ready to assemble the hot dogs.

To prepare the hot dogs, grill the hot dogs, turning often until they have grill marks on all sides, 5 to 7 minutes. Meanwhile, spread ½ tablespoon of the butter inside each bun. Grill the buns butter side down on the edges of the grill, where it's not so hot. Remove the buns from the grill when they are lightly browned, 1 to 2 minutes.

To assemble, place a hot dog in each toasted bun, then top each with 1½ tablespoons of the chipotle sauce. Divide the tomato, avocados and cheese among the dogs and serve immediately.

TIPS Chipotle sauce is the sauce found in a can of chipotle peppers with adobo sauce. It's found in the Latin-American products section of your market. Add some chopped chipotles too if you really like things spicy! Save the extra chipotle peppers and sauce by dividing them among a few zip baggies and tossing them in the freezer, where they will keep for 6 months or so.

If it's not grilling season, boil or fry the hot dogs and toast the buns in the oven instead.

Cojita cheese is a round-shaped Latin-American cheese, usually found near the cream cheese in your market. You may also use feta or goat cheese.

CHANGE IT UP!

Try adding chopped fresh cilantro to your hot dogs.

prosciutto and brie monte cristo sandwiches

Makes: 4 sandwiches   Prep Time: 25 minutes   Cook Time: 5 minutes

Some time ago, I sat in a lunchtime restaurant and perused my menu choices. I spotted a sandwich called a Monte Cristo and was immediately intrigued. It had a cool name, it was battered in egg and fried, and it was served alongside jam for dipping. I had never seen anything like it, so I ordered it for lunch. I fell in love with that sandwich, and I've never been able to stop thinking about it. It's no wonder that I included a version of it here.

8	¾-inch slices challah, about three-fourths of a 1-pound loaf (see Tips)
2	tablespoons whole grain mustard
8	ounces Brie, sliced
4	slices prosciutto or thinly sliced ham
¾	cup 1% milk
3	large eggs
2	tablespoons salted butter, divided
¼	cup seedless raspberry jam

Lay out four slices of bread on a cutting board. Spread ½ tablespoon of mustard on each slice. Top each slice with the cheese and prosciutto and then top each with a second slice of bread.

In a medium bowl, whisk together the milk and eggs.

In a large skillet melt 1 tablespoon of the butter over medium heat. Dip one of the sandwiches in the egg batter and coat both sides. Add the sandwich to the hot skillet. Repeat with a second sandwich. Cook the sandwiches for 3 to 4 minutes, or until the underside of the sandwiches have turned golden brown. Flip the sandwiches and cook until the other side is golden brown as well, an additional 2 to 3 minutes. Remove the sandwiches to a platter. Repeat with the remaining butter, sandwiches and egg batter. Serve warm with raspberry jam for dipping.

TIP Good bread is part of what makes this sandwich a success. Don't be tempted to use regular, old sandwich bread. Challah, brioche or another type of herb-free, sliceable loaf will work just fine.

CHANGE IT UP!

Substitute thinly sliced turkey or ham for the prosciutto.

Substitute Havarti cheese for the Brie if you'd like. Havarti is another great melting cheese that is delicious in this sandwich.

turkey sliders with bacon, avocado and homemade barbecue sauce

Makes: 12 sliders   Prep Time: 40 minutes   Cook Time: 35 minutes

If you're not familiar with the concept of a slider, it's simply an adorable, miniature burger. Approximately three sliders is the equivalent of a larger burger, making consumption of multiples an acceptable act. These sliders are made with a combination of ground turkey and sweet Italian sausage. Topped with a smidgen of homemade barbecue sauce, a strip of crispy bacon and sliced avocado, eating only one is just not an option.

BURGERS
¾	pound ground turkey
½	pound sweet Italian sausage
⅔	cup bread crumbs
3	tablespoons milk
1	large egg, slightly beaten
2	teaspoons minced garlic
	Salt and freshly ground black pepper

TOPPINGS AND BUNS
12	2 x 2-inch slices sharp cheddar cheese
12	slider buns or 12 small dinner rolls
3	slices bacon, cut into thirds and cooked until crisp (see Tips)
1	large avocado, pitted, peeled and cut into thin slices

BARBECUE SAUCE
1	cup ketchup
¼	cup cider vinegar
1	tablespoon molasses
1	tablespoon honey
1	tablespoon Dijon mustard
1	tablespoon water
½	teaspoon Worcestershire sauce
½	teaspoon salt
½	teaspoon freshly ground black pepper

Preheat the oven to 400°F. Spray a large, rimmed baking sheet with nonstick spray.

To prepare the burgers, place all of the burger ingredients in a medium bowl. Use a fork to gently stir the ingredients together until they are well combined. Shape the meat into twelve 3- to 4-inch burgers, using about ⅓ cup per burger, and place them on the prepared baking sheet. Bake the burgers for 30 to 35 minutes, or until they are browned and cooked through.

To prepare the barbecue sauce, in a medium saucepan, combine the sauce ingredients over medium-high heat and whisk them together until they are well combined. Bring to a boil, then reduce the heat and simmer for 10 minutes. Keep warm for serving with the sliders.

To assemble the sliders, add a slice of cheese to the top of each burger and warm in the oven for an additional 1 to 2 minutes, just until the cheese has melted. Divide the sauce among the 10 buns. Top with a slider, a slice of bacon and a slice or two of avocado. Serve immediately.

TIP While the burgers are in the oven, cook the bacon in a medium skillet over medium heat until crisp, 6 to 8 minutes. Remove the bacon to a paper towel–lined plate to drain.

MAKE-AHEAD TIP Prepare the barbecue sauce up to 2 days ahead. Keep it covered and refrigerated. On the same day of serving, shape the burger patties and place them on the baking sheet. Cover it with plastic wrap and refrigerate the patties until you are ready to bake them.

QUICK AND EASY TIP Use purchased barbecue sauce instead of making homemade.

CHANGE IT UP!

Throw the sliders on the grill instead of baking. Grill them over medium heat for 3 to 4 minutes per side, or until they are cooked through.

Consider other toppings for the sliders, such as grilled onions, tomatoes, peperoncini and different cheeses.

buffalo chicken wraps

Makes: 4 wraps   Prep Time: 25 minutes   Cook Time: 7 minutes

Buffalo wings make me think of college. There was a dive-restaurant near campus that was dedicated to serving up the most delicious spicy wings with accompaniments like blue cheese dressing and celery sticks. College makes me think of how many of those wings I consumed in those days, which most definitely contributed to my Freshman Fifteen. Thinking of that wing consumption makes me wish I still had access to those wings, and this Buffalo Chicken Wraps recipe is my wish come true in a sandwich.

BLUE CHEESE DRESSING
⅓   cup blue cheese crumbles
⅓   cup mayonnaise
2   tablespoons freshly
      squeezed lemon juice
      Salt and freshly ground
      black pepper, to taste

REMAINING INGREDIENTS
1   cup water
½   cup white rice
1   pound chicken tenders, cut
      into 1-inch pieces
⅓   cup cayenne pepper sauce
      (see Tips)
4   large flour tortillas or wraps,
      warmed
1½ cups chopped iceberg
      lettuce
1   cup chopped celery
1   cup finely chopped tomato
      Additional cayenne pepper
      sauce, optional

To prepare the dressing, in a medium bowl, mash together the blue cheese, mayonnaise, lemon juice and a sprinkle of salt and pepper. Set the dressing aside, or refrigerate until you're ready to assemble your wraps.

To prepare the remaining ingredients, bring the water to boil in a small saucepan over high heat. Add the rice. Cover, reduce the heat to medium and cook until the rice is tender and has soaked up all of the water, about 20 minutes.

Spray a medium skillet with nonstick spray and heat over medium heat. Add the chicken to the hot skillet and cook until lightly browned on all sides and no longer pink on the inside, 3 to 4 minutes per side. Remove the chicken from the pan and toss it in a medium bowl with the cayenne pepper sauce.

To assemble the wraps, wrap the tortillas in damp paper towels and microwave about 40 seconds. Lay the tortillas on a flat work surface and divide the chicken among them, placing the tenders down the middle of each tortilla. Divide the rice, lettuce, celery and tomato evenly among the tortillas. Add 1½ tablespoons of dressing to each wrap. Drizzle with more hot sauce, if desired.

Fold the bottom of the tortilla up and over the bottom fourth of the wrap. Then fold the left and right sides over the filling and hold to keep together (see Tips).

TIPS For the cayenne pepper sauce, I recommend Frank's brand, or you can also substitute a sauce that is specifically for Buffalo wings.

Iceberg lettuce adds a nice crunch to this wrap, but you can certainly use another kind of chopped lettuce if you'd like.

As you wrap each sandwich, you can take a piece of foil and wrap it around the bottom half of each wrap to help keep it together. This aids with eating as well since eaters won't have to battle with filling trying to squeeze out of the bottom of the tortillas.

CHANGE IT UP!

If you're not a fan of blue cheese, replace the blue cheese dressing with Ranch dressing and add shredded cheddar cheese to your wrap too.

Avocado fans: You might like to add in some freshly sliced avocado.

slow cooker french dip sandwiches with peppers and caramelized onions

Makes: 8 large sandwiches   Prep Time: 45 minutes   Cook Time: 12 hours

I learned how to roast beef when I was about 12 years old. Mom would lightly season the roast and leave it in the refrigerator for me to stick into the oven when I came home from school. She'd get home from work and whip up mashed potatoes, gravy and steamed peas or corn, and then we had a dinner that would fill up my older, teenage brother. We almost always made French Dip Sandwiches with the leftovers, getting at least two meals out of the same roast. This recipe makes roasting beef even easier. All done in the slow cooker, the meat comes out pull-apart tender as can be.

BEEF

4 pounds boneless beef roast, trimmed of excess fat
1 tablespoon minced garlic (2 large cloves)
1 tablespoon minced fresh rosemary (or 1 teaspoon dried)
1 tablespoon minced fresh thyme (or 1 teaspoon dried)
1 teaspoon kosher salt
½ teaspoon freshly ground black pepper
2 14.5-ounce cans low-sodium beef broth
1 teaspoon Worcestershire sauce
10 whole peppercorns
1 bay leaf
½ large onion, cut into chunks

CARAMELIZED ONIONS

2 tablespoons olive oil
2 large onions, thinly sliced
1 teaspoon kosher salt

PEPPERS

1 large red bell pepper, seeded, ribs removed and cut into thin strips
1 large green bell pepper, seeded, ribs removed and cut into thin strips

REMAINING INGREDIENTS

8 6-inch crusty French sandwich rolls
4 tablespoons (½ stick) salted butter, softened
8 slices provolone cheese

Place the roast in your slow cooker. In a small bowl, mix the garlic, rosemary, thyme, salt and pepper. Use clean hands to rub the spice mixture into the roast. Pour the beef broth around the sides of the roast. If the roast is not submerged in the broth, add just enough water to the slow cooker to cover the roast. Add the Worcestershire sauce, peppercorns and bay leaf. Place the onion on top of the roast. Cover and cook on low until the meat flakes apart easily with a fork, 11 to 12 hours.

In the last hour of cooking, prepare the caramelized onions and peppers. In a large skillet, heat the olive oil over medium heat. Add the onions and salt and cook until they turn golden brown, stirring often, reducing heat as needed if the onions are burning or browning too quickly, about 30 minutes. Add 1 tablespoon of water to the pan if it becomes too dry. The onions will

CHANGE IT UP!

Turn these into French Dip Sliders by serving these up in dinner rolls instead.

Keep a bottle of hot sauce nearby for those who like things spicy.

turn a deep golden brown and they will taste sweet. Transfer the onions to a serving bowl and wipe out the pan. Heat the pan over medium heat and add the bell peppers. Cook, stirring often, until the peppers have softened, about 7 minutes. Transfer the peppers to another serving bowl.

Remove the meat from the slow cooker to a cutting board. Cut the beef into slices against the grain, or pull into shreds with a fork. Pour the broth from the slow cooker through a fine sieve and into a bowl. Let the broth stand at room temperature to give the fat a chance to separate.

Preheat the oven to broil. Split the rolls. Spread ½ tablespoon butter on the cut side of the rolls. Lay the rolls open-faced on a rimmed baking sheet. Broil the rolls for 2 to 3 minutes, or until they begin to turn golden brown. Remove the rolls from the oven and add meat, caramelized onions, peppers and a slice of cheese. Return the sandwiches to the oven and broil for an additional 1 to 2 minutes, just until the cheese has melted. Use a spoon to skim any accumulated fat off the top of the broth. Scoop the broth into cups. Serve toasted sandwiches with cups of broth for dipping.

TIPS The caramelized onions and peppers are delicious additions to the sandwich, but they are certainly not mandatory. For a simpler option, serve sandwiches with just meat and cheese.

To serve these up midday (great for sporting events!), get them started late at night so they'll be finished cooking by lunchtime the following day.

flank steak tacos with avocado-chimichurri sauce

Makes: 12 tacos   Prep Time: 25 minutes + marinating time   Cook Time: 10 minutes

My Peruvian friend Millie and her husband David frequently host dinner parties in their California backyard where they feature an abundance of South American cuisine. They know how to prepare and enjoy good food. Millie taught me how to make empanadas, and her husband shares tips for slow-grilling the most perfectly seasoned meats that I've ever eaten. David grills an endless amount of vegetables and meats in his wood-fired oven. My favorite is his simply grilled flank steak topped with chimichurri sauce. That's the inspiration for these tacos.

STEAK

1 tablespoon olive oil
  Grated zest and juice from
    2 medium limes
3 medium garlic cloves,
    minced
2 teaspoons honey
2 teaspoons ground cumin
½ teaspoon salt
½ teaspoon freshly ground
    black pepper
2 pounds flank or skirt steak,
    fat trimmed and discarded

CHIMICHURRI SAUCE

1 cup chopped cilantro
¼ cup red wine vinegar
2 tablespoons olive oil
2 medium garlic cloves,
    minced
1 teaspoon honey
½ teaspoon ground cumin
½ teaspoon crushed red pepper
½ teaspoon sea salt
½ large avocado, pitted and
    peeled

FOR SERVING

12 corn or taco-size flour
    tortillas, warmed or fried
    (see Tips)
3 cups chopped iceberg
    lettuce
1½ cups shredded Monterey
    Jack cheese
1½ cups salsa

To marinate the steak, in a large zip baggie or glass dish, combine the olive oil, lime zest, lime juice, garlic, honey, cumin, salt and pepper. Add the steak and flip it over a few times to coat it with the marinade. Marinate the steak at room temperature for 30 minutes while you prepare the sauce.

To prepare the sauce, in a blender or small food processor, combine the cilantro, vinegar, oil, garlic, honey, cumin, crushed red pepper and sea salt. Process the mixture until it is well combined, about 1 minute. Add the avocado and continue to process until the sauce is smooth. Pour the sauce into a bowl and set it aside until you're ready to assemble the tacos.

Preheat the grill to medium-high heat. Remove the steak from the marinade. Discard the marinade. Grill the steak until it is medium rare, 4 to 6 minutes per side. Transfer the steak to a cutting board and let it rest for 10 minutes. Thinly slice the steak at an angle against the grain with a long, sharp knife.

To assemble the tacos, fill each tortilla with a couple of slices of steak,

CHANGE IT UP!

If you'd like to serve up some steak—not inside a taco—grill and slice the steak as instructed and serve it topped with the avocado-chimichurri sauce.

1 tablespoon chimichurri sauce, ¼ cup lettuce, 1 tablespoon cheese and 1 tablespoon salsa. Serve immediately.

GF GLUTEN-FREE ADAPTABLE Use brands of salsa and corn tortillas that are known to be gluten-free.

DF DAIRY-FREE ADAPTABLE Leave off the cheese.

TIPS To warm flour tortillas: Wrap a stack of 3 at a time in damp paper towels and microwave them for 25 seconds until they are warmed and softened. Alternatively, wrap them in foil with a few sprinkles of water and heat them in the oven at 350°F for 10 to 15 minutes, until they are warm and pliable.

To fry corn tortillas, in a small pan, heat ⅓ cup vegetable oil over medium heat. Fry the tortillas one at a time, about 10 seconds on each side. Place them on paper towels to drain, adding a paper towel in between each tortilla.

Flank steak is most tender when it's served as medium rare. Poke the steak with your finger while it's still raw and you'll find that it's squishy. It will begin to firm up as it cooks, so you can give it another poke as it cooks. You don't want it to get too firm or the meat will be well done and tough. If you have an instant-read thermometer, take it off the grill when it reaches 135°F.

penguin burgers (a.k.a. nostalgic burgers)

Makes: 4 burgers   Prep Time: 25 minutes   Cook Time: 10 minutes

When I was 15, I talked my way into a job at a little mom and pop ice cream and fast food shack called The Penguin. It was one of those places where you stop when you're driving through the middle of a small town on a long road trip, flashing frostie sign luring you in. It was also a place that was very popular with the residents. The malts, dipped cones and finger-size French fries were among the favorite menu items. But the burgers were what kept people coming back. The Penguin Burger was by far the best burger the town of Carson City, Nevada has ever seen. I grilled up my share of Penguin Burgers working there as a young high school student, and I topped them all with a secret special sauce that made them so delicious. The Penguin was torn down several years ago to make room for a gas station conglomerate, but my Penguin Burgers' recipe is a nod to what those burgers were all about.

SPECIAL SAUCE

½	cup mayonnaise
2	tablespoons ketchup
1	tablespoon white vinegar
2	teaspoons sweet pickle relish
1	teaspoon granulated white sugar
1	teaspoon finely grated onion
⅛	teaspoon salt
	Dash of freshly ground black pepper
	Dash of cayenne pepper

BURGERS

1½	pounds ground beef (see Tips)
3	slices bacon, finely chopped (see Tips)
½	teaspoon Worcestershire sauce
½	teaspoon salt
¼	teaspoon freshly ground black pepper

REMAINING INGREDIENTS

4	thin slices cheddar cheese
4	regular-size hamburger buns
4	tablespoons (½ stick) salted butter, melted
4	slices onion
4	large slices tomato
4	lettuce leaves

To prepare the special sauce, in a small bowl, whisk together all of the sauce ingredients. Refrigerate the sauce until the burgers are ready to assemble (see Tips).

To prepare the burgers, preheat the grill to medium-high. Place all of the burger ingredients in a medium bowl. Use your hands to gently mix the ingredients together just until they are well combined. Divide the meat into four equal parts and form burgers that are 1 inch thick. Press your thumb into the center of each burger to create an indentation (it will help prevent the burger from puffing up on the grill). Oil the grill grate. Grill the burgers, covered, until the blood in the meat begins to appear on the surface of the burger, about 3 minutes. Flip the burgers and top with the cheese. Cover and continue to cook until an instant-read thermometer inserted into a burger registers 130°F for medium rare, about 4 minutes more, or 145°F for medium, about 6 minutes more. Transfer the burgers to a platter and let them sit while you prepare the buns. Brush the buns with the melted butter. Grill the buns, butter side down, about 1 minute to obtain some toasty grill marks.

To assemble the burgers, place the bun bottoms on a platter. Spread each bun with 2 tablespoons of the special sauce and then layer the onion, burger, tomato and lettuce. Top with the bun tops. Serve immediately.

TIPS Ground chuck is the best type of ground beef to use for hamburgers. It has a fat content that ranges from 15 to 20%, it has rich flavor and it turns out a tender and moist burger.

You can use any bacon for this recipe, but my bacon of choice for these burgers is the ever-so-flavorful applewood smoked bacon. Avoid the extra-thick kind of bacon as it may be tough to cook all the way through on the grill.

MAKE-AHEAD TIP Prepare the sauce up to 2 days in advance. The burgers may be formed up to a few hours in advance. Keep them wrapped and refrigerated.

Happy Hour

It's the time of day when stomachs start rumbling, eager for dinner or at least a pre-dinner treat. I don't even have to look at a clock at this time of day and I'm well aware of what time it is. It could be a California thing—our more relaxed lifestyle finds us headed to the beach more often than not to watch the sunset with Strawberry Lemonade in hand and a big bowl of Chipotle-Mango Guacamole for chip-dunking. Friends often get together after work to enjoy a cocktail and share appetizers. For me, it's the most enjoyable, relaxed sort of party to host, making a large pitcher of Red Wine Sangria, and then asking everyone to bring a dish to share. Happy Hour should be just that—an hour (or more) of relaxed happiness with plenty of food to sample.

Recipes

W WEB FAVORITE   V VEGETARIAN *(or adaptable)*   GF GLUTEN-FREE *(or adaptable)*   DF DAIRY-FREE *(or adaptable)*

strawberry lemonade

Makes: 4 servings   Prep Time: 15 minutes + cooling/chilling time   Cook Time: 5 minutes

My son set up a lemonade stand once. He and his friend raked in about $50 serving up freshly squeezed lemonade and home-baked goodies. I'm pretty sure if we had added up how much it actually cost to buy the ingredients for all of that stuff, we may have broken even. Regardless, I let them keep the cash since they worked so hard. Next time, they'll have to serve up this strawberry version, which is sure to be an even bigger hit.

1   tablespoon grated lemon zest (see Tips)
1   cup freshly squeezed lemon juice
2   cups thin simple syrup (see Tips)
2   cups sliced fresh strawberries
2   cups sparkling water
    Ice
    Mint sprigs for garnish, optional
    Additional sliced strawberries for garnish, optional

Stir the lemon zest and lemon juice into the cooled simple syrup.

In a blender, puree the strawberries with ½ cup of the simple syrup. Pour the pureed strawberries into a medium bowl and combine with the remaining simple syrup. Pour the mixture through a fine sieve into a pitcher. Refrigerate the mixture until it is well chilled.

When you're ready to serve up the lemonade, add the sparkling water to the pitcher and stir. Pour into ice-filled glasses. Serve with a sprig of mint and sliced strawberries for garnish, if desired.

TIPS Zest your lemons before you squeeze the juice out of them.

To prepare thin simple syrup, in a small saucepan, bring 2 cups water and 1 cup granulated white sugar to a boil. Reduce the heat to low and simmer, stirring the mixture until the sugar has dissolved. Remove the pan from heat and let cool. Prepare the simple syrup up to several days ahead of time and keep chilled.

This recipe can be easily doubled or tripled.

CHANGE IT UP!

Substitute raspberries for the strawberries to make raspberry lemonade.

Add a splash of vodka to individual servings to turn this into a cocktail.

sweet southern california sun tea

Makes: 8 servings   Prep Time: 4 hours + chill time   Cook Time: 5 minutes

In Southern California, we definitely don't get the sweltering heat that folks get down there in those lovely Southern states. I traveled through those states one summer. I adored the people, admired the gorgeous scenery, and chowed down on some of the best food I've ever come across. But that overbearing heat that they experience for days on end—oh my! It's pretty brutal. We get summer heat in SoCal too, but the heat is a little nicer with no humidity. Iced tea has a permanent place in my refrigerator to keep us cool. This lightly sweetened tea is my favorite.

7   cups water
      Juice from 2 large lemons
4   tea bags (Earl Grey, English breakfast or original)
1   cup loosely packed fresh mint leaves
1   cup thin simple syrup (see Tips)
      Ice
      Additional mint leaves for garnish, optional

In a large pitcher, combine the 7 cups water and the lemon juice. Drop in the tea bags and mint leaves and cover the top of the pitcher with plastic wrap. Place the pitcher in the sun for 4 to 6 hours for sun brewing.

Remove the tea bags from the pitcher and pour the tea through a strainer into another pitcher. Discard the mint leaves. Add the simple syrup. Stir, cover and refrigerate until well chilled. Serve the tea in tall glasses over ice. Add a mint leaf to each glass for garnish, if desired.

TIPS To prepare thin simple syrup, in a small saucepan, bring 1 cup water and ½ cup granulated white sugar to a boil. Reduce the heat to low and simmer, stirring the mixture until the sugar has dissolved. Remove the pan from heat and let cool.

Amounts of tea, water and sugar may be adjusted for your preferred stronger, weaker or sweeter taste.

If you don't wish to make this a sweet tea, leave out the syrup entirely and add an extra cup of water to the pitcher for sun brewing. Stir sweetener into individual glasses, as desired.

CHANGE IT UP!

Choose a flavored tea. Try orange-spice, cranberry, lemon-ginger or your favorite.

cherry limeade

Makes: 4 to 6 servings   Prep Time: 20 minutes   Cook Time: 5 minutes

I'll never forget my first Cherry Limeade. I was visiting friends in Dallas in the very heart of summer. It was hotter in Dallas that summer than any other place I'd ever been. We headed to a Sonic Drive-In for lunch one day, and I spotted Cherry Limeade on the menu. It sounded like a fun drink, and seemed like it would be totally refreshing on such a warm day. That is when my obsession with Cherry Limeade began. I drank one, and then I drank another. I made excuses to visit Sonic again many times before we left Dallas, and now I make my own Cherry Limeade at home. Double or triple this recipe if you have a thirsty crowd.

1 cup thick simple syrup (see Tips)
4 to 6 cups chilled club soda
1 cup freshly squeezed lime juice
½ cup maraschino cherry juice
½ cup maraschino cherries
  Ice
  Lime slices

In a pitcher, combine the simple syrup with 4 cups of the club soda, the lime juice, cherry juice and cherries. Stir and taste. If it's a little too sweet for your taste, add in an additional 1 to 2 cups club soda. If it tastes just right, go ahead and pour it into ice-filled glasses, making sure that a few cherries make it into each glass. Garnish with lime slices.

GF **GLUTEN-FREE ADAPTABLE** Use a brand of maraschino cherries that is known to be gluten-free.

TIP To prepare thick simple syrup, in a small saucepan, bring 1 cup water and 1 cup granulated white sugar to a boil. Reduce the heat to low and simmer, stirring the mixture until the sugar has dissolved. Remove the pan from heat and let cool.

MAKE-AHEAD TIP Prepare the simple syrup up to several days ahead of time and keep chilled.

CHANGE IT UP!

This recipe also makes wonderful, plain-old limeade. Just leave out the cherries and juice and serve garnished with lime slices.

shirley temple

Makes: 1 drink   Prep Time: 5 minutes

This nonalcoholic, childhood favorite was always a favorite of mine but we most certainly never made it at home. When I was a kid, my Dad ordered me a Shirley Temple at restaurants before I could even tell him what I wanted. There is something about the simple sparkle, the pink hue and the taste of a maraschino cherry that makes this drink irresistible. On special occasions, I make Shirley Temples at home for my son. They're so easy to do, and kids really think they're a treat.

1   cup ice cubes
1   can lemon-lime soda
       (7-Up or Sprite)
     Dash of grenadine
1   maraschino cherry

Fill a glass with the ice cubes. Add the soda and a dash of grenadine. Garnish the drink with a maraschino cherry.

GF GLUTEN-FREE ADAPTABLE Use brands of soda, Grenadine and maraschino cherries that are known to be gluten-free.

TIP Shirley Temples are most fun to drink with a straw.

CHANGE IT UP!

For those maraschino cherry fans out there, be generous with your cherries and add more.

the best red wine sangria

Makes: 6 servings   Prep Time: 20 minutes

I'm referring to this recipe as "the best" because it truly is the best. Sangria shouldn't be sickeningly sweet, and this one is perfectly sweetened. It should be full of juicy and colorful fruits like lemons and oranges and limes. Grapes are tossed into this sangria too because they're easy fruit to munch while sipping. Added lemon juice and a small amount of club soda help smooth out the flavors, leaving you with a full-bodied cocktail that isn't too heavy-tasting on the alcohol.

1	750-milliliter bottle of red wine (see Tips)
¾	cup orange juice
½	cup thick simple syrup + more to taste (see Tips)
¼	cup brandy
¼	cup orange liqueur (such as Grand Marnier)
1	tablespoon freshly squeezed lemon juice
2	cups red and/or green grapes
1	medium lemon, thinly sliced
1	medium orange, thinly sliced
1	medium lime, thinly sliced
10	ounces chilled club soda

In a large pitcher or glass bowl, combine all ingredients (except the club soda). Chill the sangria and let it marinate for at least 8 hours, or preferably for 24 hours. Just before serving, stir in the club soda. Serve the sangria in glasses accompanied by a ladleful of fruit.

TIPS Expensive wine is not needed for this recipe. Use a dry wine like a Rioja or Syrah.

To prepare thick simple syrup, in a small saucepan, bring ½ cup water and ½ cup granulated white sugar to a boil. Reduce the heat to low and simmer, stirring the mixture until the sugar has dissolved. Remove the pan from heat and let cool.

CHANGE IT UP!

Change up the fruits in this Sangria—add strawberries and/or red or green apple slices.

Add pomegranate juice into the mix.

raspberry and peach lemonade sangria

Makes: 8 servings   Prep Time: 15 minutes

Wine is always my choice of beverage when it comes around to the happy hour time of day. Winter or summer, when five o'clock rolls around, I sure do love a glass of ice-cold white wine. When fruit is at its freshest in the middle of the summer, and I can't seem to get enough of the juicy peaches and red ripe raspberries, I like to turn my white wine into fruity sangria instead. This recipe is most fun for summer since there's added lemonade in the mix.

1	750-milliliter bottle dry white wine (Sauvignon Blanc or Pinot Grigio)
2	cups lemonade
¾	cup limoncello
⅓	cup thick simple syrup (see Tips)
1	cup peeled, pitted and sliced fresh peach
1	cup fresh raspberries or strawberries
1	lemon, thinly sliced
3	cups chilled club soda

In a large pitcher or glass bowl, combine all ingredients (except club soda). Chill the sangria and let it marinate for at least 8 hours, or preferably for 24 hours. Just before serving, stir in the club soda. Serve the sangria in glasses accompanied by a ladleful of fruit.

TIP To prepare thick simple syrup, in a small saucepan, bring ⅓ cup water and ⅓ cup granulated white sugar to a boil. Reduce the heat to low and simmer, stirring the mixture until the sugar has dissolved. Remove the pan from heat and let cool.

CHANGE IT UP!

Make this a pretty pink sangria by using rose wine and pink lemonade.

V DF

sparkling pomegranate party punch

Makes: 16 servings   Prep Time: 15 minutes

My mother had a Christmas cocktail party every year when I was growing up. All of her work friends and the entire neighborhood converged upon our little house to sample Mom's famous stuffed mushrooms and copious amounts of party punch. I'll never forget that punch because Mom always added an ice ring with maraschino cherries floating inside of it. I made a game of swirling it around with the ladle before the guests arrived. This recipe isn't Mom's party punch, but it's just as popular. Pomegranate juice and ginger ale are combined with white wine, vodka and lemonade to create a delicious, bubbly drink.

2 750-milliliter bottles dry white wine (see Tip)
2 cups pomegranate juice
1 cup vodka
1 12-ounce can frozen lemonade concentrate
   Pomegranate seeds, sliced lemons and sliced oranges, for garnish (as desired)
1 2-liter bottle ginger ale

In a large pitcher or bowl, combine all ingredients (except ginger ale). Add desired fruit garnishes and chill for several hours or overnight. Stir in the ginger ale just before serving.

GF GLUTEN-FREE ADAPTABLE Use brands of lemonade concentrate and ginger ale that are known to be gluten-free.

TIP There is no need to purchase expensive wine for this recipe. A nice, moderately priced dry wine (such as Sauvignon Blanc or Pinot Grigio) is perfect.

CHANGE IT UP!

Easily change this punch into a different flavor by substituting another juice flavor for the pomegranate.

blueberry-pineapple tequila punch

Makes: 8 servings   Prep Time: 25 minutes

Here's one for the record books. My friend Libbie was having a get-together of sorts for some friends of ours who were moving. I arrived at Libbie's house early in the day to assist with preparing some of the food and beverages for the party. This Tequila Punch with floating chunks of pineapple and fresh blueberries was one of those beverages. Excited to try it, I arrived at the party early that night only to find out that the punch was already gone. First arrivals poured themselves a glass of this punch, sipped it quickly and then poured themselves another. I guess the good news is that the punch was declared a major favorite.

½   cup thick simple syrup (see Tips)
½   cup freshly squeezed lime juice
1   cup blueberries
¾   cup lightly packed fresh mint leaves
3   cups silver tequila (see Tips)
3   cups pineapple juice
1½ cups sliced pineapple (canned or fresh)
    Crushed ice
    Additional mint leaves for garnish, optional
    Fresh pineapple wedges for garnish, optional

In a large pitcher or punch bowl, combine the simple syrup, lime juice, blueberries and mint. Muddle them gently together with a wooden spoon, crushing the blueberries and mint in the bottom of the pitcher. Stir in the tequila, pineapple juice and pineapple. Refrigerate for at least 4 hours before serving. Serve over crushed ice. Garnish with mint leaves and/or pineapple wedges, if desired.

GF GLUTEN-FREE ADAPTABLE Use brands of pineapple and juice that are known to be gluten-free.

TIPS To prepare thick simple syrup, in a small saucepan, bring ½ cup water and ½ cup granulated white sugar to a boil. Reduce the heat to low and simmer, stirring the mixture until the sugar has dissolved. Remove the pan from heat and let cool.

Silver tequila is a clear spirit that is best for using to mix with fruit in cocktails. Gold tequila is sweet and smooth and flavored with caramel. It's best for shots and mixing into margaritas.

CHANGE IT UP!
Fun serving idea: serve this cocktail in mason jars.

orange-basil mojito

Makes: 4 servings   Prep Time: 10 minutes

I had this drink once while lounging poolside in Vegas, and I loved it so much that I had to come home and create a version for myself. If you're already familiar with mojitos, you know that they usually incorporate mint and lime juice. For the Orange-Basil Mojito, I simply substitute basil for fresh mint and fresh orange juice for lime. Muddled together and mixed with rum and club soda, this makes for a totally unique and refreshing sort of cocktail.

1	cup freshly squeezed orange juice
½	cup thick simple syrup (see Tips)
10	large fresh basil leaves, stems removed and discarded
1	cup white rum
1	cup club soda
	Crushed ice
	Orange slices, for garnish
	Additional basil leaves, for garnish

In a medium pitcher, combine the orange juice, simple syrup and basil. Use a wooden spoon or a muddler to crush the basil leaves in the bottom of the pitcher. Stir in the rum and club soda. Serve immediately in individual glasses over crushed ice. Garnish with orange slices and fresh basil.

TIP To prepare thick simple syrup, in a small saucepan, bring ½ cup water and ½ cup granulated white sugar to a boil. Reduce the heat to low and simmer, stirring the mixture until the sugar has dissolved. Remove the pan from heat and let cool.

CHANGE IT UP!

Turn this cocktail into a Strawberry-Basil Mojito. Substitute ¼ cup freshly squeezed lime juice for the orange juice and add in 1½ cups sliced strawberries. Muddle together the basil, simple syrup, lime juice and strawberries. Stir in the rum and 2 cups of club soda.

mango margaritas

Makes: 6 drinks   Prep Time: 15 minutes

I'm just gonna admit it right here and now. I'm not really and truly a margarita person. The salt has never appealed to me, the tequila is always overpowering, and I'm just not into the flavor. But add strawberries or blueberries or peaches or mango to a margarita, and my story will change very quickly. I guess it's something about adding sweet things to a drinky-drink that make it more appealing and desirable. Mango happens to be my favorite in a margarita, and this is a margarita that I will (happily) consume.

Ice
1 cup fresh or frozen sliced mango
1 6-ounce can frozen limeade concentrate
6 ounces mango nectar (see Tips)
4 ounces tequila
3 ounces triple sec or Cointreau
2 ounces Grand Marnier
   Margarita salt, optional
   Lime wedges for garnish, optional

Fill a blender half-full with ice. Add the mango, limeade concentrate, mango nectar, tequila, triple sec, and Grand Marnier to the blender. Blend until smooth (about 1 minute). Dip the rims of 6 glasses in water or mango nectar and then dip in salt, if desired. Pour the margaritas into the glasses and serve, garnishing with lime wedges, if desired.

GF GLUTEN-FREE ADAPTABLE Use brands of limeade and mango nectar that are known to be gluten-free.

TIP Mango nectar can usually be found in your market's bottled juice aisle.

> **CHANGE IT UP!**
>
> This cocktail may also be served "on the rocks." Leave the ice out of the blender and place it in the glasses instead, pouring the blended cocktail over the ice.

baked brie with gingered peach sauce

Makes: 8 servings   Prep Time: 20 minutes   Cook Time: 20 minutes

When I worked for a caterer back in college, one of my favorite appetizers to see on the client's list was the baked Brie. We purchased these humongous rounds of Brie and warmed them slowly in large chafing dishes. They were simply garnished with dried cranberries and almonds. I'd watch guests dunk baguette slices into that hot, melted Brie and pray that there would be some left for me to sample. This Brie recipe is also hot and melted, it's accompanied by a sweet, gingery peach sauce, and it's even more appealing than that Brie that I so fondly remember.

1   cup fresh, frozen or canned peeled, pitted and diced peaches
¼   cup packed light brown sugar
2   tablespoons finely chopped shallots
2   tablespoons cider vinegar
1½ tablespoons cornstarch
1   tablespoon grated fresh ginger (or ½ teaspoon ground)
1   stick cinnamon
⅛   teaspoon salt
1   8-ounce round Brie cheese (see Tips)
    Baguette slices or crackers, for serving

In a large saucepan, combine all of the ingredients (except cheese and baguette). Bring the mixture to a boil over medium heat and simmer until the peaches are softened, 3 to 5 minutes. Remove the cinnamon stick. Let the peach sauce sit, covered, at room temperature while you prepare the cheese.

Preheat the oven to 300°F. Place the cheese in a pie plate or a similar size, oven-safe serving dish. With a sharp knife, cut all the way around the rind at the top edge of the cheese (don't remove the rind). Bake for 15 minutes, or until the cheese is soft and melted. Use a sharp knife to carefully cut under the top of the cheese (underneath the rind) to remove the rind. Discard the rind. Spoon the peach sauce on top of the cheese. Serve immediately with baguette slices.

GF GLUTEN-FREE ADAPTABLE Serve with gluten-free crackers in place of the baguette slices.

TIP The large warehouse stores usually carry a nice-size round Brie, as do some regular grocery stores and specialty markets.

MAKE-AHEAD TIP Prepare the peach sauce up to 1 day ahead. Keep it covered in the refrigerator. Warm it over low heat in a medium saucepan before serving.

CHANGE IT UP!

Substitute fresh blueberries for the peaches.

buffalo chicken dip

Makes: 12 servings   Prep Time: 20 minutes   Cook Time: 30 minutes

Inspired by the classic combination of buffalo wings, celery and blue cheese dressing, this dip combines all of that good stuff into one. It's the kind of dip that is perfect for displaying at sports-themed parties, or any other parties where men are hovering around the food table. I might add that women will most definitely enjoy this too.

1	cup shredded cooked chicken
¾	cup Frank's RedHot™ Original Cayenne Pepper Sauce
1	8-ounce package cream cheese (see Tips)
1	5-ounce package blue cheese crumbles
1	cup finely chopped celery
1	cup shredded cheddar-Jack cheese (blended cheddar and Monterey Jack cheeses)
¾	cup halved small cherry or pear tomatoes
½	cup chopped green onion Celery sticks and tortilla chips, for serving

Preheat the oven to 350°F. Spray an 8-inch square pan with nonstick spray.

In a medium bowl, mix the chicken and cayenne pepper sauce. Spread the mixture in the bottom of the prepared pan.

In a small saucepan, melt the cream cheese over medium heat. Stir until smooth, then add the blue cheese crumbles and stir until well combined. Remove from heat and spoon the cheese mixture over the chicken. Sprinkle the celery on top.

Bake, uncovered, for 20 minutes. Remove the pan from the oven and sprinkle the hot dip with the cheddar-Jack cheese. Return the pan to the oven and bake about 10 minutes, or until the cheese has melted. Remove the dip from the oven and sprinkle with the cherry tomatoes and green onion before serving. Serve with celery sticks and tortilla chips.

TIPS It's completely okay to use lower fat cream cheese in this recipe, but don't use low-fat cheese to sprinkle on top as it does not melt well enough.

Look for multicolored cherry tomatoes to make this dip extra colorful.

If you don't have access to the Frank's brand sauce, any variety of Buffalo Sauce will do.

CHANGE IT UP!

Change things up in this dip by substituting a spicy barbecue sauce instead. It will give the dip a different flavor, but still wonderful, indeed!

hot seafood dip in a bread bowl

Makes: 12 servings   Prep Time: 30 minutes   Cook Time: 1 hour and 45 minutes

Clam chowder is excellent when served in a bread bowl, so why not seafood dip too? When the bread bowl is carved out to make room for the dip, the resulting bread chunks are available for dipping, and as the bread chunks disappear, people seem to enjoy manhandling the bowl, tearing off pieces to dunk into this hot and creamy dip.

1	8-ounce package cream cheese, at room temperature
8	ounces sour cream
1	cup freshly grated Parmesan cheese
1	cup finely chopped celery
¼	cup beer
¼	cup grated sweet onion
1	tablespoon prepared horseradish
1	tablespoon Worcestershire sauce
2	teaspoons freshly squeezed lemon juice
1	teaspoon hot sauce
½	teaspoon garlic salt
¼	teaspoon sea salt
2	6.5-ounce cans minced clams, squeezed dry + 2 tablespoons juice reserved
1	6-ounce can small shrimp, drained and squeezed dry
1	20-ounce round French or sourdough bread
¼	cup chopped green onion Baguette slices for dunking, optional

Preheat the oven to 300°F. Spray an 8-inch square pan with nonstick spray.

In a large bowl, whisk together the cream cheese and sour cream until smooth. Stir in the Parmesan cheese, celery, beer, onion, horseradish, Worcestershire sauce, lemon juice, hot sauce, garlic salt and salt. Add the clams and reserved clam juice and the shrimp and stir to combine. Scrape the creamy seafood mixture into the prepared dish and cover with foil. Bake for 1½ hours.

Use a serrated knife to cut around the top edge of the bread. Remove the top and cut it into bite-size pieces. Scoop out the bread to create a bowl. Tear the scooped out bread into bite-size pieces. Transfer all of the bread pieces and the bowl to a sealed container or zip baggie. Set aside.

Remove the dip from the oven and carefully spoon it into the bread bowl. Place the bread bowl on a baking sheet and return it to the oven for an additional 15 minutes before serving. Place the bread bowl dip on a serving platter, sprinkle it with the green onion, surround it with the bread chunks and additional baguette slices, if desired, and serve immediately.

TIP Substitute 1½ cups of fresh clams and tiny shrimp for the canned, if desired.

> **CHANGE IT UP!**
> Turn this into a decadent lobster dip. Substitute 1½ cups of lobster meat for the clams and shrimp.

caramelized onion dip

Makes: 3 cups   Prep Time: 25 minutes   Cook Time: 30 minutes

There's nothing like having a tub of that store-bought onion dip by your side with a bag of your favorite potato chips when you're watching your favorite teams play on TV, right? But when you can replace it with something that is homemade and sweet and delicious and incredible, I guarantee that you won't want that tub stuff ever again.

2   tablespoons olive oil
3   cups finely diced sweet
        onion
¾   teaspoon kosher salt,
        divided
1½   cups sour cream
¾   cup mayonnaise
½   teaspoon garlic powder
¼   teaspoon white pepper
        Dash of hot sauce (Tabasco
        or something similar), to
        taste
⅛   teaspoon red pepper flakes,
        optional
        Sturdy potato chips, for
        serving

In a large skillet, heat the olive oil over medium heat. Add the onion and ¼ teaspoon of the salt. Cook, stirring every so often, until the onion begins to caramelize and turn golden brown, about 30 minutes. Don't stir the onions constantly because you want them to brown, but do watch that they aren't browning too quickly or burning and adjust the heat as needed. Remove the onions from heat and set aside to cool.

In a medium bowl, mix the remaining ½ teaspoon salt, the sour cream, mayonnaise, garlic powder, white pepper, hot sauce and red pepper flakes, and then add the cooled onions. Taste and adjust seasoning, adding additional garlic powder, salt and/or hot sauce, as desired. Refrigerate until ready to serve. Stir before serving. Serve with sturdy potato chips.

GF GLUTEN-FREE ADAPTABLE Use brands of mayonnaise and potato chips that are known to be gluten-free.

TIPS Prepare this dip a day in advance so the flavors really have a chance to come together.

Make this a lower fat dip by using low-fat sour cream and low-fat mayonnaise.

CHANGE IT UP!

Use red onions instead of sweet onions.

Try mixing in chopped roasted red peppers.

warm artichoke and bacon dip

Makes: 12 servings   Prep Time: 25 minutes   Cook Time: 45 minutes

Here's a rich and creamy dip with chunks of artichoke hearts and crispy bacon. It's one of those dips where it's hard to stop after just a couple of bites. Serve this appetizer on a day where warmth and comfort are needed and a large, hungry crowd is ready and waiting. It's all-around good comfort food.

8	ounces cream cheese, cut into pieces
1	14-ounce can artichoke hearts, drained and finely chopped
1	cup jarred roasted red peppers, drained and finely chopped
½	cup mayonnaise
½	cup finely diced celery
4	ounces Gorgonzola or blue cheese crumbles
⅓	cup white wine
1	large egg, beaten
½	teaspoon garlic powder
½	cup cooked and crumbled bacon (about 8 slices; see Tips)
	Pita chips or baguette slices, for serving

Preheat the oven to 350°F. Spray a 9-inch pie plate with nonstick spray.

In a small saucepan, melt the cream cheese over low heat. Stir until smooth. Scrape the melted cream cheese into a large bowl. Whisk in the remaining ingredients (except bacon and chips). Pour the mixture into the prepared pie plate. Cover it with foil and bake for 25 minutes. Remove the foil and bake an additional 25 minutes, or until the dip is baked through and bubbly. Sprinkle the bacon on top. Serve immediately with pita chips or baguette slices.

GF GLUTEN-FREE ADAPTABLE Use goat or feta cheese in place of the Gorgonzola cheese, and use brands of mayonnaise and bacon that are known to be gluten-free. Serve with gluten-free crackers.

V VEGETARIAN ADAPTABLE Leave out the bacon.

TIP For easy clean-up, cook your bacon in the oven. Preheat the oven to 400°F. Line a large, rimmed baking sheet with foil and place a rack on top. Spray the rack with nonstick spray. Lay the bacon slices on the rack. Bake for 15 to 20 minutes, or until the bacon is crisp. Timing will vary depending on the thickness of your bacon.

CHANGE IT UP!

Turn this into a spinach-artichoke dip by mixing in a 10-ounce package of frozen spinach (thawed and squeezed dry).

layered mediterranean spinach dip

Makes: 12 servings   Prep Time: 25 minutes

The simplicity of picking up a tub of store-bought hummus is all too familiar and comfortable for many people. Add carrots and a handful of chips for dipping and you've got yourself a very easy, no-fuss appetizer. But if you'd like to go the extra mile and tack on just a few more minutes into your prep time, you'll have that hummus and a whole lot more to offer your guests. This recipe layers a spinach dip with hummus, tomato, feta cheese and Kalamata olives to create something a little more special than the usual old store-bought tub.

1½ cups packed fresh spinach leaves
1 5-ounce can sliced water chestnuts, drained
4 ounces cream cheese, at room temperature
½ cup sour cream
1 tablespoon freshly squeezed lemon juice
½ teaspoon salt
⅛ teaspoon freshly ground black pepper
10 ounces plain prepared hummus (store-bought is fine)
1 cup chopped tomato
½ cup roughly chopped Kalamata olives
½ cup crumbled feta cheese
⅓ cup chopped green onion, white and light green parts
Pita chips, for serving

In a food processor, combine the spinach, water chestnuts, cream cheese, sour cream, lemon juice, salt and pepper. Pulse until the mixture is well combined and pureed. Spread the puree onto a 9-inch round or 9-inch square serving dish (or something similar). Spoon the hummus on top of the spinach puree and spread to create the second layer of the dip. Sprinkle the second layer with tomato, olives and feta cheese. Scatter the green onion on top. Refrigerate until ready to serve. Serve with pita chips for dipping.

GF GLUTEN-FREE ADAPTABLE Use brands of hummus and Kalamata olives that are known to be gluten-free. Serve with gluten-free crackers.

TIP This dip can be prepared up to 4 hours in advance. Cover it lightly with plastic wrap and keep refrigerated until ready to serve.

CHANGE IT UP!

Add finely chopped cucumber into the layers.

Use an alternative variety of hummus, such as roasted garlic or roasted red pepper.

so-cal 7-layer mexican dip

Makes: One 9 x 13-inch pan of dip   Prep Time: 30 minutes   Cook Time: 18 minutes

The concept of a 7-layer Mexican dip has been around forever. You can actually now purchase the simple-to-make dip already layered in a plastic tub at most grocery stores. With its congealed sour cream and fake guacamole, I find the plastic tub version to be rather unappealing. It's really quite simple to make your own layer dip. I've jazzed up the classic version using crispy bacon, corn, crumbled Mexican Cojita cheese and, of course, real guacamole. It's easy to make, and I promise it will be 100 percent better than a plastic tub dip.

10	slices bacon
3	large avocados, pitted, peeled and cored
1¾	cup sour cream, divided
1	tablespoon freshly squeezed lime juice
	Salt and freshly ground black pepper, to taste
1	large ear corn on the cob, shucked, rinsed and dried
1	30-ounce can refried beans
2	cups chopped Roma tomato (about 4 large)
1	cup crumbled Cojita cheese (see Tips)
	Tortilla chips, for dipping

Cook the bacon in the oven (see Tips). While the bacon is cooking, prepare the rest of the dip.

To prepare a simple guacamole, mash the avocados in a medium bowl and stir in ¼ cup of the sour cream and the lime juice. Season the guacamole with salt and pepper, to taste.

Cut the corn kernels off of the cob (see Tips).

To assemble the dip, spray a 9 x 13-inch dish lightly with nonstick spray. Spread the refried beans in the bottom of the dish. Add the remaining 1½ cups sour cream on top and spread to cover. Spoon the guacamole on top of the sour cream and gently spread it to the edges to cover the sour cream. Sprinkle the tomato over. Crumble the bacon over the tomato. Layer the corn and cheese. Cover the dip with plastic wrap and refrigerate until ready to serve. Serve with tortilla chips.

GF GLUTEN-FREE ADAPTABLE Use brands of bacon, refried beans and tortilla chips that are known to be gluten-free.

V VEGETARIAN ADAPTABLE Leave out the bacon.

TIPS For easy clean-up, cook your bacon in the oven. Preheat the oven to 400°F. Line a large, rimmed baking sheet with foil and place a rack on top. Spray the rack with nonstick spray. Lay the bacon slices on the rack. Bake for 15 to 20 minutes, or until the bacon is crisp. Timing will vary depending on the thickness of your bacon.

To cut the corn kernels off the cob: Cut a small slice off of the end of the cob to create a flat surface. Set the flat end of the corn upright inside of a bowl, holding it at the top. Cut down the sides of the cob with a sharp knife and the corn kernels will collect inside of the bowl.

Cojita cheese is a crumbly Mexican cheese. It can usually be found in the specialty cheese section of your market. Feta cheese may be substituted.

This dip may be prepared up to 2 hours in advance.

CHANGE IT UP!

Add in more layers: fresh chopped cilantro, black olives and/or chopped green onions.

curry-dill vegetable dip

Makes: 3 cups   Prep Time: 15 minutes + chill time

For some not-entirely odd reason, I have a curry-dill dip recipe stuck in my head. Whenever my mother served fresh vegetables as an appetizer for guests, she whipped up a very simple herbed curry and dill dip to serve alongside them. Because of that, I just always think of curry as the base for a vegetable dip. This recipe is along the same lines as Mom's dip, but it includes some fresh herbs and spinach, and it packs a creamier punch. The curry taste is mild but you can certainly add more if you prefer.

1   cup mayonnaise
1   cup sour cream
1   cup packed fresh spinach
      leaves
4   ounces crumbled goat
      cheese
2   tablespoons chopped fresh
      parsley
1   tablespoon chopped fresh
      dill
1   teaspoon curry powder
½   teaspoon celery salt
½   teaspoon onion powder
1   tablespoon chopped fresh
      chives for garnish, optional
      Assorted vegetables for
      dipping (see Tips)

In a food processor, combine all of the ingredients (except chives and dipping vegetables) and process until smooth. Keep refrigerated until ready to serve. When ready to serve, transfer the dip to a serving bowl and sprinkle with chives, if desired. Serve with assorted vegetables.

GF GLUTEN-FREE ADAPTABLE Use a brand of mayonnaise that is known to be gluten-free.

TIPS Suggested vegetables for dipping: sliced cucumber, broccoli, zucchini, radish, cauliflower, cherry or pear tomatoes, carrots and celery.

This dip may be prepared up to 2 days in advance.

CHANGE IT UP!

Leave out the spinach if you don't have a food processor or if you'd like a more streamlined herb-only dip.

Add in 1 teaspoon freshly squeezed lemon juice.

strawberry-avocado salsa

Makes: 2½ cups salsa   Prep Time: 15 minutes

Sometimes it's the simple things in life that fill your tummy and make you smile. This super simple fruit salsa is one of those things. It's best for making in the middle of extra-juicy and sweet strawberry season, and all you need is a few chips for scooping.

1   cup finely diced fresh
      strawberries
1   cup finely diced avocado
      (1 medium)
½   cup finely chopped sweet
      onion
2   teaspoons freshly squeezed
      lime juice
2   teaspoons finely chopped
      jalapeño (seeds and ribs
      removed)
    Tortilla chips, for dipping

Combine all of the ingredients (except tortilla chips) in a medium bowl. Serve immediately with the tortilla chips.

GF GLUTEN-FREE ADAPTABLE Use a brand of tortilla chips that is known to be gluten-free.

TIP This isn't a recipe that you want to make well in advance of serving. When avocado is exposed to air, it begins the process of oxidation, which turns the avocado brown. The addition of lime juice slows the oxidation process but it does not prevent it entirely. Plan to prep the salsa and serve right away.

CHANGE IT UP!

Avocado pairs nicely with other fruits too. Try substituting peach, nectarine or mango for the strawberries.

sweet smokin' hot mango-chipotle guacamole

Makes: 2 cups   Prep Time: 20 minutes

When I first became interested in cooking so much, I used to enter recipes into contests at the San Diego County Fair. One year I scored a second place ribbon in the cheesecake contest with my strawberry-coconut variety. A few years later I was excited to see that they were having a guacamole competition. Having always considered myself a guacamole connoisseur, I worked really hard to perfect this recipe—adding in chopped mango, chipotle and bacon—with the intention of entering it into the contest at the Fair. My dreams of winning the grand prize were shattered when I realized that I was no longer eligible (as a food professional) to enter. So I'm sharing it with my cookbook readers instead. So what do you think—prize-winning capability?

2	medium perfectly ripe avocados (see Tips)
½	medium lime, divided
2	tablespoons sour cream
1	teaspoon chopped canned chipotle peppers in adobo sauce, seeds removed + ½ teaspoon sauce (see Tips)
¾	cup chopped fresh mango, divided
3	slices bacon, cooked until crisp and crumbled, divided
3	tablespoons fresh salsa
	Salt and freshly ground black pepper, to taste
	Tortilla chips and/or jicama slices, for serving

In a medium bowl, mash the avocado roughly with a fork, leaving some chunks. Squeeze the juice from ¼ of the lime on top. Add the sour cream and chipotles and sauce. Stir gently until combined. Mix in ½ cup of the mango, 2 slices of the crumbled bacon and the salsa. Add salt and pepper to taste. Drizzle the guacamole with the juice of the remaining ¼ of the lime. Sprinkle with the remaining crumbled bacon and mango.

Serve immediately (or soon) with tortilla chips and/or jicama slices. If you need to store the guacamole in the refrigerator for an hour or so before serving, place a piece of plastic wrap on top so that the plastic wrap is touching the guacamole. This will prevent air from getting in and turning your guacamole brown.

GF GLUTEN-FREE ADAPTABLE Use brands of bacon, chipotles in adobo and tortilla chips that are known to be gluten-free.

DF DAIRY-FREE ADAPTABLE Leave out the sour cream.

V VEGETARIAN ADAPTABLE Leave out the bacon.

TIPS To determine if an avocado is ripe or not, hold it in your hand and press lightly. A perfectly ripe avocado has a little bit of give to it when you press down. If it's easy to squish, it's too ripe. If there are any soft (or hollow) spots, it's too ripe. If you can't find avocados that are ready to use because they're not quite ripe enough, bring them home and let them sit on your counter for a day or two. Place them in a paper bag to speed up the ripening process.

Chipotle peppers in adobo sauce are sold canned, and you should be able to find them in your market's Latin-American products section. If you open a new can of chipotles in adobo, you'll have lots left over. They freeze really well. Just scoop a chipotle pepper and some sauce into individual zip baggies and throw them into the freezer. Simply let them thaw out when you need them again.

Fresh salsa can usually be found in your market's deli section, where they carry other refrigerated Latin-American products.

blt polenta squares

Makes: 24 to 30 appetizers   Prep Time: 40 minutes   Cook Time: 10 minutes

I'm fairly new to polenta, and if you're new to it as well, then you should definitely consider opening up to the idea of trying it. When it's served in solid form as it is in this appetizer, the texture is certainly interesting—not unlike a damp, whole-grain cube of cornmeal. It takes on the flavors of whatever you add to it, so in this case the polenta takes on flavors of bacon, fresh herbs and sun-dried tomatoes. Then it's topped with soft cheese, bacon and watercress. How could that be anything but wonderful? It's a rather unique appetizer that you don't see every day.

5   slices center-cut bacon, cut into 1-inch pieces
½   cup finely chopped sweet onion
3   cups chicken broth
1   sprig fresh rosemary
1   sprig fresh thyme
1   large garlic clove, crushed
1   cup polenta (not instant)
½   cup chopped sun-dried tomatoes packed in oil, drained
     Salt and freshly ground black pepper, to taste
½   tablespoon olive oil
½   cup soft garlic and herb cheese (such as Boursin; see Tips)
½   cup watercress, torn into small pieces

Spray a 9 x 13-inch glass dish with nonstick spray.

In a medium saucepan, fry the bacon over medium-high heat until crisp, 6 to 8 minutes. Remove the bacon to a paper towel–lined plate to drain. Spoon out and discard all but 1 tablespoon of the bacon fat. Add the onion to the pan and cook over medium heat, stirring, until golden, 3 to 4 minutes. Add the chicken broth, rosemary, thyme and garlic. Turn the heat to high and bring the broth to a boil. Use a slotted spoon to remove the herbs and garlic and discard. Whisk in the polenta in a slow and steady stream. Reduce the heat to medium and cook, stirring constantly, for 10 to 15 minutes, or until the polenta becomes very thick and begins to come away from the sides of the pan. Stir in the sun-dried tomatoes and season with salt and pepper to taste.

Pour the polenta into the prepared dish and smooth the top with a rubber spatula. Set it aside to cool completely.

Cut the cooled polenta into 1-inch squares. Heat the olive oil in a medium skillet over medium heat. Add the polenta squares to the pan and fry until lightly browned, 1 to 2 minutes on each side. Remove the polenta squares to a paper towel–lined plate to drain. Top each polenta square with 1 teaspoon cheese, 1 piece bacon and a small sprig of watercress. Serve at room temperature.

GF GLUTEN-FREE ADAPTABLE Use brands of bacon, chicken broth and polenta that are known to be gluten-free.

DF DAIRY-FREE ADAPTABLE Use hummus or another substitute for the cheese.

TIPS Make your own garlic and herb cheese: Mix 4 ounces softened cream cheese with ½ tablespoon freshly squeezed lemon juice, ½ teaspoon dried Italian seasoning and 1 large garlic clove, minced.

Substitute baby arugula or flat-leaf parsley for the watercress, if desired.

CHANGE IT UP!

Cut rounds or triangles instead of squares, or use holiday cookie cutters to cut desired polenta shapes—hearts, shamrocks, stars, trees, etc.

pizzette with goat cheese, pear and caramelized shallots

Makes: 18 appetizers   Prep Time: 35 minutes   Cook Time: 25 minutes

There is an unwritten rule in the world of food that caramelizing anything makes something taste better. Are you familiar with this rule? These simple mini pizza appetizers are covered with goat cheese, pear and fresh thyme, and then they're given a generous pinch of caramelized shallots to top it all off and make them worthy of eating at least four. I love that unwritten rule.

1   tablespoon + 2 teaspoons olive oil, divided
6   medium shallots, peeled and thinly sliced
¼   teaspoon salt
1   pound pizza dough (see Tips)
1   4-ounce log goat cheese
1   large, ripe pear, unpeeled and thinly sliced into 2-inch wedges
1   tablespoon chopped fresh thyme leaves

In a medium skillet, heat 1 tablespoon of the olive oil over medium heat. Add the shallots and salt. Reduce the heat to medium-low and cook, stirring often, until the shallots are soft and lightly browned, 15 to 20 minutes. Set aside.

Preheat the oven to 475°F. Line a baking sheet with parchment paper or a Silpat mat.

On a lightly floured surface, roll out the pizza dough to ¼-inch thickness. Use a 2½-inch round biscuit cutter to cut 18 rounds of dough, rerolling the dough as needed (see Tips). Place the rounds on the prepared baking sheet and brush them lightly with the remaining 2 teaspoons olive oil. Spread each round with about ½ tablespoon of the goat cheese and then top with 2 overlapping slices of pear. Bake 8 to 10 minutes, or until the dough is golden brown.

Place the pizzette on a serving platter and top each with ½ tablespoon of the caramelized shallots and a sprinkle of thyme.

TIPS Make your own pizza dough (page 248), purchase premade pizza dough from your market, or ask a pizza shop to sell you a 1-pound ball of dough.

If you do not own a biscuit cutter, use the top of a drinking glass that has about a 2½-inch diameter.

CHANGE IT UP!

Substitute sweet onions or red onions for the shallots, increasing cooking time to 20 to 25 minutes, and substitute soft, spreadable herb cheese for the goat cheese.

balsamic-marinated zucchini and cheese-stuffed mushrooms

Makes: 24 mushrooms   Prep Time: 35 minutes   Cook Time: 25 minutes

I don't quite understand why my son won't eat mushrooms. I was brought up eating my Mom's "famous" stuffed mushrooms, which were just mushrooms stuffed with mushroom pieces and sausage. So simple, but they worked and they were always devoured pretty much immediately upon being removed from the oven. Since sausage is used in so many stuffed mushroom recipes nowadays, I decided to go a different route with my recipe. These are marinated with balsamic vinegar and stuffed with zucchini, onion and Swiss cheese. I think you'll find that they're pretty popular at a party. But no matter what I try to do to mushrooms, I still can't get my own kid to go anywhere near them. I guess that just means I'll have more of these for myself.

MARINADE

3 tablespoons balsamic vinegar
1½ teaspoons minced garlic
1½ teaspoons Dijon mustard

MUSHROOMS AND STUFFING

24 medium to large (2½-inch diameter) white mushrooms, stems discarded, rinsed and dried
1 cup packed shredded zucchini (about 1½ large zucchini), squeezed of excess moisture
1½ cups grated Swiss or Gruyère cheese
½ cup Italian-style bread crumbs
⅓ cup finely chopped sweet onion
¼ teaspoon freshly ground black pepper
2 to 3 tablespoons heavy whipping cream
1 tablespoon olive oil
2 tablespoons finely chopped flat-leaf parsley, optional

Preheat the oven to 375°F.

In a small bowl, whisk together the marinade ingredients.

Place the mushrooms stem side up in a 9 x 13-inch glass dish. Drizzle ½ teaspoon of the marinade into each mushroom.

To prepare the stuffing, in a medium bowl, mix together the zucchini, cheese, bread crumbs, onion and pepper. Drizzle in 2 tablespoons of the cream and the olive oil and stir to combine. The mixture should be slightly moist and should come together when a spoon is pressed against it. Add in any remaining marinade and add another tablespoon of cream, if needed, to add more moisture.

Spoon the filling into the mushroom cavities, mounding the stuffing slightly. Add 3 tablespoons of water into the bottom of the pan. Bake the mushrooms for 25 to 30 minutes, or until the mushrooms are tender and the stuffing is heated through and golden on top. Sprinkle the mushrooms with flat-leaf parsley, if desired, and serve immediately.

GF GLUTEN-FREE ADAPTABLE Use a brand of Dijon that is known to be gluten-free. Substitute gluten-free bread crumbs for the regular bread crumbs.

TIP Stuffed mushrooms are best served fresh out of the oven. Tray serve them with toothpicks and napkins for your guests and distribute them quickly while they are still warm.

CHANGE IT UP!

Substitute 1 cup shredded Parmesan or provolone for the Swiss/Gruyère.

Chop the tender parts of the mushroom stems and include some of those in the stuffing.

smoked salmon–topped cucumber rounds

Makes: 30 appetizers   Prep Time: 40 minutes

Thank goodness for smoked salmon when you need to make a quick and easy, elegant appetizer. It's sold in a little package at your market, all ready to serve with no cooking needed, and it's such a pretty addition to your appetizer display. In this recipe, cucumber slices are spread with a creamy caper and horseradish cheese and then topped with a slice of smoked salmon and fresh dill.

⅓ cup sour cream
3 ounces cream cheese, at room temperature
2 tablespoons chopped capers
1 tablespoon prepared horseradish
  Salt and freshly ground black pepper, to taste
1 large English hothouse cucumber, cut crosswise into thirty ¼-inch slices
½ pound smoked salmon, cut into 1½-inch pieces
30 ½-inch pieces dill

In a medium bowl, stir together the sour cream, cream cheese, capers and horseradish until smooth. Add salt and pepper, to taste.

Spread a heaping teaspoonful of the cheese mixture onto each cucumber slice. Top the cheese with a folded-over piece of salmon and garnish with a piece of dill. Refrigerate for up to 2 hours before serving.

GF GLUTEN-FREE ADAPTABLE Use brands of horseradish and smoked salmon that are known to be gluten-free.

QUICK AND EASY TIP Purchase a soft herb tub cheese and use that in place of the cream cheese mixture.

CHANGE IT UP!
Serve this appetizer, cucumber and all, placed on top of square-shaped cocktail bread.

sweet nectarine bruschetta

Makes: 24 appetizers   Prep Time: 30 minutes   Cook Time: 10 minutes

In this fun-take on a no-tomato-needed bruschetta, sweet nectarines are combined with the tangy flavor of feta cheese to make a delicious summer appetizer. It's best when nectarines are sweet and ripe. This is one appetizer that the kids will gobble up too.

2	medium ripe nectarines, pitted and finely diced (about 1 cup)
½	medium red bell pepper, diced (about ⅔ cup)
3	green onions, chopped, white parts only
3	tablespoons olive oil, divided
1	tablespoon freshly squeezed lime juice
1	teaspoon minced Serrano chile
24	thin slices baguette
¾	cup crumbled feta cheese

Preheat the oven to 350°F and place the rack in the middle of the oven.

In a medium bowl, gently toss the nectarines, bell pepper, onions, 1 tablespoon of the olive oil, the lime juice and chile. Set aside.

Spread out the baguette slices on a baking sheet. Drizzle the bread with the remaining 2 tablespoons olive oil. Bake the baguette slices until the bread is lightly toasted, 3 to 5 minutes (watch closely so they don't overbrown or burn).

Remove the bread from the oven and top each slice with a spoonful of the nectarine mixture. Sprinkle the cheese on top. Place the baking sheet back into the oven and heat the bruschetta for an additional 3 to 5 minutes, just until the bruschetta are heated through. Serve immediately.

GF GLUTEN-FREE ADAPTABLE Serve the sweet nectarine mixture on gluten-free crackers instead of baguette slices.

DF DAIRY-FREE ADAPTABLE Leave off the cheese.

TIPS Slice the baguette on a slight diagonal to create slightly larger, more decorative slices of bread.

This recipe is also wonderful served cold on toasted baguette slices.

CHANGE IT UP!

Try using peaches or sweet plums in place of nectarines, and goat cheese in place of the feta cheese. Add chopped prosciutto into the mix.

spinach, sun-dried tomato and prosciutto puff pastry pinwheels

Makes: 36 appetizers   Prep Time: 15 minutes + chill/freeze time   Cook Time: 20 minutes

This pinwheel appetizer is another simple one to prepare. You don't have to have the skills of a TV chef, yet everyone always comments that they're festive and impressive. They're a great make-ahead option since you can keep them in the freezer to use at a moment's notice.

1	17.3-ounce package of puff pastry (2 sheets)
1	10-ounce package frozen chopped spinach, thawed and squeezed completely dry
½	cup chopped sun-dried tomatoes (see Tips)
½	cup mayonnaise
½	cup freshly grated Asiago or Parmesan cheese
1	teaspoon onion powder
1	teaspoon garlic powder
¼	teaspoon freshly ground black pepper
5	ounces thinly sliced prosciutto
1	large egg, beaten and mixed with 1 tablespoon water

Thaw the puff pastry at room temperature for 30 minutes, or until it is defrosted and easy to unfold.

Meanwhile, to prepare the filling, in a medium bowl, stir together the spinach, sun-dried tomatoes, mayonnaise, cheese, onion powder, garlic powder and pepper. Cover and refrigerate until ready to use.

Unfold 1 sheet of the pastry and place it on a lightly floured surface with a long side facing you. Spread half of the spinach mixture evenly over the pastry sheet, leaving a ½-inch border around the edge. Lay half of the prosciutto slices on top of the spinach. Starting at the long side facing you, roll up the pastry, pressing to seal the seam. Wrap the log in plastic wrap. Repeat the procedure with the remaining pastry, spinach mixture and prosciutto. Freeze the rolled up pastry logs for 45 minutes, or until they are firm but not completely frozen.

Preheat the oven to 400°F. Cut the pastry logs into ½-inch-thick slices and place on two baking sheets, leaving 1½ inches between each pinwheel. Brush each pinwheel with egg wash. Bake for 20 to 25 minutes, or until golden brown. Serve warm or at room temperature.

TIPS Use sun-dried tomatoes packed in oil (drain and pat dry), or you can rehydrate dried tomatoes in hot water until softened (drain and pat dry).

These appetizers may be cut, frozen on baking sheets and then bagged and kept frozen for up to 3 months. Remove the slices from the freezer and bake, as needed.

CHANGE IT UP!

Create a new version of a puff pastry pinwheel: Layer with 2 tablespoons honey mustard, 5 ounces thinly sliced prosciutto and ¾ cup shredded Parmesan cheese.

stuffed endive with fig, blue cheese and honeyed walnuts

Makes: 18 appetizers   Prep Time: 40 minutes   Cook Time: 10 minutes

Endive is a member of the chicory family, and it's related to things like radicchio and escarole. It's a pull-apart kind of vegetable with small, crunchy leaves that create a natural resting place for appetizer fillings. This two-bite appetizer recipe fills those leaves with a blue cheese spread, dried fig and toasted honeyed walnuts.

½   cup roughly chopped walnuts
1½   tablespoons honey
3   ounces cream cheese, softened
⅓   cup blue cheese crumbles
1   tablespoon sour cream
2   heads endive, leaves separated
9   dried figs, cut into thirds

Preheat the oven to 350°F. Spray a baking sheet with nonstick spray.

In a small bowl, mix the walnuts with the honey. Spread them out on the baking sheet and bake 10 minutes, stirring halfway through cooking. Remove from the oven and let cool.

In a medium bowl, stir together the cream cheese, blue cheese and sour cream until smooth.

Spoon 2 teaspoons of the cream cheese mixture into each endive leaf. Top each with 1 slice of fig and 1 teaspoon walnuts.

GF GLUTEN-FREE ADAPTABLE Use a brand of figs that is known to be gluten-free, and substitute feta or goat cheese for the blue cheese.

TIPS When fresh figs are in season, use those in place of the dried figs.

This recipe may be assembled 2 to 3 hours in advance. Keep refrigerated until ready to serve.

CHANGE IT UP!

Substitute pecans in place of walnuts, goat cheese in place of the blue cheese, and dried apricots for the figs.

scallops with bacon-balsamic cream sauce (for two)

Makes: 2 servings   Prep Time: 15 minutes   Cook Time: 10 minutes

Recipes designed for two are perfect for a little nibble as a prelude to your romantic (or ho-hum, we've been married forever) dinner. Scallops cook up so quickly and easily on the stove, making them a good choice for an appetizer. When you coat them with a hefty drizzle of balsamic cream sauce and a sprinkle of bacon, you're going to wish that you didn't have to share them with your partner.

2	tablespoons finely chopped shallot
2	slices bacon, finely chopped (see Tips)
4	large scallops
½	tablespoon minced garlic
2	tablespoons white wine
¼	cup heavy whipping cream
1	tablespoon balsamic vinegar
¼	cup seeded and diced tomato
	Chopped fresh chives or flat-leaf parsley for garnish, optional

In a medium skillet, cook the shallot and bacon over medium heat for 5 to 6 minutes, or until the shallots begin to soften and brown and the bacon is crisp. Add the scallops and continue to cook until the scallops are lightly browned underneath, 2 to 3 minutes. Stir in the garlic and cook for 30 seconds. Flip the scallops and add the wine to the pan. Continue to cook until the wine is nearly evaporated. Add the cream and vinegar. Simmer the scallops in the sauce until cooked through, 2 to 3 more minutes.

For serving, place two scallops each on two plates, and top with a drizzle of the balsamic cream sauce and 2 tablespoons of the tomato. Sprinkle with chives or parsley, if desired.

GF GLUTEN-FREE ADAPTABLE Use a brand of bacon that is known to be gluten-free.

TIP I prefer to use center-cut bacon for this recipe since you'll get more bacon out of it and less fat.

CHANGE IT UP!
Turn this into a main dish for one by serving the scallops and sauce over hot cooked pasta.

chilled strawberry and coconut milk soup shooters

Makes: 10 soup shooters   Prep Time: 15 minutes + marinating time

Chilled soup might be viewed as a bit of an odd commodity, but it really shouldn't be. It's a fun and fancy little appetizer, but it's not so fancy to prepare. All of it can be done in the blender and the prep time is minimal. Serve it up in small plastic cups or tall shot glasses accompanied by a small strawberry to garnish the glass and a sprinkle of toasted coconut. This one has "fun summer appetizer" written all over it. Kids will enjoy it too.

8   ounces strawberries, rinsed and sliced
2   tablespoons granulated white sugar
1   tablespoon freshly squeezed lime juice
1   cup low-fat canned coconut milk
     Additional small strawberries, for garnish
¼   cup toasted shaved coconut, for garnish (optional; see Tips)

Toss together the strawberries, sugar and lime juice in a medium bowl. Let the mixture marinate for 30 minutes.

In a blender or food processor, combine the strawberries and coconut milk. Process until smooth. Pour into small serving glasses and garnish with strawberries and toasted coconut, if desired.

TIP To toast the coconut: Preheat the oven to 350°F. Spread the coconut onto a rimmed baking sheet and bake until golden, 4 to 6 minutes (stirring halfway through). If the coconut is sweetened, it will brown more quickly, so keep an eye on it.

CHANGE IT UP!

Add white rum or coconut rum to make this a cocktail instead of an appetizer.

chorizo and cheese—stuffed jalapeños

Makes: 20 appetizers   Prep Time: 30 minutes   Cook Time: 15 minutes

Back in college, my roommates and I frequented happy hour at many fine local establishments. Our mission was to piece together a cheap dinner off of the "Happy Hour Appetizer Specials" menu, and we proceeded to consume as many calories as is entirely possible in one sitting. One of the appetizers that contributed to that ultimately bad decision was the infamous deep-fried jalapeño popper. I think I'm still working off the long-term damage those deep-fried appetizers did to my thighs. My recipe for stuffed jalapeños is not anywhere near as evil as those college treats. They're stuffed with cheesy goodness and a little bit of chorizo mixed with corn tortilla crumbs, and they're baked instead of fried.

10	medium fresh jalapeño peppers
6	ounces pork chorizo, cooked and crumbled
4	ounces cream cheese, softened
½	cup tortilla crumbs (see Tips)
½	cup finely shredded extra sharp cheddar cheese
¼	teaspoon garlic powder
¼	teaspoon onion powder
⅛	teaspoon freshly ground black pepper
¼	cup chopped fresh cilantro + additional sprigs for garnish

Preheat the oven to 400°F.

Cut the jalapeños in half lengthwise, keeping the stem intact on one half. Scrape out the seeds and ribs and discard (see Tips).

To prepare the filling, in a medium bowl, mix the chorizo with the remaining ingredients (except cilantro). Stuff each jalapeño half with the filling, mounding it slightly. Place the stuffed jalapeños on a baking sheet.

Bake 15 to 20 minutes, or until the peppers have softened and the filling is hot. Move the jalapeños to a serving platter and sprinkle them with the chopped cilantro. Garnish the platter with sprigs of cilantro and serve immediately.

GF GLUTEN-FREE ADAPTABLE Use brands of chorizo and corn tortillas that are known to be gluten-free.

TIPS Be careful with handling the jalapeños since they'll impart burning spice to your hands. Wear gloves while handling to prevent this from happening. Be sure to discard all of the ribs and seeds since those are the extra spicy parts of the pepper.

Grind 2 corn tortillas in a food processor or blender to create about ½ cup of crumbs. There is no need to purchase fresh. If you have older, semi-stale tortillas around, they'll grind up just fine.

CHANGE IT UP!

Substitute hot Italian sausage for the chorizo and bread crumbs for the tortilla crumbs.

sticky-sweet chicken wings

Makes: 8 servings   Prep Time: 25 minutes + marinating time   Cook Time: 15 minutes

Between my hunky husband and my sports-obsessed son, there is an awful lot of football-watching that goes on in our house. The boys sit down to watch their favorites (Chargers, Patriots and Green Bay) and all of the others too. They don't want to talk much while the game is on, but I often hear mumblings of, "I'm hungry," and "Hey, are you planning on whipping up some munchies for the game?" This recipe was inspired by one of those football-watching Sundays when my boys were craving chicken wings of the sweet variety. These are definitely sweet and a little sticky. The fresh cilantro sprinkled on top gives them an extra boost of flavor.

MARINADE

⅔ cup soy sauce
¼ cup packed dark brown sugar
¼ cup honey
1 tablespoon minced garlic (about 3 large cloves)
1 tablespoon freshly squeezed lemon juice
1 tablespoon minced fresh ginger
1 teaspoon freshly ground black pepper

REMAINING INGREDIENTS

4 pounds chicken wings, trimmed (see Tips)
¼ cup chopped fresh cilantro

In a large zip baggie, combine all of the marinade ingredients. Add the trimmed chicken wings and drumsticks, seal the bag and move them around to coat with the marinade. Refrigerate the marinating wings for at least 12 hours or overnight, turning the bag every so often to make sure the marinade is reaching all of the chicken pieces.

Preheat the oven to 450°F. Line a rimmed baking sheet with foil and place a baking rack onto the foil. Spray the rack with cooking spray.

Drain and discard the marinade from the bag. Place the chicken pieces on the rack. Bake 15 to 18 minutes, or until the chicken skin is dark brown and crispy. Juices should run clean when the wings are pierced with a knife. Move the chicken to a serving platter, sprinkle with cilantro and serve.

GF GLUTEN-FREE ADAPTABLE Use a brand of soy sauce that is known to be gluten-free.

TIP To trim chicken wings: Use a sharp knife or kitchen scissors to trim off and discard the tips. Cut each wing at the joint so you'll end up with a drumstick and a flat wing.

> **CHANGE IT UP!**
>
> The marinade in this recipe is also delicious when used as a marinade for larger chicken drumsticks. Bake at 350°F for 50 to 60 minutes, until the chicken is cooked through.

bacon-wrapped tater tots

Makes: 24 appetizers   Prep Time: 25 minutes   Cook Time: 15 minutes

The best thing about "Game Day" (besides watching those guys in tight pants running around the field with a football) is definitely the food. It's usually about comfort food of all sorts, food you're willing to sacrifice extra time at the gym for, and food that you only treat yourself to once a year on Super Bowl Sunday. Here's a quick and easy appetizer recipe for you that requires only 4 ingredients. It's great for a football-type party, but it's also fun for other times when good ol' comfort food is needed.

12 slices center-cut bacon, cut in half crosswise
24 tater tots, partially defrosted (15 minutes at room temperature)
24 ½-inch chunks sharp cheddar cheese
Tabasco sauce
24 toothpicks

Preheat the oven to 450°F. Line a baking sheet with parchment paper or spray with nonstick spray.

Lay a piece of bacon on a flat surface. Place a tater tot on top. Using a sharp knife, gently cut a slit down the center of the tater tot. Wiggle a piece of cheese into the slit. Sprinkle Tabasco sauce on top. Wrap the bacon tightly around the stuffed tater tot and secure it with a toothpick. Repeat with the remaining ingredients.

Bake for 15 minutes, or until the tater tots are cooked through and the bacon is crispy. Serve immediately.

GF GLUTEN-FREE ADAPTABLE Use brands of tator tots and bacon that are known to be gluten-free.

TIP Try serving these with a spicy sour cream dip—sour cream mixed with a little bit of Tabasco sauce.

MAKE-AHEAD TIP Assemble these a few hours ahead of time and place them on a baking sheet. Cover with plastic wrap, refrigerate, and bake when ready.

CHANGE IT UP!

Add a piece of pickle on top of the cheese.

Roll the bacon-wrapped tater tot in brown sugar before baking to add a sweet flavor—just make sure you don't overbake them or the sugar will cause them to burn.

Replace the cheddar cheese with cream cheese and a piece of peperoncini.

corn dog mini muffins

Makes: 24 mini muffins   Prep Time: 25 minutes   Cook Time: 10 minutes

In our neighborhood, we tend to have a lot of parties outdoors in a common area where the adults can socialize and the kids are running amok. I always bring along dozens of these handheld mini muffins to contribute, and they disappear from the table rather quickly. Dads often enter into battle with their children over who gets the last corn dog muffin.

1   cup cornmeal
½   cup all-purpose flour
2   tablespoons packed light
     brown sugar
1   tablespoon baking powder
1   teaspoon salt
½   teaspoon baking soda
1   cup buttermilk
½   cup milk
2   tablespoons unsalted butter,
     melted
1   large egg
1   cup shredded extra-sharp
     cheddar cheese
5   hot dogs, diced
     Ketchup, mustard, sour
     cream, and/or honey
     mustard for dipping,
     optional

Preheat the oven to 400°F. Grease a 24-cup mini muffin pan generously with shortening or nonstick spray.

In a medium bowl, whisk together the cornmeal, flour, sugar, baking powder, salt and baking soda.

In a large bowl, combine the buttermilk, milk, butter and egg. Stir in the dry ingredients and cheese just until combined. Spoon a generous tablespoonful of batter into each muffin tin. Add a few pieces of hot dog to each muffin cup.

Bake for 10 to 12 minutes, or until golden brown. Let the muffins cool for 10 to 15 minutes in the pan before removing (see Tips). Serve warm with desired dipping sauces.

TIP For easy removal from the pan, slide a sharp knife between the outsides of the muffins and the pan, working the knife around the pan, then tip the pan upside down onto a large cutting board and urge the muffins out of the pan using the knife to tap the bottoms of the muffin tins. They should slide right out.

CHANGE IT UP!

Use your favorite cornbread mix in place of homemade. Follow the instructions on the box, add in 1 cup of cheddar cheese and mix in chopped hot dogs too. If your favorite cornbread mix doesn't have a sweet element to it, add in 2 tablespoons brown sugar.

cheesy pepperoni pizza
pull-apart bread

Makes: 1 large bread loaf appetizer   Prep Time: 20 minutes   Cook Time: 30 minutes

Food blogs exploded in experimenting with pull-apart round bread loaf recipes in 2012. It was an Internet craze as people sliced open their sourdough rounds and stuffed in cheese, caramelized onions, mushrooms and even ranch dressing, and then baked them up to a big cheesy, delicious mess of an appetizer. I admit to jumping on the pull-apart bread bandwagon myself. It's the perfect appetizer to place in front of a circle of hungry people and let them go at it. My version includes chopped pepperoni and pizza sauce, along with an appropriate amount of cheese and melted garlic butter to hold it all together.

1   20-ounce round loaf of
     French or sourdough bread
1   cup jarred pizza sauce
2   cups (8 ounces) shredded
     mozzarella cheese
1   cup (4 ounces) shredded
     cheddar cheese
1   3.5-ounce package sliced
     pepperoni, chopped (about
     1 cup)
2   tablespoons salted butter,
     melted
½   teaspoon garlic powder
¼   teaspoon Italian seasoning
     Additional pizza sauce,
     warmed for dipping,
     optional

Preheat the oven to 350°F.

Place the bread on a cutting board. Use a bread knife to cut a crisscross pattern in the bread, ½ inch between cuts, slicing down toward the bottom of the bread loaf without cutting through the bottom crust.

Place the bread loaf inside a large piece of foil, one that will be large enough to wrap around the entire loaf. Spoon the pizza sauce into the cuts. In a medium bowl, combine the cheeses. Stuff the cheese and pepperoni into the cuts, too. It will be messy and imperfect, and that's okay. Continue stuffing until you've used up all of the cheese and pepperoni, filling as many cuts as you can. Mix the butter, garlic powder and Italian seasoning in a small bowl. Drizzle over the top of the bread. Wrap the foil around the loaf and bake for 15 minutes. Unwrap the foil and bake for an additional 15 to 20 minutes, or until the bread is toasted and the cheese is melted. Move the bread to a platter and serve immediately accompanied by a side dish of warmed pizza sauce for dipping, if desired.

TIP If you're unable to locate a round loaf, it's okay to use a rectangular-shaped loaf. Just purchase one that is unsliced and cross-cut it the same way.

CHANGE IT UP!

Leave out the pizza sauce and the pepperoni and substitute ½ pound chopped and cooked bacon instead. Drizzle with 4 tablespoons melted butter + ½ teaspoon garlic powder and sprinkle ½ cup green onions on top.

roasted spicy maple almonds

Makes: 2 cups   Prep Time: 25 minutes   Cook Time: 15 minutes

If I were stuck on a desert island and all that was available to eat was almonds, I think I'd probably be okay with that. Almonds are my nemesis. I'd eat them all day long and every which way if it were okay to do so. Whether they're plain, naked, Marcona, roasted, spiced, sweet . . . all varieties are appealing to me. Place a bowl of almonds in front of me, and I'm not likely to share. I'll share these with you though. These almonds are roasted with a bit of sugared sweet maple syrup and melted butter, and there's some cayenne thrown in there for a little kick.

1	tablespoon granulated white sugar
1	teaspoon fine sea salt, divided
2	tablespoons unsalted butter
2	tablespoons maple syrup
2	cups blanched or raw almonds
½	teaspoon cayenne pepper

Preheat the oven to 350°F. Spray a 20-inch piece of foil with nonstick spray. Spray a baking sheet with nonstick spray.

In a small bowl, stir together the sugar and ½ teaspoon of the salt. Set aside.

In a large skillet, heat the butter and syrup over medium-high heat until it's bubbling. Remove from the heat and stir in the almonds, cayenne, and remaining ½ teaspoon salt. Toss to coat. Spread the almonds onto the prepared baking sheet. Sprinkle the almonds evenly with the sugar mixture. Bake, stirring halfway through, for 15 to 20 minutes, or until golden brown. Scoop the almonds onto the prepared foil and spread them out as much as possible. Let them cool completely and then store in a covered container.

GF GLUTEN-FREE ADAPTABLE Use a brand of maple syrup that is known to be gluten-free.

TIPS This recipe works with other nuts too—walnuts, cashews, pecans, etc.

Prepare these almonds up to 3 days ahead. Store them in a covered container.

CHANGE IT UP!

Don't like it spicy? Add ground cinnamon in place of the cayenne.

Add herbs! Try adding 1 tablespoon finely chopped rosemary to the skillet.

Salads & Sides

Oftentimes my favorite part of a meal when we're out to eat is one of the lesser-known side dishes on the menu. When salads are made just right, with a light coating of dressing and the proper embellishments to the greens, we might find ourselves wishing we could have seconds. When potatoes are baked just-so or when rice or vegetables are blended with unexpected ingredients, that's sometimes what keeps us remembering that meal. Side dishes aren't meant to take on the starring role in a dinner, but sometimes they accidentally do. If my family let me get away with it, I'd have side dishes for dinner and that's it!

Recipes

W WEB FAVORITE   V VEGETARIAN *(or adaptable)*   GF GLUTEN-FREE *(or adaptable)*   DF DAIRY-FREE *(or adaptable)*

avocado–pine nut salad

Makes: 8 servings   Prep Time: 15 minutes

This salad has served several purposes in my life for a number of years. It has found a spot on the buffet table at nearly every family get-together, and it has been brought to the needy, both to celebrate new babies and to mourn those lost. It has netted the coveted salad slot at my Thanksgiving dinner, and it's the only salad that is repeated in my kitchen time and time again. Everyone (literally, everyone) loves this salad. I hope you do too.

DRESSING

- 4 tablespoons white wine vinegar
- 3 tablespoons extra-virgin olive oil
- 1½ tablespoons Dijon mustard
  Salt and freshly ground black pepper, to taste

SALAD

- 1 head green leaf lettuce, chopped (4 to 5 cups)
- 1 head red leaf lettuce, chopped (4 to 5 cups)
- 2 medium vine-ripened tomatoes, chopped
- 1 large avocado, pitted, peeled and chopped
- ⅓ cup toasted pine nuts (see Tip)
- ¼ cup shredded mozzarella cheese

In a shaker jar or a plastic tub, add the dressing ingredients and shake well.

In a large salad bowl, add all of the salad ingredients and drizzle the dressing on top. Toss gently to combine and coat the salad. Serve immediately.

GF **GLUTEN-FREE ADAPTABLE** Use a brand of Dijon that is known to be gluten-free.

DF **DAIRY-FREE ADAPTABLE** Leave out the cheese.

TIP A simple way to toast the pine nuts is to dry roast them in a small skillet over medium heat. Stir them often so that they do not burn (they'll burn easily if they're not tended to). Pull them from the heat as soon as they begin to turn golden brown and pour them onto a paper towel to cool off.

MAKE-AHEAD TIP The dressing may be made 2 to 3 days in advance. Just keep it in a covered container in the refrigerator until it is ready to use.

CHANGE IT UP!

Turn this into a main dish salad by adding grilled chicken or shrimp.

DF

kale and bacon salad with strawberry jam vinaigrette

Makes: 4 servings   Prep Time: 15 minutes   Cook Time: 10 minutes

While dining in Atlanta on a business trip, I discovered the beauty and deliciousness of raw kale in the form of a kale salad. The restaurant was called Terrace, and I will forever be indebted to the chefs there for putting this idea of a salad in my head. Kale can be tough and gritty and not-so-pleasant to eat unless you treat it just right. If you do, then it happens to be wonderful and healthy and very pleasant to eat. The trick with a salad is to cut the kale into thin strips, dress it and then give the kale some time to absorb the vinaigrette and take in all of that flavor.

SALAD

3	slices bacon, cut into ½-inch pieces
½	cup thinly sliced red bell pepper
½	cup thinly julienned carrot (see Tips)
¼	cup sliced shallot
5	to 6 cups thinly sliced kale strips (ribs removed and discarded, see Tips)

VINAIGRETTE

1	tablespoon red wine vinegar
1	tablespoon whole grain Dijon mustard
1	tablespoon extra-virgin olive oil
1	tablespoon strawberry jam

In a medium skillet, fry the bacon over medium heat until crisp, 6 to 8 minutes. Remove the bacon to a paper towel–lined plate to drain. Discard all but 1 tablespoon of bacon fat. Add the bell pepper, carrot and shallot to the reserved bacon fat in the pan. Turn the heat to medium and cook, stirring, until the vegetables have softened slightly, 3 to 4 minutes. Remove the pan from heat and let the vegetables cool, about 5 minutes.

Place the kale strips into a serving bowl and add the cooled vegetables.

In a small bowl, whisk together the vinaigrette ingredients. Pour the vinaigrette over the salad and toss. Let the kale and vegetables marinate in the vinaigrette for at least 15 minutes, tossing now and then to redistribute the vinaigrette. Serve immediately.

GF GLUTEN-FREE ADAPTABLE Use brands of bacon, Dijon and strawberry jam that are known to be gluten-free.

 VEGETARIAN ADAPTABLE Leave out the bacon.

TIPS A "julienne" is a type of cut that makes a long thin strip (like a matchstick). Start with a 2-inch piece of peeled carrot. Cut down the sides to create a rectangular shape, and then cut thin slices lengthwise. Stack those slices and then cut long, thin strips from the stack.

Use the green, leafy Tuscan (or similar kind) of kale for this recipe. Remove the center ribs and carefully chiffonade (thinly slice) the kale into strips.

Don't be tempted to eat this salad as soon as you toss it. Kale needs time to marinate in the vinaigrette, and then it will be more tender and ready for eating.

> **CHANGE IT UP!**
>
> Add a sweet element of sliced strawberries to the salad, leaving out the red bell pepper and carrot and adding in toasted, sliced almonds instead.

triple berry salad with sugared almonds

Makes: 6 to 8 servings   Prep Time: 25 minutes   Cook Time: 5 minutes

If you've never had fresh berries in a green salad before, now is the time to try it out. My sister Susie was visiting one summer and she shared her secret for losing an entire dress size over the period of a couple of months: she ate salad with berries and sugared nuts for dinner almost every night! Okay, so she's a fanatic on the elliptical machine too, but in any case, this is a darn good salad, and it's healthy too. Sister Susie helped me create this one. (And FYI, no guarantees on that dress-size thing.)

ALMONDS
3   tablespoons granulated white sugar
½   cup slivered almonds

DRESSING
3   tablespoons strawberry jam
2   tablespoons white balsamic vinegar (see Tips)
1   tablespoon chopped flat-leaf parsley
½   teaspoon salt
½   teaspoon Dijon mustard
    Dash of freshly ground black pepper
¼   cup extra-virgin olive oil

SALAD
1   pound mixed salad greens
1½   cups blackberries
1½   cups sliced strawberries
1½   cups blueberries
1   large avocado, pitted, peeled and chopped
2   green onions, white and green parts, finely chopped
¾   cup Gorgonzola cheese crumbles

To prepare the almonds, in a small skillet, heat the sugar over medium heat until it begins to melt. Add the almonds to the pan and toss rapidly until the sugar coats all of the almonds and the almonds are lightly browned. Pour them into a glass dish and separate the almonds with a fork. Cool until hardened and break into pieces.

To prepare the dressing, in a small bowl or shaker jar, whisk together all of the dressing ingredients (except olive oil). Add the olive oil in a slow stream, whisking constantly, until the dressing thickens.

To assemble the salad, in a large bowl, combine the greens, berries, avocado and onions. Add the dressing and toss the salad. Add the sugared almonds and cheese. Toss again lightly and serve.

GF GLUTEN-FREE ADAPTABLE Use brands of strawberry jam and Dijon mustard that are known to be gluten-free. Substitute goat or feta cheese for the Gorgonzola (unless you are sure that the gorgonzola you're using is gluten-free).

DF DAIRY-FREE ADAPTABLE Leave out the cheese.

TIPS This recipe calls for white balsamic vinegar, which makes the salad look clean and nice. White wine vinegar may be substituted. You're certainly welcome to use regular balsamic vinegar too but it adds brown color to the pretty berry salad.

The almonds and the dressing can be made 2 to 3 days in advance. Keep the almonds in a covered container, and keep the dressing covered and refrigerated.

CHANGE IT UP!

Use whatever kinds of berries you'd like, and feel free to switch out the gorgonzola crumbles for goat cheese or feta.

Add in some grilled chicken to turn this into a main-dish salad.

caprese salad with burrata cheese

Makes: 4 servings   Prep Time: 25 minutes   Cook Time: 15 minutes

At some time in your lifetime of visiting Italian food establishments, you've very likely come across the classic caprese salad—the version of this salad that utilizes slices of fresh mozzarella cheese. Using Burrata cheese in this salad turns it into an entirely different salad altogether. Burrata means "buttered" in Italian (and for good reason!). Rounds of Burrata have an exterior of mozzarella and an interior of mozzarella strands mixed with cream. It happens to be soft and rich and creamy. When Burrata is paired with fresh tomatoes and basil, that's just about all it needs to create a wonderful, new version of the caprese.

⅔   cup balsamic vinegar
2   large red tomatoes, each cut into 4 slices
4   2.5-ounce rounds Burrata cheese, each cut into 3 slices (see Tips)
12 large fresh basil leaves
2   large yellow tomatoes, each cut into 4 slices
4   tablespoons extra-virgin olive oil
    Salt and freshly ground black pepper, to taste

In a small saucepan, bring the vinegar to a boil over medium heat. Reduce the heat to low and simmer until the vinegar is reduced by at least half, 15 to 20 minutes. It becomes a little bit thicker as it reduces. Remove the vinegar from heat and let it cool at room temperature until you are ready to assemble the salads (see Tips).

To assemble the salads, on each of four plates, layer 1 slice red tomato, 1 slice of cheese, 1 basil leaf, 1 slice yellow tomato, 1 slice cheese, 1 basil leaf, 1 slice red tomato, 1 slice cheese, 1 basil leaf and 1 slice yellow tomato. Drizzle 1 tablespoon of olive oil over each salad. Drizzle 1 tablespoon of the reduced balsamic on each salad. Top with a sprinkle of salt and a couple of grinds of pepper.

TIPS Burrata can usually be found in the gourmet cheese section of your market (in the same place where you'd find fresh mozzarella) or in Italian or specialty markets.

Reduce the balsamic vinegar up to 2 days in advance. Keep it covered and refrigerated. Let it come to room temperature before using in the salad.

If you can get your hands on some heirloom tomatoes, they are wonderful as the star of this salad.

CHANGE IT UP!

Substitute fresh mozzarella for the Burrata cheese, if you prefer to make a classic caprese salad.

Spoon a drizzle of pesto sauce onto the salads instead of using fresh basil.

Sprinkle toasted pine nuts on top.

mexican salad with sweet honey-lime vinaigrette

Makes: 6 servings   Prep Time: 25 minutes

We eat a whole lot of Mexican food here in Southern California. The little fast-food shacks are great, but we serve up an awful lot of it at home too. The problem with Mexican food is that it can be terribly heavy and filling. It's nice to have a side dish to serve alongside it that adds a splash of greenery to the meal. That's where the idea of this salad came into play. Cheese is purposefully left out since there is usually a fair amount of cheese in a Mexican main dish. Now you can eat your tacos and get your veggies in too.

VINAIGRETTE

- ¼ cup freshly squeezed lime juice (about 2 large limes)
- 2 tablespoons extra-virgin olive oil
- 1 teaspoon honey
- 1 medium garlic clove, minced
- ½ teaspoon salt
- ⅛ teaspoon cayenne pepper
- ⅛ teaspoon ground cumin

SALAD

- 4 cups chopped romaine lettuce
- 1 15.5-ounce can black beans, rinsed and drained
- ¾ cup chopped tomato
- ¾ cup chopped, peeled jicama
- ¾ cup corn kernels (see Tips)
- 1 large avocado, peeled, cored and chopped
- 1 large red bell pepper, seeded, ribs removed and diced
- 2 tablespoons chopped fresh cilantro

In a small bowl, whisk together the vinaigrette ingredients.

In a large bowl, toss together the salad ingredients. Add the vinaigrette and toss lightly. Serve immediately.

GF GLUTEN-FREE ADAPTABLE Use a brand of black beans that is known to be gluten-free.

TIP I like to use raw corn kernels (cut right off the cob) for this recipe. To cut the corn kernels off the cob: Cut a small slice off of the end of the cob to create a flat surface. Set the flat end of the corn upright inside of a bowl, holding it at the top. Cut down the sides of the cob with a sharp knife and the corn kernels will collect inside of the bowl. You can certainly use canned corn kernels or defrosted frozen corn too.

CHANGE IT UP!

Leave out the lettuce, chop the salad ingredients finely, toss with the dressing, and serve as a chunky salsa with tortilla chips.

Add in grilled chicken or shrimp, crumbled Mexican Cojita cheese and crushed tortilla chips to create a hearty, main-dish salad.

classic greek salad

Makes: 6 servings   Prep Time: 15 minutes

I included this salad for my mother-in-law (who I happen to like very much, by the way), since she whips up Greek salads often at her house. It's your typical Greek salad with crunchy lettuce, tomato, red onion and cucumber, and additions of feta cheese and Greek Kalamata olives are a must. Tossed in a lemony red wine vinaigrette, this salad is finished off with a generous sprinkle of fresh dill.

VINAIGRETTE

6	tablespoons extra-virgin olive oil
3	tablespoons red wine vinegar
3	tablespoons freshly squeezed lemon juice
1	tablespoon granulated white sugar
1	medium garlic clove, minced
½	teaspoon dried oregano
½	teaspoon salt
¼	teaspoon freshly ground black pepper

SALAD

1	head romaine lettuce, rinsed and chopped
1	cup chopped tomato (about 1 medium)
¾	cup chopped cucumber
½	cup sliced red onion (about ½ medium)
½	cup halved Kalamata olives
4	ounces crumbled feta cheese
2	tablespoon chopped fresh dill (see Tips)

In a small bowl, whisk together the vinaigrette ingredients.

In a large bowl, toss together the lettuce, tomato, cucumber and red onion. Add the vinaigrette and toss again. Add olives and cheese and lightly toss. Sprinkle dill on top and serve immediately.

GF GLUTEN-FREE ADAPTABLE Use a brand of Kalamata olives that is known to be gluten-free.

DF DAIRY-FREE ADAPTABLE Leave out the feta cheese.

TIPS Don't be tempted to use dried dill. The fresh dill is what really brings this salad to life.

Serve with wedges of warmed pita bread and a spoonful of hummus for dipping.

CHANGE IT UP!

Some aficionados of Greek salad prefer to use iceberg lettuce instead of romaine.

Try using goat cheese in place of the feta and add in chopped red and green bell peppers.

insalata romantica ("romantic italian salad" for two)

Makes: 2 servings   Prep Time: 15 minutes

I was fortunate enough to travel to Italy with my husband for our 10-year wedding anniversary. We searched out the best restaurants by asking the waiters where they liked to eat. As a result, we ended up in dark alley bungalows where no one spoke a lick of English and we could merely point to things on the menu and hope we were ordering something good. It turns out that the local Italians ate pretty basic stuff, just fresh pasta with a hearty, flavorful sauce, and very simple salads without a lot of adornment. That's what this salad is all about.

2   cups torn arugula, rinsed and dried
¼   cup pine nuts, toasted (see Tips)
¼   cup shaved Parmigiano Reggiano cheese (see Tips)
2   tablespoons extra-virgin olive oil
4   teaspoons balsamic vinegar
     Salt and freshly ground black pepper, to taste

Divide the arugula equally between two salad bowls. Sprinkle each with 2 tablespoons pine nuts and 2 tablespoons cheese. Drizzle each with 1 tablespoon olive oil and 2 teaspoons vinegar. Sprinkle with salt and pepper and serve immediately.

DF DAIRY-FREE ADAPTABLE Leave off the cheese.

TIPS A simple way to toast the pine nuts is to dry roast them in a small skillet over medium heat. Stir them often so that they do not burn (they'll burn easily if they're not tended to). Pull them from the heat as soon as they begin to turn golden brown and pour them onto a paper towel to cool off.

Parmigiano Reggiano is aged according to strict, centuries-old laws in Italy regarding the making of the cheese. Production of American Parmesan cheese is not subject to the same laws, nor is it aged in the same manner. Therefore, Parmigiano Reggiano has a superior quality and taste that cannot be found in regular Parmesan cheese. Splurge for the good stuff if your budget allows for it, but you can also use Parmesan.

Use white balsamic vinegar if you'd prefer your salad to maintain a cleaner look.

CHANGE IT UP!

Add in some roasted tomatoes. Preheat the oven to 400°F. Spread cherry tomatoes onto a rimmed baking sheet. Drizzle the tomatoes with olive oil and sprinkle them with salt and pepper. Roast for 15 to 20 minutes, until soft. Serve on top of the salad.

not-your-mama's macaroni salad

Makes: 8 servings   Prep Time: 15 minutes

I'm not a huge fan of raw onion and my family isn't either. But when you soak red onion in cold water for a few minutes and then give it a rinse, it loses that super-sharp onion taste and it'll give your salad a little more crunch and flavor and color. Mom definitely doesn't like onion in her macaroni salad, she despises celery, and she'd probably balk at the addition of tomato and bacon too. You'll have to trust me though. This is probably not close to any of our mama's methods of making macaroni salad, but it's one to add to the must-make list.

2   cups dry elbow macaroni, cooked according to package directions
1   cup diced vine-ripened tomato
⅔   cup diced celery
½   cup minced red onion, soaked in cold water for 5 minutes then drained
2   tablespoons minced flat-leaf parsley
⅔   cup mayonnaise
⅓   cup sour cream
2   tablespoons apple cider vinegar
1   teaspoon dry mustard
1   teaspoon granulated white sugar
1   teaspoon salt
    Freshly ground black pepper, to taste
8   slices bacon, cooked and crumbled (see Tips)

In a large bowl, combine the macaroni, tomato, celery, onion and parsley.

In a small bowl, combine the mayonnaise, sour cream, vinegar, mustard, sugar and salt.

Use a rubber spatula to scrape the dressing into the pasta mixture and stir to combine. Season the salad with pepper, to taste. Sprinkle crumbled bacon on top.

TIPS For easy clean-up, cook your bacon in the oven. Preheat the oven to 400°F. Line a large, rimmed baking sheet with foil and place a rack on top. Spray the rack with nonstick spray. Lay the bacon slices on the rack. Bake for 15 to 20 minutes, or until the bacon is crisp. Timing will vary depending on the thickness of your bacon.

This recipe can be easily cut in half to accommodate a smaller meal.

Keep this salad covered and refrigerated until ready to serve. It may be prepared up to 6 hours ahead.

CHANGE IT UP!

Turn this salad into a BLT salad by serving it on top of iceberg or Boston lettuce leaves.

If you don't care for a mayonnaise-based macaroni salad, substitute your favorite Italian dressing instead.

three bean salad

Makes: 8 servings   Prep Time: 20 minutes + refrigeration time   Cook Time: 3 minutes

For as long as I can remember, I've loved the sweet vinegar-soaked salad known to many as the 3-Bean Salad. It has always been welcome at summer potlucks, and it's probably rarely made homemade. It's such an easy salad to make though, since most versions are quickly assembled by combining three cans of beans with a sweet, vinegar-based dressing. I've jazzed things up a bit in my recipe, utilizing lightly blanched fresh green beans and adding in fresh red pepper too. It's still as sweet and vinegary as can be, and it will be most welcome at any potluck.

VINAIGRETTE
¼ cup apple cider vinegar
3 tablespoons granulated white sugar
2 tablespoons canola or vegetable oil (see Tips)
1½ teaspoons salt
¼ teaspoon pepper

SALAD
1½ cups fresh green beans, trimmed and cut into 1-inch pieces
1 15.5-ounce can garbanzo beans (chickpeas), rinsed and drained
1 15.5-ounce can kidney beans, rinsed and drained
⅔ cup chopped red bell pepper
½ cup chopped red onion
¼ cup chopped flat-leaf parsley

In a small bowl, whisk together the vinaigrette ingredients.

Bring a medium pot of water to boil. Add the green beans and cook them just until slightly tender, about 3 minutes. Pour the green beans through a strainer and run cold water over them until they no longer feel hot.

Place the cooled green beans, beans, bell pepper, onion and parsley in a large bowl. Add the vinaigrette and toss. Cover and refrigerate the salad, tossing often, for at least 2 hours and up to 8 hours before serving.

GF GLUTEN-FREE ADAPTABLE Use brands of garbanzo and kidney beans that are known to be gluten-free.

TIPS Don't be tempted to use olive oil as it's too strong-tasting for this salad.

Leftovers of this salad will be delicious for 2 to 3 days after preparation.

QUICK AND EASY TIP Leave out the green beans and substitute another canned bean (such as white or black beans) instead.

> **CHANGE IT UP!**
>
> Modify the flavor of the vinaigrette by using white balsamic vinegar or white wine vinegar in place of the apple cider vinegar.
>
> Add in chopped cucumber or chopped celery for added crunch.

grilled corn salad

Makes: 8 servings   Prep Time: 20 minutes + soaking time   Cook Time: 9 minutes

Nibbling cob after cob of sweet fresh corn in the summer time is a given. So why not make a salad out of it? Giving corn a few char marks by tossing it briefly on the grill will give your salad a delicious smoky flavor, and by soaking the corn for a half hour before grilling, you'll be giving it enough moisture to prevent it from drying out on the grill.

VINAIGRETTE

- 3 tablespoons extra-virgin olive oil
- 3 tablespoons apple cider vinegar
- 1 tablespoon freshly squeezed lemon juice
- ½ teaspoon kosher salt
  Freshly ground black pepper, to taste

SALAD

- 5 ears corn, shucked and rinsed
- 1½ cups halved cherry or pear tomatoes
- ½ cup fresh basil, cut into thin strips
- ¼ cup diced red onion
  Salt and freshly ground black pepper, to taste

In a small bowl, whisk together the vinaigrette ingredients.

Soak the corn in a large bowl of water for 30 minutes. Preheat the grill to medium. Drain the corn and place on the hot grill grates, grilling for 3 to 4 minutes on each side, or just until char marks begin to appear. Remove the ears of corn from the grill and let them cool. Cut the corn kernels off the cobs (see Tips).

In a large bowl, mix the corn kernels, tomatoes, basil and red onion.

Add the vinaigrette to the salad and toss. Season the salad with salt and pepper to taste. Cover and refrigerate until ready to serve.

TIPS To cut the corn kernels off the cob: Cut a small slice off of the end of each corn cob to create a flat surface. Set the flat end of the corn upright inside of a bowl, holding it at the top. Cut down the sides of the corn with a sharp knife and the corn kernels will collect inside of the bowl.

Using multicolored cherry tomatoes gives this salad a colorful bonus.

This salad may be prepared up to 4 hours before serving.

CHANGE IT UP!

Make a raw-corn salad instead. Just cut the corn kernels off of the cleaned cobs and proceed with the salad directions as written, omitting the steps for grilling.

Turn this salad into a Mexican-themed corn salad. Substitute lime juice for the lemon in the vinaigrette and substitute fresh cilantro for the basil.

perfect potato salad

Makes: 10 servings   Prep Time: 25 minutes   Cook Time: 10 minutes

No pickles or celery or mustard ever graced the bowl of my mother's homemade potato salad. She was a basic potato salad kind of girl, and us kids got used to eating it without any sort of added crunch or flavor bang. I've updated Mom's potato salad somewhat with a tangy mayonnaise and mustard dressing. I still don't care for crunch in my potato salad, but there always must be plenty of hard-boiled eggs. See Change It Up! below for adding in crunch, if you like that sort of thing.

4	pounds red potatoes, cleaned and cut into 1½-inch cubes
1	cup mayonnaise
½	cup sour cream
2	tablespoons white wine vinegar
1	teaspoon prepared mustard
¼	teaspoon celery salt
4	large hard-boiled eggs, chopped (see Tips)
⅓	cup chopped flat-leaf parsley
⅓	cup finely chopped green onion
	Salt and freshly ground black pepper, to taste
	Paprika

Place the potato cubes in a large pot. Add enough water to cover the potatoes. Bring the water to a boil over high heat. Reduce the heat to medium-high and continue to boil the potatoes until they are tender, 8 to 10 minutes (see Tips). Drain the potatoes in a colander and let them cool. Place the cooled potatoes in a large bowl.

To make the dressing, in a medium bowl, mix the mayonnaise, sour cream, vinegar, mustard and celery salt.

Pour the dressing over the potatoes and gently toss to coat. Add the eggs, parsley and onion and gently toss again. Season the salad with salt and pepper to taste. Sprinkle with a light dusting of paprika. Cover and refrigerate the salad for at least 2 hours and up to 6 hours before serving.

GF GLUTEN-FREE ADAPTABLE Use brands of mayonnaise and mustard that are known to be gluten-free.

TIPS To make perfect hard-boiled eggs, place your eggs into a pot and fill it with enough water to cover the eggs. Bring the water to a boil over high heat, then cover the pan and turn off the heat. Let the eggs sit in the covered pan for 15 minutes, then rinse and peel them under cold water.

When boiling the potatoes, it's important that you don't overcook them. Keep an eye on them while they are cooking and take one out to test it. You want them to be tender, but you also want them to maintain their shape and not turn into mush.

To speed up the potato-cooling process, place them in bowl and refrigerate them until ready to use (can be done up to 1 day ahead).

CHANGE IT UP!

Add crunch to this potato salad by adding in chopped pickles or celery. Add fresh dill to create a different flavor.

creamy dijon mashed potatoes

Makes: 6 servings   Prep Time: 30 minutes   Cook Time: 12 minutes

Yukon gold potatoes are my potato-of-choice for mashing. They boil up tender and fluffy, and they impart a slight, natural butter flavor to your potato dish, and since too much butter is never a bad thing, these potatoes work well with just about everything. I've added some Dijon mustard into the mashing process. The Dijon doesn't make these spicy. Instead it gives the potatoes a bit of tang and flavor, leaving little need or desire for gravy. These potatoes are good all on their own, with a smidge of butter floating on top and spooned up with whatever meat you're serving alongside (meatloaf is my favorite).

3   pounds Yukon gold or russet potatoes, peeled and cut into 1-inch pieces
½   tablespoon kosher salt
3   tablespoons salted butter
2   ounces cream cheese
½   cup whole milk, heated to warm, divided (see Tips)
3   tablespoons Dijon mustard
¼   cup chopped green onion (green parts only)
     Salt and freshly ground black pepper, to taste
3   tablespoons salted butter for topping, optional

Place the potatoes in a large pot and add enough water to cover them. Add the salt to the water and bring it to a boil. Boil the potatoes until they are very tender when pierced with a fork, 12 to 15 minutes. Drain the potatoes in a colander.

Place the drained, cooked potatoes in a large bowl (see Tips) and mash with a potato masher. Add the butter, cream cheese and ¼ cup of the warmed milk. Use an electric mixer to combine. Add the Dijon, green onion and the remaining ¼ cup milk and beat the potatoes until there are few lumps left and they have a creamy texture. Add salt and pepper, to taste. Serve immediately topped with butter, if desired.

GF GLUTEN-FREE ADAPTABLE Use a brand of Dijon mustard that is known to be gluten-free.

TIPS If you happen to own a potato ricer gadget, it works wonders for getting a good-textured mashed potato. If not, go ahead and use a potato masher, and if you don't possess either of these gadgets, an electric mixer should do a pretty good job of mashing them up.

To warm the milk, just pour it into a glass measuring cup and heat it in the microwave or in a small saucepan on the stove. It should only take a short time, but watch it closely so it doesn't bubble up and over the cup.

MAKE-AHEAD TIP Make these potatoes early in the day and keep them warmed in a slow cooker until you are ready to serve them. They also warm up nicely after refrigeration if you need to make them a day ahead.

CHANGE IT UP!

Mascarpone cheese is also wonderful in these potatoes. Use it in place of the cream cheese for a richer flavor and more luxurious texture. Alternatively, sour cream used in place of the cream cheese will add a tangy flavor.

gorgonzola smashed potatoes

Makes: 6 servings   Prep Time: 20 minutes   Cook Time: 10 minutes

What's great about these potatoes is that they're smashed rather than mashed. With mashed potatoes, you need to be concerned with getting them just right, with no chunks floating around and creating a nice and smooth texture. Smashed potatoes are just smashed. That's it, nothing fancy. Add in cream and butter and those smashed potatoes will soak it right up. Add in Gorgonzola too, and now you've got something fancy!

2½ pounds baby red potatoes, cut into 1½-inch chunks (unpeeled)
¾ to 1 cup half-and-half, warmed (see Tips)
1 tablespoon salted butter
4 ounces crumbled Gorgonzola cheese
   Salt and freshly ground black pepper, to taste

Bring a large pot of water to a boil and add the potato chunks. Boil the potatoes just until they are tender, 10 to 15 minutes. Drain the potatoes in a colander. Place them in a large bowl. Mash them lightly with a fork. Stir ¾ cup of the half-and-half and the butter into the potatoes. Add more half-and-half, as needed, if the potatoes seem too dry. Stir in the cheese and season with salt and pepper, to taste.

GF GLUTEN-FREE ADAPTABLE Make sure that the brand of Gorgonzola cheese you're using is known to be gluten-free, or use a substitute such as feta or goat cheese.

TIP To warm the half-and-half, just pour it into a glass measuring cup and heat it in the microwave or in a small saucepan on the stove. It should only take a short time, but watch it closely so it doesn't bubble up and over the cup.

CHANGE IT UP!

The potato peels add color and nutrients to this dish. If you don't care for the peel on the potatoes, go ahead and peel the potatoes before boiling.

Not a fan of Gorgonzola? Substitute another crumbled cheese instead, such as feta or goat cheese.

V DF

twice-baked crispy greek fingerling potatoes

Makes: 6 servings   Prep Time: 30 minutes + cooling time   Cook Time: 1 hour

This is the perfect, easy potato dish to make for a dinner party. You can do the first roasting of the potatoes ahead of time, let them cool to room temperature, then throw them in for a quick heat and crisp while you're getting the rest of your meal ready to serve. They're tossed with a lemony dressing just before serving to lend fresh flavor to crispy potatoes.

½ cup extra-virgin olive oil
¼ cup freshly squeezed lemon juice (see Tips)
2 tablespoons chopped shallots
1½ tablespoons chopped fresh dill
1 tablespoon chopped flat-leaf parsley
1 teaspoon finely grated lemon zest
   Salt and freshly ground black pepper, to taste
4 medium garlic cloves, thinly sliced
2½ pounds fingerling potatoes, halved lengthwise
½ cup low-sodium chicken broth

Preheat the oven to 425°F.

In a small bowl, whisk together the olive oil, lemon juice, shallots, dill, parsley and lemon zest. Add salt and pepper, to taste. Toss the garlic and ½ cup of the dressing in another small bowl. Set the rest of the dressing aside to use for serving (don't refrigerate).

On a large, rimmed baking sheet, toss the potatoes with the garlic dressing. Pour the chicken broth around the potatoes and sprinkle with salt and pepper. Roast the potatoes for 45 minutes, or until they are tender and golden, turning occasionally. Remove them from the oven and let them cool completely. Slide a spatula underneath the potatoes to loosen any potatoes that are clinging to the baking sheet.

Once the potatoes have cooled completely (see Tips), bake them again for 15 minutes (at 425°F), or until they are crisp. Toss the potatoes in a serving bowl with the reserved dressing. Serve immediately.

GF GLUTEN-FREE ADAPTABLE Use a brand of chicken broth that is known to be gluten-free.

TIP Zest your lemon before you squeeze the juice out of it.

MAKE-AHEAD TIP Prepare the first roasting of the potatoes up to 3 hours ahead. Just let them sit at room temperature until you're ready to finish them up.

CHANGE IT UP!

Use fresh chopped oregano in place of the dill.

Fingerling potatoes come in white, red and purple. Use all three for a more colorful side dish!

rainbow couscous

Makes: 4 servings   Prep Time: 15 minutes   Cook Time: 10 minutes

I've always heard that if your diet includes eating a rainbow of foods, then you're eating healthy. This side dish is full of color with some finely chopped veggies mixed into couscous. If the veggies are small, those vegetable-resistant children don't notice them as much and just might gobble them up with the rest of their dinner.

2   tablespoons salted butter
1   large shallot, minced
1   cup low-sodium chicken or
        vegetable broth
½   cup thinly sliced snow peas
½   cup shredded carrot
½   cup finely diced red bell
        pepper
½   cup finely diced yellow
        squash
1   cup dried couscous
1   tablespoon freshly squeezed
        lemon juice
½   teaspoon sea salt
2   tablespoons chopped fresh
        chives, optional

In a medium saucepan, melt the butter over medium heat. Add the shallot and cook until softened, about 2 minutes. Stir in the broth, snow peas, carrot, bell pepper and squash. Increase the heat to medium-high and bring to a boil.

Stir in the couscous, cover, remove from heat and let sit for 5 minutes. Remove the lid and stir in the lemon juice and sea salt. Sprinkle with chives, if desired. Serve immediately.

DF DAIRY-FREE ADAPTABLE Substitute oil for butter.

TIP Chop all of your veggies well ahead of dinner so putting this dish together is a snap.

CHANGE IT UP!

Try adding in other vegetables such as zucchini, yellow or green bell peppers or mushrooms.

coconut-ginger rice

Makes: 8 servings   Prep Time: 20 minutes   Cook Time: 20 minutes

I've always told my son that if I lined up all of the little boys in the world, I'd still pick him as my favorite. It's the same with this rice recipe. If I lined up all of the rice side dishes in the world, I'd choose this one hands-down. It's simmered with creamy coconut milk, which gives the rice incredible tenderness and flavor. Added pesto lends the spice to the dish, and chopped sushi ginger sets it apart from other rice dishes. If I've got a day with my son and a bowl of Coconut-Ginger Rice, well, then that's a good day.

4   tablespoons (½ stick) salted
    butter
½   cup finely diced sweet onion
2   tablespoons minced garlic
    (about 4 large cloves)
2   tablespoons sushi (pickled)
    ginger, drained and
    chopped (see Tips)
2   cups white jasmine rice
4   cups water
½   cup coconut milk
1   teaspoon kosher salt
⅛   teaspoon ground white
    pepper
1   tablespoon prepared basil
    pesto

In a medium saucepan, melt the butter over medium heat. Add the onion, garlic and ginger and cook, stirring frequently, until the onion is softened and transparent, 4 to 5 minutes. Add the rice, stirring until coated. Add the water, coconut milk, salt and pepper. Increase the heat to medium-high and bring to a boil. Cover and reduce the heat to low. Simmer until the liquid is absorbed, about 20 minutes. Remove the pan from heat and let it sit for 5 minutes.

Scoop the rice into a serving bowl, add the pesto and toss. Serve immediately.

GF **GLUTEN-FREE ADAPTABLE** Use a brand of pesto that is known to be gluten-free.

TIPS At markets where they make their own sushi, ask the sushi chef if you can take home a small container of their pickled ginger (or offer to buy it). Otherwise, look for sushi ginger in the Asian products aisle of your market.

You may substitute freshly grated ginger for the sushi ginger if you must (use ½ tablespoon). I highly recommend the pickled ginger though for the unique flavor addition.

CHANGE IT UP!

Add in ½ cup shredded or flaked coconut for added coconut flavor and texture.

lemony brown rice pilaf with toasted pine nuts

Makes: 8 servings   Prep Time: 15 minutes   Cook Time: 45 minutes

I never really liked brown rice until I experimented with mixing things into it. This recipe adds a subtle lemon flavor and a small handful of toasted pine nuts. It goes with just about anything. Leftovers (if there are any) are just as good reheated.

½	tablespoon olive oil
1	large shallot, peeled and finely chopped
1	cup brown rice (not instant)
2¼	cups water
¼	cup freshly squeezed lemon juice (see Tips)
⅓	cup pine nuts, toasted (see Tips)
½	teaspoon finely grated lemon zest

In a medium saucepan, heat the olive oil over medium heat. Add the shallot and cook, stirring constantly, until it is soft, about 5 minutes. Stir in the rice. Add the water and lemon juice. Turn the heat to medium-high and bring to a boil. Cover and reduce the heat to low. Simmer until the liquid is absorbed and the rice is fluffy and tender, 40 to 45 minutes. Stir in the pine nuts and lemon zest. Serve immediately.

TIPS Zest your lemon before you squeeze the juice out of it.

A simple way to toast the pine nuts is to dry roast them in a small skillet over medium heat. Stir them often so that they do not burn (they'll burn easily if they're not tended to). Pull them from the heat as soon as they begin to turn golden brown and pour them onto a paper towel to cool off.

CHANGE IT UP!

To use white rice in place of brown rice, use 2 cups of water and reduce the cooking time to 20 minutes (using white rice will serve 4 instead of 8).

Use almonds in place of pine nuts.

cilantro rice

Makes: 8 servings   Prep Time: 15 minutes   Cook Time: 20 minutes

My mother always served up a tomato-based Spanish rice for our family's weekly taco night. I love Mom's Spanish rice, but nowadays I prefer to have something with a little more flavor-kick. Here's a diversion from the rice that I've always known to go with any sort of Mexican food. This Mexican-themed rice recipe is simply steamed white rice with a tangy cilantro sauce mixed in.

2½ cups water
2 cups white rice
1 teaspoon sea salt
1 cup loosely packed fresh cilantro
¼ cup freshly squeezed lime juice
2 tablespoons extra-virgin olive oil
2 medium garlic cloves

In a medium saucepan, bring 2½ cups water to a boil over high heat. Add the rice and salt. Cover and reduce the heat to low. Simmer until the rice has absorbed all of the liquid, about 20 minutes.

Meanwhile, prepare the sauce. In a mini food processor, add the cilantro, lime juice, olive oil and garlic. Process until smooth.

Stir the sauce into the hot rice. Serve immediately.

TIP Use leftover rice as a filling for chicken or shrimp burritos.

CHANGE IT UP!

Make it spicy: Stir in 1 tablespoon chopped canned chipotle chiles in adobo sauce

Make it creamy: Stir in ½ cup Mexican crema.

creamy coconut polenta

Makes: 4 servings   Prep Time: 25 minutes   Cook Time: 30 minutes

I was first introduced to polenta in its solid form. When cooked a certain way, it can be poured into a dish where it eventually solidifies, allowing you to cut out rounds, place goodies on top and enjoy it as a handheld appetizer. I soon found that polenta can also be served creamy, in a most delicious way. In this recipe, the polenta is cooked much like risotto, adding a little bit of liquid at a time to allow the polenta to fully absorb the liquid before adding more. The natural cream in coconut milk helps give this polenta its creamy texture and great flavor.

1   13.66-ounce can coconut milk (see Tips)
¾   cup whole grain polenta (see Tips)
2   cups whole milk, warmed (see Tips)
1   tablespoon salted butter
1   teaspoon kosher salt
½   teaspoon freshly ground black pepper
2   tablespoons fresh chives

In a medium saucepan, bring the coconut milk to a boil. Whisk in the polenta and reduce the heat to low. Simmer for 5 minutes, stirring often. Add 1 cup of the milk and stir. Continue to stir and simmer for 6 to 7 more minutes. Stir in the remaining 1 cup milk and continue to simmer, still stirring often, until the polenta is thick and creamy, 6 to 7 minutes. Stir in the butter, salt and pepper. Serve immediately and top with chives.

GF GLUTEN-FREE ADAPTABLE Use a brand of polenta that is known to be gluten-free.

TIPS Using regular coconut milk for this recipe instead of a low-fat version turns out a much more delicious and flavorful polenta with a creamy texture.

Do not use instant or quick-cooking polenta for this recipe as it is not cooked in the same manner.

To warm the milk, just pour it into a glass measuring cup and heat it in the microwave or in a small saucepan on the stove. It should only take a short time, but watch it closely so it doesn't bubble up and over.

CHANGE IT UP!

Make this dish even more creamy by stirring in ½ cup softened cream cheese or ¼ cup heavy whipping cream.

tomato-mascarpone risotto

Makes: 8 side-dish servings (or 4 main-dish)   Prep Time: 25 minutes

Cook Time: 35 minutes

Risotto is a high-starch, short-grain rice that has the ability to absorb liquids and release starch, which makes it stickier than regular long-grain rice. When it's properly cooked, it will be creamy and the rice will still have a slight bite to it. You must tend to it with frequent stirring during the process of adding a little bit of broth at a time to the rice while it's cooking. But your labor will be one of love in the end when you have a tomato-based, mascarpone-infused, creamy bowl of rice to sample.

3   cups low-sodium chicken or vegetable broth
1   8-ounce can tomato sauce
2   tablespoons olive oil
1   cup finely chopped onion (about ½ large)
1½   cups shredded zucchini
1   large garlic clove, minced
1½   cups Arborio rice
1   cup dry white wine (Sauvignon Blanc or Pinot Grigio)
½   teaspoon kosher salt
½   cup mascarpone cheese (see Tips)
2   tablespoons freshly chopped basil
     Freshly ground black pepper, to taste

In a medium saucepan, combine the broth and tomato sauce and heat over low heat until just warmed, 4 to 5 minutes.

In a large saucepan, heat the olive oil over medium-high heat. Add the onion and cook, stirring, until softened, 3 to 4 minutes. Add the zucchini and garlic and continue to cook, stirring, until those are softened too, 3 to 4 minutes. Stir in the rice and cook, stirring occasionally, until it is glossy in appearance, 2 to 3 minutes. Add the wine, stir and let the liquid evaporate. Stir in the salt. Add the warmed tomato broth ½ cup at a time, stirring occasionally. When the broth has just about been completely absorbed by the rice, add another ½ cup. Continue to cook and stir and add broth in ½ cup increments until all of the broth has been absorbed and the risotto is tender, but still firm to the bite, 20 to 25 minutes.

Remove the pan from heat and stir in the cheese, basil and pepper to taste. Serve immediately.

GF GLUTEN-FREE ADAPTABLE Use a brand of broth that is known to be gluten-free.

DF DAIRY-FREE ADAPTABLE Leave out the cheese.

TIPS If you don't have access to mascarpone cheese, use softened cream cheese instead.

Be sure to stir often during the cooking process to keep the rice from sticking to the bottom of the pan.

Serve this as a side dish alongside roasted chicken or grilled Italian sausages.

CHANGE IT UP!

The mascarpone cheese makes the risotto creamy and rich. Leave it out if you would just like a tomato-zucchini risotto.

bacon and brown sugar
slow cooker baked beans

Makes: 8 servings   Prep Time: 15 minutes   Cook Time: 4 hours and 10 minutes

Folks usually like to have a barbecue or three in the summer time, when it's toasty-warm outside and probably inside your house too. The outdoor air absorbs the heat of your grill, but using the oven is likely to heat up your house even more. The slow cooker is a good option for sweltering hot days. These baked beans are slow cooked anywhere from 4 to 6 hours, and they'll keep the heat inside the pot without releasing it into your kitchen.

6   slices bacon, cut into 1-inch pieces (see Tips)
1   large onion, peeled and chopped
1   large green bell pepper, seeded, ribs removed and chopped
¾   cup bottled barbecue sauce
¼   to ½ cup packed light brown sugar (see Tips)
2   tablespoons tomato paste
2   tablespoons spicy brown mustard
2   tablespoons apple cider vinegar
3   15-ounce cans white beans, drained and rinsed
½   cup low-sodium chicken broth
    Salt and freshly ground black pepper, to taste

In a large skillet, cook the bacon over medium-high heat until it is slightly browned, about 4 minutes. Add the onion and pepper and cook, stirring occasionally, until they are softened and the bacon is crisp, 4 to 5 additional minutes.

Scrape the bacon and vegetables into a slow cooker. Add the barbecue sauce, sugar, tomato paste, mustard, vinegar, beans and broth to the slow cooker and stir to combine. Add salt and pepper, to taste. Cover and cook for 4 to 6 hours on low heat.

GF GLUTEN-FREE ADAPTABLE Use brands of bacon, barbecue sauce, mustard, beans and chicken broth that are known to be gluten-free.

TIPS This recipe will turn out best using regular bacon instead of turkey bacon. The bacon grease contributes to the flavor of the dish.

The amount of brown sugar you use depends on how sweet you like your baked beans. It also depends on how sweet your barbecue sauce is. Start with ¼ cup brown sugar and add more, if desired.

OVEN OPTION Bake, covered, at 350°F for 45 minutes, or until heated through and bubbling. Remove the cover and bake an additional 15 minutes.

CHANGE IT UP!

The flavor of the barbecue sauce you decide to use can have a profound effect on the flavor of your baked beans. Use something spicy and you'll have spicier baked beans. Use a smoky sauce and you'll have smoky baked beans. You get the idea.

It's perfectly okay to change up the beans in this recipe to kidney, black beans, pinto—whatever you'd like. Mix and match, or use all of one type.

brown butter and smoked gouda skillet cornbread

Makes: 12 servings   Prep Time: 20 minutes   Cook Time: 20 minutes

There is nothing on this earth that I love more than brown butter. Okay, maybe that's not true, but it comes darn near close. It's nutty aroma and flavor are intoxicating and addictive. If it were proper to drink it with a straw, I just might consider it. In any case, it's delicious to add to recipes. This cornbread is baked in a small puddle of brown butter, which gives it a crisp and buttery crust. Smoked Gouda cheese and fresh corn are mixed in to create a cornbread worthy of serving to company.

4	tablespoons (½ stick) unsalted butter
1½	cups yellow cornmeal
½	cup all-purpose flour
3	tablespoons granulated white sugar
1	tablespoon baking powder
½	teaspoon kosher salt
¼	teaspoon baking soda
1¼	cups buttermilk
2	large eggs, lightly beaten
2	tablespoons vegetable or canola oil
1	cup corn kernels (see Tips)
1	cup shredded smoked Gouda cheese
½	teaspoon smoked paprika

Preheat the oven to 425°F.

In a 10-inch cast-iron skillet, melt the butter over medium heat (see Tips). Continue to cook and stir until the butter has foamed and turned a light tan color, 3 to 5 minutes. Remove the skillet from heat and set it aside to cool. It will continue to brown slightly in the hot skillet.

In a medium bowl, whisk together the cornmeal, flour, sugar, baking powder, salt and baking soda. Make a well in the center and add the buttermilk, eggs and oil. Stir just until the batter is incorporated. Gently stir in the corn and cheese.

Scrape the batter into the skillet on top of the brown butter and smooth the top. Sprinkle with the paprika. Bake for 20 minutes, or until a toothpick inserted in the center of the cornbread comes out clean. Cut into wedges and serve.

GF GLUTEN-FREE ADAPTABLE Use brands of cornmeal and cheese that are known to be gluten-free. Substitute a gluten-free all-purpose flour blend for the regular all-purpose flour.

TIPS Use frozen, canned or fresh corn on the cob. If you're using fresh, to

continued on page 184

continued from page 183

cut the corn kernels off the cob: Cut a small slice off of the end of each corn cob to create a flat surface. Set the flat end of the corn upright inside of a bowl, holding it at the top. Cut down the sides of the corn with a sharp knife and the corn kernels will collect inside of the bowl.

If you don't have a cast-iron skillet, you may bake this cornbread in a 9 x 9-inch pan. Brown the butter in a saucepan instead and then pour it into the bottom of the pan.

When browning butter, it can change from browned to burnt very quickly. Be sure to pull the skillet off the heat at the first sign of browning (you'll see a few specks of brown) and let the indirect heat of the skillet do the rest of the work on a cool surface.

CHANGE IT UP!

You can easily change the flavor of the cornbread by using a different type of cheese. I recommend sharp cheddar, smoked provolone or fontina.

Great additional add-ins: cooked and crumbled bacon or canned green chiles.

cheese and herb beer bread

Makes: 8 servings   Prep Time: 15 minutes   Cook Time: 50 minutes

If you're one who fears yeast and therefore fear the idea of making bread in general, you need not fear beer bread. There is no yeast or kneading or rising involved in making a loaf of beer bread. It's a simple, stir-and-bake bread that turns out pretty fabulous. Flavor variations are endless (see Change It Up!), but this version calls for sharp cheddar cheese and a spoonful of chopped chives, and just in case you're wondering about the kids, it's perfectly fine to let them eat beer bread. The alcohol evaporates during the baking process.

3   cups all-purpose flour
¼   cup granulated white sugar
1   tablespoon baking powder
1   teaspoon salt
12 ounces beer, at room
    temperature (see Tips)
1   cup shredded extra-sharp
    cheddar cheese
2   tablespoons chopped fresh
    chives or finely chopped
    green onion
3   tablespoons salted butter,
    melted

Preheat the oven to 350°F.

In a large bowl, whisk together the flour, sugar, baking powder and salt. Stir in the beer, cheese and chives. Scrape the batter into a 5 x 9-inch loaf pan. Drizzle the melted butter on top. Bake for 50 to 60 minutes, or until the bread feels firm to the touch and a toothpick inserted into the center of the loaf comes out clean.

TIP Use beer that you typically enjoy drinking on its own. The flavor of the beer will come out in the bread—the darker the beer, the heavier the flavor.

CHANGE IT UP!

Substitute fresh dill for the chives to create Cheddar-Dill Beer Bread. Substitute Gruyère cheese and fresh thyme for the cheddar and chives to create Gruyère-Thyme Beer Bread. Experiment with other cheese and herb substitutions!

buttery asiago and rosemary cloverleaf rolls

Makes: 24 rolls   Prep Time: 45 minutes + rising time   Cook Time: 12 minutes

Three little balls of dough snuggled together in a muffin cup and baked to perfection. That's how a cloverleaf roll is created. A good dose of butter makes these pull-apart rolls tender and delicious. They're best served fresh, hot-baked from the oven.

1   cup milk, warmed (105°F to 115°F; see Tips)
¼   cup granulated white sugar
1   .25-ounce package (2¼ teaspoons) active dry yeast
1   large egg
2   tablespoons unsalted butter, melted and cooled
¾   teaspoon salt
3   cups bread flour, or more as needed
1   cup freshly grated Asiago cheese
1½   tablespoons finely chopped fresh rosemary
¾   cup (1½ sticks) salted butter, melted and cooled slightly

In the bowl of a stand mixer, combine the milk, sugar and yeast. Let the mixture sit until it bubbles, about 5 minutes (see Tips).

Add the egg, butter, salt and 1 cup of the flour. Use the dough hook attachment to mix on medium speed and continue adding the bread flour ½ cup at a time until it is all incorporated. Add the cheese and rosemary and continue to mix. The dough should be pulling away from the sides and bottom of the mixing bowl (scrape the sides once in a while with a rubber spatula, if needed). It will be sticky, but it's okay to add a little bit more flour if the dough appears too wet. Let the dough hook knead on medium speed for 4 minutes (see Tips for hand mixing and kneading).

Remove the dough from the mixing bowl and place it in a large bowl that has been coated with nonstick spray. Turn it to coat. Place a clean dish towel over the bowl and place it in a warm place to rise until the volume has almost doubled in size, 1 to 2 hours (see Tips).

Punch the dough down and divide it equally in half. Each half needs to be divided into 12 equal pieces. I like to gently roll each half into a log on a lightly floured surface and divide from there. You should end up with 24 equal pieces of dough.

Spray two 12-cup muffin tins with nonstick spray. Divide each piece of dough into 3 pieces. Roll each piece into a ball, dip it into the melted butter and place all three butter-dipped bread balls into the same muffin cup. Repeat with the remaining 23 pieces of dough.

Cover the muffin tins lightly with clean dish towels and place them in a warm place to rise until they are almost doubled in size, about 30 minutes.

Meanwhile, preheat the oven to 400°F.

CHANGE IT UP!

Leave out the rosemary and the cheese to create classic cloverleaf rolls.

Substitute fresh thyme and Parmesan for the rosemary and Asiago.

Remove the dish towels and bake the rolls for 12 minutes, or until they have puffed up and turned golden brown.

TIPS The temperature of the milk to mix with the yeast is important. If it's too hot, it might kill the yeast. Watch for the yeast to bubble—if it doesn't bubble, your yeast is likely no longer active and you should try again with a new packet.

If you're using a hand mixer, in a large bowl, combine the milk, sugar and yeast as described above. Then use a hand mixer to beat in the egg, butter and salt. Use a wooden spoon to stir in the flour 1 cup at a time until it's completely incorporated. Stir in the cheese and rosemary. Transfer the dough to a floured surface (it will be sticky) and continue to work the dough, kneading it for 5 to 8 minutes by hand, continuing to add flour, as needed, until the dough comes together to form a smooth ball and is not quite as sticky. Then continue with the instructions for rising.

To create a warm place for rising, use your oven. Before putting the dough in, turn the light on in the oven to give off a small amount of warmth. Turn on the oven for 30 seconds and then turn it back off again to get a warm burst of air in there.

MAKE-AHEAD TIP Before the second rise, cover the muffin tins with plastic wrap and refrigerate them until you're ready for the second rise. They'll be fine for a few hours or overnight. When you're ready to bake them, continue with the recipe as written, placing them in a warm place for the second rise.

green beans with bacon and thyme

Makes: 6 servings   Prep Time: 25 minutes   Cook Time: 10 minutes

Green beans are beautiful when they are boiled briefly—which gives them a bright green color—and slathered in bacon butter. Adding a bit of bacon butter to vegetables is a good ploy to turn veggie-haters into veggie-lovers. My son Brooks always tells me that everything is better with bacon. I've taught him, and I've taught him well, haven't I? This bacon butter is made extra special with the addition of fresh thyme.

6   slices center-cut bacon
4   tablespoons (½ stick) salted butter, at room temperature
1   tablespoon chopped fresh thyme
¼   teaspoon salt
⅛   teaspoon freshly ground black pepper
4   cups fresh green beans, trimmed and cut into 1-inch pieces

To prepare the bacon butter, in a large skillet, fry the bacon over medium heat until it is very crisp, 6 to 8 minutes. Remove the bacon to a paper towel–lined plate to drain. In a medium bowl, mix the butter, thyme, salt and pepper. Crumble the bacon into small pieces and add it to the butter mixture. Stir together until it is well combined.

To prepare the green beans, bring a large pot of water to a rolling boil. Add the green beans and cook for 4 minutes. Drain the green beans and then dump them back into the large pot. Add the bacon butter to the green beans and toss to combine. Spoon the green beans into a serving bowl, scraping out every last bit of the bacon butter to drizzle on top. Serve immediately.

GF GLUTEN-FREE ADAPTABLE Use a brand of bacon that is known to be gluten-free.

TIP This recipe turns out green beans that are a little bit on the crisp side. If you prefer them to be more tender, cook them for an additional 3 to 4 minutes.

MAKE-AHEAD TIP If you'd like to prepare this ahead, prepare the bacon butter, cover and refrigerate. Cook the green beans and then refrigerate. When you're ready to serve, heat the bacon butter in a medium saucepan, add the green beans and stir until the green beans are heated through and coated with the bacon butter.

CHANGE IT UP!

Change this into an Italian-style dish by substituting pancetta and basil for the bacon and thyme in the butter, preparing the herbed butter the same way.

broccolini with sharp cheddar sauce

Makes: 6 servings   Prep Time: 20 minutes   Cook Time: 10 minutes

When he was a child, I could never get my little boy to eat any vegetables. He shunned carrots, spit out tomatoes and refused to try broccoli. His babysitter, however, was able to get all of the kids in her care to eat broccoli. She told them that they simply had to eat up all of the trees before the big, bad giant arrived and wanted all of the trees for himself. That's a grand and swell idea and all, except that older kids don't fall for that one anymore. Nowadays we serve up taller, broccolini trees for dinner, and we top them with a generous drizzle of creamy cheese sauce.

1	tablespoon salted butter
1	teaspoon minced garlic
1	tablespoon all-purpose flour
½	teaspoon salt
¼	teaspoon mustard powder
⅛	teaspoon freshly ground black pepper
	Dash of cayenne pepper
⅔	cup milk, warmed (see Tips)
½	cup shredded sharp cheddar cheese
1	tablespoon white wine
2	bunches broccolini (about 1 pound)

Bring a large pot of water to boil. Meanwhile, prepare the cheese sauce.

In a medium saucepan, melt the butter over medium heat. Add the garlic and cook, stirring, for 1 minute. Add the flour, salt, mustard powder, black pepper and cayenne and cook, stirring, for 30 seconds. Whisk in the milk, a little at a time, until smooth. Cook until the sauce is hot and begins to thicken, 1 to 2 minutes. Add the cheese and continue to cook and stir until the cheese is melted. Remove the pan from heat and stir in the wine.

Trim the broccolini by pulling off the leaves and cutting off and discarding the tough stems. If any of the stalks are unusually thick, cut the broccolini in half vertically. Drop the broccolini into the boiling water and cook until slightly tender, 4 to 5 minutes. Drain the broccolini in a colander. Transfer to a serving dish and drizzle the cheese sauce on top. Serve immediately.

GF GLUTEN-FREE ADAPTABLE Use cornstarch, potato starch or another type of thickener in place of the all-purpose flour.

TIPS To warm the milk, just pour it into a glass measuring cup and heat it in the microwave or heat it in a small saucepan on the stove. It should only take a short time, but watch it closely so it doesn't bubble up and over.

If you don't care to use wine in the recipe, it's okay to leave it out entirely.

CHANGE IT UP!

Broccoli or cauliflower can easily be substituted for the broccolini.

The cheese sauce is versatile—try using other varieties of cheese in the sauce.

roasted cauliflower with lemon-brown butter

Makes: 6 servings   Prep Time: 20 minutes   Cook Time: 25 minutes

This recipe has a couple of things going for it. Number one: roasting cauliflower is the best way (ever) to eat the stuff. If you've never roasted cauliflower, you've been missing out big time. It turns into this nutty and wonderful-tasting vegetable, and you'll have a tough time not going back for seconds. Number two: adding brown butter to vegetables is another of those "tricks" for getting people to eat and enjoy vegetables. Brown butter is so good that it's difficult not to eat by the spoonful, and it's incredibly simple to make too.

1   **large cauliflower head, cut into florets (about 6 cups)**
2   **tablespoons olive oil**
½   **teaspoon salt**
¼   **teaspoon freshly ground black pepper**
½   **medium lemon**
2   **tablespoons salted butter**
1   **tablespoon finely chopped fresh chives**

Preheat the oven to 500°F.

On a large baking sheet, spread out the cauliflower florets. Drizzle with the olive oil and toss until the florets are well coated. Sprinkle with salt and pepper. Add the lemon half to the baking sheet. Bake for 20 to 25 minutes, or until the cauliflower is lightly browned.

Meanwhile, prepare the brown butter. In a small skillet, melt the butter over medium heat. Continue to cook, stirring often, until it begins to turn light brown, 4 to 5 minutes. The butter is perfect when you can lift a spoonful of it out of the pan and see lots of brown pieces floating around. Remove it from the heat.

Place the roasted cauliflower in a serving bowl and toss with the brown butter. Squeeze lemon juice from the roasted lemon on top. Sprinkle with chives and serve immediately.

TIP If you'd prefer not to have a lemon flavor in the dish, just leave out the lemon.

CHANGE IT UP!

Serve the brown butter with steamed cauliflower or broccoli instead. Add the lemon to the steaming water.

roasted butternut squash with garlic, sage and pine nuts

Makes: 6 servings   Prep Time: 15 minutes   Cook Time: 45 minutes

Since my husband and I both work from home, I'm often scurrying about the kitchen looking for creative things to put together for lunch. Oftentimes it's a unique take on grilled cheese or a salad filled with whatever I happen to have in the fridge. On one chilly winter day, I roasted some butternut squash and discovered that it pairs perfectly with sage. Adding in toasted pine nuts and garlic was also a good idea. A big bowl of this squash with a sprinkle of goat cheese and a glass of chilled white wine makes for a perfectly delicious, light lunch. Of course the other option is to serve it as a side dish too.

3	pounds butternut squash, peeled, seeded and cut into ¾-inch cubes
2	tablespoons olive oil, divided
1	teaspoon kosher salt
½	teaspoon freshly ground black pepper
⅓	cup pine nuts
2	tablespoons finely chopped fresh sage
2	large garlic cloves, minced

Preheat the oven to 450°F. Line a baking sheet with parchment paper or spray lightly with cooking spray.

In a medium bowl, toss the butternut squash cubes with 1½ tablespoons olive oil. Spread out the butternut squash on the prepared baking sheet and sprinkle with the salt and pepper. Roast the squash for 35 to 45 minutes, or until tender.

While the squash is roasting, in a small skillet, heat the remaining ½ tablespoon oil over medium-low heat. Add the pine nuts, sage and garlic and cook, stirring constantly, until the pine nuts are lightly browned, 3 to 4 minutes (see Tips).

Scoop the butternut squash into a large bowl. Scrape the pine nut mixture onto the butternut squash and gently toss. Serve immediately.

TIPS Pine nuts can turn from brown to burnt fairly quickly. Keep a close eye on them and keep stirring.

You can substitute any other type of winter squash for the butternut squash.

CHANGE IT UP!

Add crumbled goat cheese on top.

Chop the squash into very small pieces and you can serve this same mixture on top of toasted baguette slices for an appetizer.

tomato-zucchini gratin

Makes: 6 servings   Prep Time: 30 minutes   Cook Time: 1 hour and 10 minutes

This recipe is best when made in the heart of summer, when tomatoes are red, ripe and at their best and the squash are overflowing in your garden. If you're without a vegetable garden, hit the local farmers' market for the absolute freshest selections of summer produce.

1   tablespoon olive oil
1   large onion, sliced
2   teaspoons chopped fresh
      thyme, divided
1   cup freshly grated Parmesan
      cheese, divided
2   medium zucchini, sliced,
      divided
2   medium yellow squash,
      sliced, divided
2   large tomatoes, sliced,
      divided
     Salt and freshly ground
       black pepper, to taste

Preheat the oven to 375°F. Spray a 9-inch square pan with nonstick spray.

Heat the olive oil in a large skillet over medium-high heat. Add the onion and cook, stirring, until softened and lightly browned, 10 to 12 minutes. Remove the pan from heat. Set aside to cool.

Spread half of the onion in the bottom of the prepared pan. Sprinkle 1 teaspoon thyme and 2 tablespoons of the cheese of top. Layer half of the zucchini and yellow squash (overlapping is okay), then another 2 tablespoons of the cheese. Add a layer with half of the tomatoes. Top with 2 tablespoons of cheese and a sprinkle of salt and pepper. Repeat layers with the remaining ingredients, sprinkling the remaining cheese on top.

Bake for 1 hour, or until the gratin has browned all over and is bubbling with juices. Let cool for at least 15 minutes before serving.

DF DAIRY-FREE ADAPTABLE Use dried bread crumbs in place of the cheese (1 cup bread crumbs moistened with 2 tablespoons olive oil).

TIPS Look for multicolored heirloom tomato varieties to make this dish even more colorful.

Serve individual portions on top of a couple of large fresh basil leaves.

CHANGE IT UP!

Try using other hard cheeses for this dish: Asiago, Parmigiano Reggiano, Pecorino or Romano.

baked barbecued onion rings

Makes: 6 servings   Prep Time: 20 minutes   Cook Time: 12 minutes

My son plays a lot of sports, and by a lot, I mean that every day we're at either a practice or a game, and it's not entirely unusual for him to be active in two sports at the same time. I love to watch my kiddo in action, but there happens to be a lot of sitting around, twiddling-my-thumbs time too. One day, I was browsing through a few cookbooks on the soccer field when I came across a recipe for onion rings, and then I flipped a few more pages and saw a recipe for barbecued chicken. It was then that I realized the fate of onion rings meeting barbecue sauce. With sauce built inside the onion ring, there is no need for ketchup.

1	cup bottled barbecue sauce (see Tips)
2	large eggs, lightly beaten
¼	cup all-purpose flour
3	cups panko bread crumbs (see Tips)
2	large sweet onions, sliced into ½-inch rings

Preheat the oven to 450°F. Place two baking sheets in the oven to preheat. Line a cutting board or flat surface with parchment paper.

In a medium bowl, whisk together the barbecue sauce, eggs and flour. Pour the bread crumbs into a separate bowl.

Use tongs (or your fingers) to dip an onion slice into the barbecue mixture, shake off the excess and then dunk on all sides into the bread crumbs. Lay the coated onion on the prepared cutting board. Repeat with the remaining onion slices, using a second cutting board, if needed.

Remove the hot baking sheets from the oven. Grab the edges of the parchment paper onions and carefully slide them (paper and all) onto the hot baking sheet. Repeat with the other baking sheet. Spray the onion rings lightly with cooking spray.

Bake the onions for 6 minutes, or until they are golden. Use tongs or a metal spatula to gently turn each onion ring over. Spray the other side with cooking spray and bake for an additional 4 to 6 minutes. Watch the onion rings closely to make sure the crumbs are not browning too quickly. Remove them from the oven and serve immediately.

GF GLUTEN-FREE ADAPTABLE Use a brand of barbecue sauce that is known to be gluten-free, use a gluten-free all-purpose flour blend or potato starch and turn gluten-free pretzels or bread into crumbs to coat the rings.

TIPS Use your favorite flavored barbecue sauce for this recipe, the thicker the better.

Panko bread crumbs can be found in your market's Asian products section. Regular bread crumbs may be substituted.

CHANGE IT UP!

Serve these onion rings as condiments to add to burgers instead of using regular onions.

peas with basil and bacon

Makes: 6 servings   Prep Time: 25 minutes   Cook Time: 12 minutes

To me, peas feel like a big treat. They have such a subtle, sweet flavor that I'm completely drawn to them. Set a big bowl of peas in front of me and I'm a happy camper. I'm perfectly content eating spoonfuls of peas all on their own, but adding just a little bit of bacon into the mix makes them simply irresistible. This dish is so simple to assemble and it's always a favorite on the dinner table.

2   slices thick bacon, cut into ¼-inch pieces
½   tablespoon salted butter, at room temperature
2   tablespoons chopped shallot
2   medium garlic cloves, minced
16   ounces frozen peas, thawed
½   cup fresh basil leaves, cut into very thin strips
    Salt and freshly ground black pepper, to taste

In a large skillet, cook the bacon over medium heat until crisp, 5 to 6 minutes. Remove the bacon to drain on a paper towel–lined plate. Discard all but 1 tablespoon of the bacon drippings in the pan. Add the butter, shallot and garlic to the pan and cook, stirring, over medium heat just until softened, about 2 minutes. Add the peas and the basil and cook until the peas are heated through, 4 to 5 minutes. Crumble the bacon into the peas and add salt and pepper, to taste. Serve immediately.

GF GLUTEN-FREE ADAPTABLE Use a brand of bacon that is known to be gluten-free.

DF DAIRY-FREE ADAPTABLE Use olive oil in place of the butter.

V VEGETARIAN ADAPTABLE Leave out the bacon.

TIPS The type of bacon you use affects the taste of this dish. Try using applewood-smoked bacon, maple-smoked bacon or peppered bacon for a variation in flavor.

Try this recipe using fresh peas in the summer time.

CHANGE IT UP!
Substitute thyme and pancetta for the basil and bacon.

garlicky swiss chard and chickpeas

Makes: 6 servings   Prep Time: 20 minutes   Cook Time: 20 minutes

Before I started working in food, chickpeas (otherwise known as garbanzo beans) were never much more than a salad add-in for me. I've since discovered that they are fabulous when roasted, they can be turned into hummus for dip, and they're quite delicious when stir-fried too. This dish of tender-cooked Swiss chard mixes in garlic and chickpeas, and it's topped off with a light drizzle of lemon. Since it's one of my son's favorite things to eat, I guess you can call it kid-friendly too.

2   tablespoons olive oil, divided
2   bunches Swiss chard,
     center stems cut out and
     discarded and leaves
     coarsely chopped
2   cups low-sodium chicken
     broth
2   medium shallots, finely
     chopped (about ½ cup)
6   medium garlic cloves,
     minced
1   15.5-ounce can garbanzo
     beans (chickpeas), rinsed
     and drained
2   tablespoons freshly
     squeezed lemon juice
     Salt and freshly ground
     black pepper, to taste
½   cup crumbled feta cheese,
     optional

In a large skillet, heat 1 tablespoon of the olive oil over medium-high heat. Add half of the chard and cook, 1 to 2 minutes. When the first half has wilted, add the remaining chard. When all of the chard is wilted, add the chicken broth. Cover the skillet and cook the chard until tender, about 10 minutes. Drain the chard through a fine sieve (strainer) and set it aside (see Make-Ahead Tip).

Wipe out the skillet and heat the remaining 1 tablespoon olive oil over medium-high heat. Add the shallots and garlic and cook, stirring, until they are softened, about 2 minutes. Add the chard and chickpeas and cook until heated through, 3 to 4 minutes. Drizzle the lemon juice over the mixture and season with salt and pepper, to taste. Sprinkle cheese on top just before serving, if desired.

GF GLUTEN-FREE ADAPTABLE Use brands of chicken broth and chickpeas that are known to be gluten-free.

DF DAIRY-FREE ADAPTABLE Leave out the cheese.

V VEGETARIAN ADAPTABLE Use vegetable broth instead of chicken broth.

MAKE-AHEAD TIP The chard may be cooked up to 2 hours ahead. Just let it sit at room temperature until you are ready to complete the dish.

CHANGE IT UP!

White beans may be substituted for the chickpeas.

Use rainbow chard to add more color to the dish.

Dinner at 6

Dear Family,

What would you like for dinner? For once, I'd actually like you to give me an answer, which will at least give me an idea, a springboard, a little knowledge about what you're craving, so I can plan something that we'll all enjoy and there will be few complaints. Dear husband, I know that you cringe when I tell you we're having chicken, so please let me know what it is that you want, and my sweet son, you know that we can't have ravioli every night for dinner. Just an idea, please. That's all I ask. This chapter has been written just for you, so you can point to your favorite and then I'll get to work.

XO   Recipe Girl

Recipes

 WEB FAVORITE   VEGETARIAN *(or adaptable)*   GLUTEN-FREE *(or adaptable)*   DAIRY-FREE *(or adaptable)*

sweet chili pulled pork

Makes: 4 servings   Prep Time: 25 minutes   Cook Time: 1 hour

Here you will find pork that is simmered in beer, rice wine vinegar, a handful of garlic cloves and a chunk of ginger. Then it's pulled and mixed with sweet chili sauce to produce a tender and flavorful meat that is terrific for piling onto sandwich rolls and, more importantly, for topping my Creamy Coconut Polenta (page 179).

1½ pounds pork tenderloin
1   12-ounce bottle beer (see Tips)
½   cup rice vinegar
¼   cup water
5   medium garlic cloves, smashed
1   2-inch piece ginger, peeled
2   teaspoons kosher salt
½   teaspoon freshly ground black pepper
¼   teaspoon ground red pepper
¾   cup Thai Sweet Chili Sauce (see Tips)

Cut the pork in half lengthwise and then cut it crosswise into 2½-inch chunks.

In a medium saucepan, bring the beer, vinegar, water, garlic, ginger, salt, black pepper and red pepper to a boil over medium-high heat. Add the pork, cover and reduce the heat to low. Simmer for 1 hour, or until the pork is very tender.

Remove the pork from the liquid and transfer to a cutting board. Use two forks to shred the pork.

Using a slotted spoon, scoop out and discard the garlic and ginger from the pan juices. Add the shredded pork and chili sauce to the pan. Stir to combine.

GF GLUTEN-FREE ADAPTABLE Use 1½ cups chicken or vegetable broth in place of the beer and use a brand of chili sauce that is known to be gluten-free.

TIPS Choose a beer you enjoy that is fairly mild in flavor. Dark beer varieties will not be good for this recipe.

Thai Sweet Chili Sauce is commonly used in Asian cooking. Look for it in your grocery store's Asian products aisle.

SERVING TIPS Serve on sandwich rolls or slider buns as sandwiches, or serve on top of steamed rice or polenta.

CHANGE IT UP!

Turn this recipe into barbecue pulled pork. Substitute apple cider vinegar for the rice wine vinegar, leave out the ginger and substitute your favorite barbecue sauce for the sweet chili sauce.

slow cooker carnitas

Makes: 10 servings   Prep Time: 20 minutes   Cook Time: 6 hours

Southern Californians know a good taco when they see it, they can hold an avocado in their hands and know its exact moment of ripeness and they aren't afraid to eat things like carne asada and carnitas. I live in San Diego, you see—the land of really great Mexican food pretty much everywhere you look. "Carnitas" is just a big, fancy Spanish word for braised, roasted pork. It is my husband's absolute favorite Mexican dish. When cooked at a low heat for a long time, the pork shreds apart into tender chunks of meat that make a wonderful filling for tacos or burritos.

CARNITAS

3 pounds boneless country-style pork ribs or pork shoulder (Boston butt), cut into 1½-inch pieces
2 medium garlic cloves, minced
1 tablespoon dried oregano (preferably Mexican)
1 tablespoon ground cumin
2 teaspoons kosher salt
2 teaspoons freshly ground black pepper
1 large yellow onion, cut into wedges

FOR SERVING

20 corn tortillas, fried or warmed (see Tips)
Fresh cilantro, sliced red bell pepper, sliced avocado, sour cream, salsa, tomato, cheese and/or lime wedges

In a slow cooker, toss the pork with the garlic, oregano, cumin, salt and pepper. Place the onion wedges on top. Cover and cook on low heat for 6 to 8 hours, or until the pork is tender and pulls apart easily.

Just before serving, transfer the pork to a cutting board. Shred the pork with two forks, discarding any fat that remains. Scoop the shredded pork into a serving dish. Discard the onions from the juices in the slow cooker and drizzle the shredded pork with some of the juices.

To serve, fill tortillas with shredded pork and any desired condiments.

GF GLUTEN-FREE ADAPTABLE Use a brand of tortillas that is known to be gluten-free.

TIPS To fry the tortillas, in a small skillet, heat ⅓ cup canola or vegetable oil over medium heat. Fry the tortillas one at a time, about 10 seconds per side, and remove them to a paper towel–lined plate to drain, adding a paper towel in between each tortilla. To warm the tortillas, wrap a stack of 3 at a time in damp paper towels and microwave them until they are warmed and softened, 40 to 60 seconds. Alternatively, wrap them in foil with a few sprinkles of water and heat them in the oven at 350°F for 10 to 15 minutes, until they are warm and pliable.

I like to set up a carnitas serve-yourself station. Display warmed tortillas, shredded pork and a variety of the suggested condiments. Let people create their own carnitas tacos.

CHANGE IT UP!

Carnitas are also wonderful served inside a large flour tortilla as a burrito. Since burritos are much larger than tacos, I like to add steamed rice or Spanish rice as a filler along with the shredded pork and condiments.

pork loin roast with rosemary-mustard mushroom sauce

Makes: 6 servings   Prep Time: 25 minutes   Cook Time: 1 hour

Rosemary grows year-round in abundance in my backyard, and by "abundance" I mean that it has weaseled its way into a very large hedge and refuses to budge. Therefore, we must come up with many ways to utilize this great, fresh herb. It works out wonderfully in this simply roasted pork with a creamy Dijon-mushroom sauce to drizzle over the top.

PORK

1	3- to 4-pound bone-in or boneless pork loin roast
2	tablespoons minced garlic (about 5 large cloves)
1	tablespoon olive oil
1	tablespoon Italian seasoning
1	tablespoon kosher salt
1	teaspoon freshly ground black pepper

MUSHROOM SAUCE

2	tablespoons salted butter
1	pound sliced mushrooms
1	bunch green onions, chopped, white and light green parts
1¼	cups low-sodium chicken or vegetable broth
¾	cup heavy whipping cream
3	teaspoons whole grain Dijon mustard
1	teaspoon finely chopped fresh rosemary
	Salt and freshly ground black pepper, to taste

Preheat the oven to 350°F.

To prepare the pork, rinse the roast and pat it dry. Place it on a rack in a greased, shallow roasting pan. In a small bowl, mix the garlic, olive oil and Italian seasoning. Rub the garlic mixture all over the pork roast and then sprinkle with the salt and pepper. Cook the roast for 1 to 1½ hours (20 to 22 minutes per pound), or until the internal temperature reaches 145°F. Remove the roast from the oven, cover it with foil and let it rest 15 minutes before serving.

To prepare the mushroom sauce, in a large skillet, melt the butter over medium-high heat. Add the mushrooms and green onions and cook, stirring, until they begin to soften, 3 to 4 minutes. Add the broth and bring to a boil. Boil for 10 minutes to reduce the liquid. Stir in the cream, mustard and rosemary. Season the sauce with salt and pepper, to taste.

Carve thin slices of the pork roast and top with a generous spoonful of the mushroom sauce.

GF GLUTEN-FREE ADAPTABLE Use brands of broth and Dijon mustard that are known to be gluten-free.

TIP The sauce in this dish is so delicious that you'll want to plan to serve sides that can be scooped up alongside to enjoy it. Try serving with rice, roasted potatoes and/or broccoli.

CHANGE IT UP!

Substitute leeks or shallots for the green onions.

Turn the sauce into a Marsala-mushroom sauce. Use ¾ cup broth and ½ cup Marsala wine. Leave out the mustard.

swedish meatballs over egg noodles

Makes: 6 servings   Prep Time: 40 minutes   Cook Time: 30 minutes

My father gave me my blond hair, my large Scandinavian bones and my extremely stubborn personality. Yep, I'm a Swede. Dad grew up in northern Minnesota, which is where many migrating Scandinavians settled years ago. My grandmother dished out plenty of comfort food in those days to create a good layer of body insulation amidst those cold Minnesota winters. Dad had his fair share of Swedish meatballs back in the day. They had always been a favorite of Dad's and mine, and I like to think that Dad would have enjoyed my recipe too.

MEATBALLS
¾   cup bread crumbs (see Tips)
¼   cup milk
1   pound ground beef
     (85% lean)
½   pound ground pork
1   large egg
1   small onion, chopped finely
     (about ¾ cup)
½   teaspoon salt
¼   teaspoon allspice
¼   teaspoon white pepper

GRAVY
3   tablespoons all-purpose flour
¾   cup water
1   cup half-and-half
1   teaspoon beef bouillon
½   teaspoon salt

FOR SERVING
Freshly chopped flat-leaf
   parsley for garnish, optional
Hot cooked egg noodles

Preheat the oven to 350°F.

To prepare the meatballs, in a small bowl, mix the bread crumbs and milk. Let the bread crumbs soak up the milk for 5 minutes.

In a large bowl, mix the soaked bread crumbs, beef, pork, egg, onion, salt, allspice and pepper. Shape the mixture into 1-inch balls (see Tips). Place the meatballs on an ungreased, rimmed baking pan. Bake, uncovered, for about 20 minutes, or until lightly browned and cooked through. Transfer the meatballs to a serving dish, cover and keep warm.

To prepare the gravy, spoon 3 tablespoons of the meatball drippings into a medium saucepan (see Tips) and heat over low heat. Whisk in the flour. Cook, stirring constantly, until the mixture is smooth and bubbly. Whisk in the water, half-and-half, bouillon and salt. Increase the heat to medium and bring to a boil, whisking constantly. Once the gravy is boiling, cook and whisk for 1 minute, or until it begins to thicken. Remove from heat.

To serve, pour the gravy over the meatballs, sprinkle with fresh parsley, if desired, and serve over hot cooked noodles.

TIPS You can certainly use regular, store-bought bread crumbs for this recipe, or you can make your own. Leave 2 to 3 slices of bread out on your counter for 24 hours, remove the crusts and then give them a whir in the blender or food processor—instant fresh bread crumbs!

When shaping meatballs, dip your hands into cold water to prevent the meat from sticking to your hands.

If you find that you do not have enough meatball drippings, it's okay to use unsalted butter in place of the drippings.

CHANGE IT UP!

Go the traditional route and serve these Swedish meatballs with boiled potatoes instead of noodles.

mom's tacos

Makes: 12 tacos   Prep Time: 15 minutes   Cook Time: 25 minutes

Things were pretty simple in the '70s. I remember shag carpet and an avocado-colored refrigerator. I remember polyester pants and our big, green station wagon with the seat in the way-back that faced backwards. I remember playing outside for hours with kids in the neighborhood, not reliant upon any electronic toys to make us happy, and most of all I remember the dinners that my Mom used to make. We had quite a lot of canned or frozen vegetables—they were affordable and easy for working parents. Mom had her favorites that she liked to make, things like spaghetti, beef burgundy and split pea soup. But what I remember most was my favorite dinner of all: Mom's Tacos. Her secret was to add lots of beans, which extended the filling and fed a bunch of hungry kids.

1   teaspoon chili powder
1   teaspoon ground cumin
½   teaspoon garlic powder
½   teaspoon dried oregano
½   teaspoon salt
¼   teaspoon freshly ground
      black pepper
1   tablespoon olive oil
½   pound ground turkey
½   pound ground beef (see
      Tips)
1   cup chopped sweet onion
      (about 1 medium)
1   15.5-ounce can chili beans,
      drained (see Change It Up!)
1   10-ounce can Ro-Tel original
      tomatoes and chiles
12   taco-size corn tortillas, fried
      (see Tips)
      Desired taco fixings (lettuce,
      tomato, sour cream, cheese,
      avocado, salsa, etc.)

In a small bowl, mix the chili powder, cumin, garlic powder, oregano, salt and pepper. Set aside.

Heat a large skillet over medium-high heat, then swirl in the olive oil. Add the turkey, beef and onion and cook, stirring to break up the meat, until the meat is lightly browned and cooked through, 5 to 7 minutes. Tilt the pan, scoot the meat and onions to one side and spoon out any accumulated fat.

Sprinkle the mixed spices onto the cooked meat. Add the beans and tomatoes and stir. Decrease the heat to medium and heat the beans and tomatoes through, about 10 minutes.

Fill the tortillas with about ⅓ cup of the taco filling mixture plus desired taco fixings.

GF GLUTEN-FREE ADAPTABLE Use a brand of corn tortillas that is known to be gluten-free. Use chili beans that are gluten-free (or add in desired type of canned beans that are gluten-free).

DF DAIRY-FREE ADAPTABLE Leave cheese and sour cream off of your tacos.

TIPS For best results, use ground beef that is 85% lean. Trying to reduce the fat further will result in a dry meat mixture.

Mom liked to heat the corn tortillas by frying them briefly in a little bit of hot oil. In a small pan heat ⅓ cup vegetable oil over medium heat. Fry the tortillas one at a time, about 10 seconds on each side. Place them on a paper towel–lined plate to drain, adding a paper towel in between each tortilla.

CHANGE IT UP!

Chili beans are nice to use because they come canned in a lightly spiced sauce. Drain the sauce slightly but don't rinse. You can substitute kidney beans or black beans for the chili beans if you'd like.

If you don't have access to Ro-Tel (found in the canned tomatoes aisle), substitute a can of chopped tomatoes and a can of chopped chiles.

easy beef enchiladas

Makes: 12 enchiladas   Prep Time: 30 minutes   Cook Time: 35 minutes

Cinco de Mayo is a big holiday here in Southern California. Truthfully, most people don't know the origin of what this holiday really represents, but rather they use it as an opportunity to consume margaritas, overdose on guacamole and eat things like tacos, burritos and enchiladas. It doesn't have to be Cinco de Mayo to make these enchiladas. In fact, it's such a quick and easy, family-friendly recipe that you might just want to surprise the family with some good Mexican food, and then you can make it again on the fifth of May with a margarita in hand.

1   tablespoon olive oil
1   pound lean ground beef
1½ cups diced onion (about
      1 large)
1½ cups finely diced zucchini
      (about 2 medium)
2½ cups enchilada sauce, canned
      or homemade (page 249),
      divided
12 corn tortillas, fried in oil to
      soften (see Tips)
3   cups shredded cheddar-
      Jack cheese (blended
      cheddar and Monterey Jack
      cheeses)
      Shredded lettuce, avocado,
      cilantro and/or sour cream
      for serving, as desired

CHANGE IT UP!

Substitute 1½ cups shredded chicken breast for the beef to make chicken enchiladas

Preheat the oven to 350°F. Spray a 9 x 13-inch pan with nonstick spray.

In a large skillet, heat the olive oil over medium heat. Add the ground beef and use a spoon or spatula to break apart and crumble the meat. Cook the meat until browned, about 5 minutes. Tilt the pan and spoon the fat out of the pan and discard. Transfer the cooked meat to a bowl.

Return the pan to medium heat and add the onion and zucchini. Cook just until softened, 3 to 4 minutes. Transfer the vegetables to the bowl with the meat. Set aside.

Spread ½ cup of the enchilada sauce in the prepared pan to coat the bottom.

Place a tortilla on a flat work surface. Spoon ¼ to ⅓ cup of the meat mixture down the middle of the tortilla. Sprinkle 2 tablespoons of the cheese on top of the meat. Drizzle 1 tablespoon of the sauce on top of the cheese. Wrap the tortilla tightly around the filling and place it seam side down in the pan. Repeat with the remaining tortillas, filling and sauce, placing the tortillas side by side in the pan. It's okay if they are snuggled in tightly. Pour the remaining sauce over the top of the stuffed enchiladas. Cover the dish with foil and bake for 30 minutes.

Remove the pan from the oven and take off the foil. Sprinkle the remaining cheese on top and return the pan to the oven. Bake for an additional 5 minutes, or until the cheese is melted. Serve with shredded lettuce, avocado, cilantro and/or sour cream, as desired.

GF GLUTEN-FREE ADAPTABLE Use brands of enchilada sauce and corn tortillas that are known to be gluten-free.

TIP To fry the tortillas: In a small pan, heat ⅓ cup vegetable oil to medium heat. Fry the tortillas one at a time, about 10 seconds on each side. Place them on a paper towel–lined plate to drain, adding a paper towel in between each tortilla.

grilled balsamic skirt steak with grilled corn salsa

Makes: 4 servings   Prep Time: 30 minutes + marinating time   Cook Time: 18 minutes

There isn't much that I don't love about summer. Taking walks on the beach, reading a zillion books, and grilling some great steaks on the barbecue are included in that love. Skirt steak is my favorite cut of steak for many reasons. It takes on the flavor of marinade easily, it's easy to grill, and it pairs nicely with just about everything.

MARINADE

¼   cup extra-virgin olive oil
¼   cup balsamic vinegar
¼   cup chopped fresh basil
1   tablespoon packed brown sugar
2   garlic cloves, minced (about 1½ teaspoons)
1   teaspoon salt
½   teaspoon freshly ground black pepper

STEAK

1½ pounds skirt steak, fat trimmed

SALSA

2   large ears corn, shucked and rinsed (see Change It Up!)
1   cup chopped cherry tomatoes
2   tablespoons extra-virgin olive oil
1   tablespoon balsamic vinegar
2   tablespoons finely chopped fresh basil
    Salt and freshly ground black pepper, to taste

Place the marinade ingredients into a large zip baggie or a glass pan and stir them together. Add the steak to the marinade and turn it to coat. Marinate the steak for at least 4 hours or overnight in the refrigerator, turning it often to coat all sides of the steak.

When you're ready to grill, remove the steak from the refrigerator and allow it to sit at room temperature for about 30 minutes. Soak the corn in a large bowl of water for 30 minutes. Preheat the grill to medium. Place the corn on the hot grill grates, grilling until the ears are slightly charred on all sides. Remove them from the grill and let them cool. Cut the corn kernels off of the cobs (see Tips). In a large bowl, mix the corn, tomatoes, olive oil, vinegar and basil. Season with salt and pepper, to taste.

Drain the steak from the marinade and grill, covered, until it has good grill marks, 5 to 6 minutes. Flip and cook, covered, until the steak is done to your liking, 4 to 5 minutes for medium rare (cut into the steak to check). Transfer the steak to a cutting board and let it rest for 5 to 10 minutes. Thinly slice the steak against the grain. Serve the sliced steak topped with the corn salsa.

TIP To cut the corn kernels off the cob: Cut a small slice off of the end of the cob to create a flat surface. Set the flat end of the corn upright inside of a bowl, holding it at the top. Cut down the sides of the cob with a sharp knife and the corn kernels will collect inside of the bowl.

CHANGE IT UP!

Try using flank or hanger steak with this marinade too.

You can serve this steak with raw corn salsa too. Just cut the corn kernels off of the cob and mix it with the other salsa ingredients.

bacon-wrapped meatloaf
with brown sugar glaze

Makes: 8 servings   Prep Time: 30 minutes   Cook Time: 65 minutes

If I told you that this meatloaf was kid-approved, would you be convinced enough to try it? How about if I told you that my meatloaf-obsessed son—the kid who requests meatloaf for dinner more than any other dish on the planet (besides ravioli)—craves this meatloaf over any he's ever tried? And what if I told you that this meatloaf is covered in a solid layer of bacon . . . would you be convinced then? We sure love meatloaf around our house, and we love bacon too. Their partnership was meant to be, and they make a wonderful meatloaf together.

MEATLOAF

1	cup finely chopped mushrooms
¾	cup finely chopped onion
1	tablespoon Worcestershire sauce
1	tablespoon dry sherry or Dijon mustard
1	tablespoon chopped fresh thyme
2	garlic cloves, minced
1	teaspoon kosher salt
½	teaspoon freshly ground black pepper
1½	cups torn day-old bread pieces
½	cup whole milk
2	large eggs
1½	pounds 85% lean ground beef
½	pound ground pork sausage

GLAZE

½	cup chili sauce or barbecue sauce
¼	cup packed light brown sugar
2	teaspoons cider vinegar

TOPPING

8	slices bacon

Preheat the oven to 350°F. Spray a 9 x 13-inch pan with nonstick spray.

In a medium bowl, mix the mushrooms, onion, Worcestershire sauce, sherry, thyme, garlic, salt and pepper.

In a separate medium bowl, mix the bread pieces, milk and eggs.

In a large bowl, use clean hands to gently combine the ground meats. Add in the mushroom and bread mixtures and continue to gently combine. Form into a 4 x 10-inch loaf in the pan.

In a small bowl, combine the glaze ingredients. Use half of the glaze to spread over the top of the loaf. Lay the bacon strips side by side over the glaze and across the width of the meatloaf.

Bake for 60 to 70 minutes, or until an instant-read thermometer tests 160°F when inserted into the center of the loaf. Turn the oven to broil and broil the meatloaf for 3 to 4 minutes, or until the bacon is crisp. While the meatloaf is broiling, warm the remaining glaze.

Remove the meatloaf to a serving platter and drizzle the remaining glaze on top.

TIP Don't use turkey bacon for this recipe. The bacon is meant to deliver flavor to the meatloaf and give it a moist texture. Turkey bacon just won't work well for that.

MAKE-AHEAD TIP Form the meatloaf in the pan, wrap it with the bacon, cover the pan and keep it refrigerated until it is ready to bake. This can be done up to 8 hours in advance. Let the meatloaf sit at room temperature for 30 minutes before baking.

SERVING SUGGESTION Serve alongside Creamy Dijon Mashed Potatoes (page 171) for convenient dunking and scooping.

CHANGE IT UP!

Use a mixture of beef and pork or beef and veal instead of beef and sausage.

smoky joe sliders

Makes: 8 mini sliders   Prep Time: 30 minutes   Cook Time: 35 minutes

I was a Sloppy Joe kid. My mother took advantage of the Sloppy Joe–craze of the '70s and put those spiced up hamburger-meat sandwiches into the regular dinner rotation. The idea is slightly genius, really. Kids seem to love ground beef, sweet things and soft hamburger buns. It's a no-brainer, family-friendly dinner that your kids will eat. Yippee! I've changed up the Sloppy Joe a little bit to create the Smoky Joe. Smoked paprika adds a slightly smoky flavor to the dish, and piling the meat onto mini hamburger buns makes it fun for the little ones to nibble (and adults can feel like they're eating light).

1½ pounds 85% lean ground beef
½   cup finely chopped onion
½   cup finely chopped bell pepper
1   8-ounce can tomato sauce
½   cup ketchup
½   cup water
2   tablespoons cider vinegar
1   tablespoon packed light brown sugar
1   tablespoon Worcestershire sauce
1   tablespoon cornstarch
1   teaspoon dry mustard
1   teaspoon smoked paprika
½   teaspoon chili powder
½   teaspoon salt
8   mini slider buns, buttered and toasted (see Tips)

Heat a large skillet over medium-high heat. Add the beef, onion and bell pepper. Use a spatula to break the meat apart and cook for 5 to 6 minutes, or until the meat has browned and vegetables are softened. Tilt the pan and move the mixture to one side. Spoon out and discard any accumulated fat. Add the tomato sauce, ketchup, water, vinegar, sugar, Worcestershire sauce, cornstarch, mustard, paprika, chili powder and salt, and bring the mixture to a boil. Reduce the heat to low. Cover and simmer for 30 minutes, stirring every so often to reincorporate the sauce into the meat. Add in a couple of tablespoons of water, if needed, if too much sauce evaporates while simmering.

Divide the meat mixture among the slider buns and serve.

GF GLUTEN-FREE ADAPTABLE Use brands of ketchup and Worcestershire sauce that are known to be gluten-free. Use gluten-free bread in place of slider buns.

DF DAIRY-FREE ADAPTABLE Don't butter your slider buns.

TIP To toast the buns, spread each with a little bit of butter and heat them for a minute or two under the broiler, just until lightly browned.

CHANGE IT UP!

Turn these into regular-size Joes by using 4 regular-size hamburger buns.

Get really crazy and make these even smokier. Melt a slice of smoked provolone or smoked Gouda on top.

pan-fried lemon-garlic rib eye steaks

Makes: 2 servings   Prep Time: 25 minutes + marinating time   Cook Time: 5 minutes

Romantic dinners for two should involve things that are easy to cook and a snap to clean up. They shouldn't involve messy grills and a million dishes to wash, and they should be deliciously simplistic and fresh. I think a good steak falls into that category. Since I've never been skilled at grilling steaks to perfection, pan-frying them is an option that works fantastically for me. They sear up nicely, they cook quickly, and it's easy to keep an eye on them. Just a few fresh ingredients are added for flavor to create a perfectly prepared steak.

2   8-ounce rib eye steaks, trimmed of excess fat
2   large garlic cloves, peeled and cut in half
    Freshly ground black pepper
2   tablespoons extra-virgin olive oil, divided
1   tablespoon finely chopped fresh oregano, divided
1   tablespoon salted butter
2   teaspoons kosher salt
½   medium lemon

Rub both sides of the steaks with the split garlic halves. Coat both sides of the steaks with a generous sprinkle of pepper. Coat each steak with ½ tablespoon olive oil and press on ½ tablespoon oregano. Wrap the steaks in plastic wrap and let them sit at room temperature for 1 hour (see Tips).

Preheat a large skillet to medium heat. Add the butter and the remaining 1 tablespoon olive oil. Remove the steaks from the plastic wrap and sprinkle each with 1 teaspoon of the salt. Add the steaks to the hot pan and cook 2 minutes on the first side, or until they are seared a nice, deep brown. Turn the steaks over and add the lemon to the pan, cut side down. Turn heat to medium-low and cook for 2½ minutes more, or until the steaks become browned on the bottom. Your steaks will be medium rare at this point. Add a little more cooking time if you prefer your steak more well done. Remove the steaks to a cutting board and let them rest for 5 to 10 minutes before serving. Squeeze the pan-fried lemon over the two steaks. Serve immediately.

DF DAIRY-FREE ADAPTABLE Leave out the butter and substitute 1 tablespoon olive oil.

TIPS Cooking a steak at room temperature will allow for it to cook more evenly and quickly.

You'll get a better result in pan-frying your steaks if you avoid using a nonstick skillet. The steaks will brown more nicely and hold a better texture if you opt for a stainless steel or cast-iron skillet.

MAKE-AHEAD TIP Wrap the steaks in plastic wrap and let them marinate in the refrigerator for several hours or up to 1 day. Remove the steaks from the refrigerator and let them sit at room temperature for 1 hour before cooking.

CHANGE IT UP!

Of course, grilling is definitely an option for this steak as well. Preheat your grill to medium and grill the steaks 3 to 4 minutes per side for medium rare. Grill the lemon cut side down.

slow cooker italian pot roast

Makes: 6 servings   Prep Time: 20 minutes   Cook Time: 6 hours

When you come home after a day of running around all over tarnation and you'd just like to sit down and let someone else make you a really nice dinner, this is the recipe for you. This roast is cooked up by the good ol' slow cooker. It's slowly simmered in canned San Marzano tomatoes, and it turns out just as tender and comforting as you could imagine. I recommend serving it with polenta or boiled potatoes and a nice, crusty bread to soak up all of the red sauce that will accompany the meat.

3	pounds rump or chuck beef roast
4	garlic cloves, peeled and cut in half
1	tablespoon olive oil
1	large onion, cut into wedges
1	28-ounce can crushed San Marzano tomatoes (see Tips)
1	tablespoon chopped fresh rosemary or ½ tablespoon dried Italian seasoning
1	teaspoon kosher salt
½	teaspoon freshly ground black pepper

Trim any excess fat from the roast and discard. Cut eight 1-inch slits into the roast (four on the top and four on the bottom). Tuck a garlic half into each slit.

In a large skillet, heat the olive oil over medium-high heat. Add the roast and cook 1 to 2 minutes on on each side, achieving a deep brown color before turning to the next side.

Add the onion wedges to the slow cooker and place the browned roast on top. Pour the crushed tomatoes on top of the roast and sprinkle with the rosemary, salt and pepper. Cover and cook on high heat for 6 hours or on low heat for 10 hours. Skim the top of the liquid in the slow cooker for any accumulated fat and discard. Use two forks to pull apart the meat. Serve the meat topped with sauce.

TIPS San Marzano tomatoes can usually be found in your market's canned tomatoes section. If you're unable to locate them, purchase the best quality crushed tomatoes available.

If you'd like this dish to be ready to go in the morning when you're taking off for work, do all of the precooking and place it in the slow cooker insert along with the sauce and onions, etc. Cover and keep it refrigerated. In the morning, simply place the insert in the slow cooker, turn it on and you're good to go!

CHANGE IT UP!

Serve the shredded meat in sandwiches instead. Pull apart the meat and pile it into Italian sandwich rolls along with some of the sauce.

rosemary and garlic leg of lamb roast

Makes: 6 to 8 servings   Prep Time: 15 minutes   Cook Time: 2 hours and 30 minutes

My grandma and grandpa lived on a ranch as I was growing up. There were cows, chickens, sheep, a mean rooster and horses that were too old to ride. Grandma drove a bright pink jeep around that ranch, she baked endless pies and jam with fruit from her orchards and she made the most tender lamb roast I've ever tasted. Memories of time spent on that ranch are indeed treasured. I like to think that Grandma would be proud of my lamb roast recipe. It's roasted slowly and seasoned just enough to bring out the brilliant flavor of the lamb itself.

4- to 5-pound boneless leg of lamb roast, fat trimmed to ¼ inch thick
1 tablespoon freshly squeezed lemon juice (see Tips)
1 tablespoon olive oil
8 medium garlic cloves, minced
3 tablespoons chopped fresh rosemary
1 tablespoon kosher salt
2 teaspoons freshly ground black pepper
1 teaspoon finely grated lemon zest

Preheat the oven to 425°F. Place the lamb on the rack of a foil-lined roasting pan.

In a small bowl, whisk together the lemon juice and olive oil and use clean hands to rub it all over the lamb roast.

In a small bowl, combine the garlic, rosemary, salt, pepper and lemon zest. Rub this mixture into the surface of the roast, making sure that you cover all sides.

Place the lamb in the oven and roast for 20 minutes. Reduce the oven temperature to 325°F and continue to roast 2 to 2½ hours, or until the meat thermometer inserted into the center of the roast registers 145°F to 150°F (see Tips).

Remove the lamb from the oven and allow it to rest for about 15 minutes before carving. The temperature will continue to rise 5 or 6°F.

TIPS Zest your lemon before you juice it.

The general rule for roasting lamb is to cook it 30 minutes per pound, so be sure to check your measurements and do the math.

Sliced lamb makes for wonderful, next-day sandwich leftovers.

CHANGE IT UP!

Substitute fresh oregano or thyme for the rosemary.

home-roasted (no-brainer) lemon, herb and garlic chicken

Makes: 4 servings   Prep Time: 15 minutes   Cook Time: 1 hour and 15 minutes

Food writer and cookbook author Michael Ruhlman once wrote a post on his blog called, "America: Too Stupid to Cook." The post was about the popularity of buying prepared foods (like cake mixes and rotisserie chickens) so that people don't have to be inconvenienced with the time-consuming experience of making something from scratch. His point was that Americans are being taught that cooking is so difficult that we need others to do it for us. He then proceeded to show the world how incredibly easy it is to make a roasted chicken at home. Bravo to Ruhlman and others who are showing people that cooking does not have to be time-consuming or difficult. Here's another chicken for you, with flavors of herbs and lemon, roasted to perfection with a crispy skin, and it happens to be much better than any you'd buy at the store.

1   whole chicken (about
      5 pounds)
1   tablespoon olive oil
2   large garlic cloves, minced
2   teaspoons chopped fresh
      thyme
1   teaspoon freshly grated
      lemon zest (about
      ½ lemon)
    Kosher salt and freshly
      ground black pepper

Preheat the oven to 450°F. Spray a Dutch oven or broiler pan with nonstick spray.

Remove the giblets and neck from the inside of your chicken. Rinse the chicken and pat it dry. Place the chicken in the prepared pan.

In a small bowl, combine the olive oil, garlic, thyme and lemon zest. Use clean hands to rub it all over the chicken and underneath the skin. Sprinkle the chicken generously with salt and pepper.

Roast for 30 minutes, then reduce the oven temperature to 400°F and roast for an additional 45 minutes, or until a thermometer inserted into the meaty part of the thigh registers 165°F. Transfer the chicken to a cutting board. Cover it with a piece of foil, let it rest for 10 minutes and then slice and serve.

TIP Tie the legs together with string up and over the breasts. This helps keep the breast meat moist while roasting.

CHANGE IT UP!

Other ways to roast your chicken: Cover the bird with 2 tablespoons grated orange zest, 1 tablespoon oil, salt and pepper. Or rub a paste of 1 tablespoon bacon fat, 1 tablespoon butter and 2 minced garlic cloves underneath the skin.

chicken and black bean enchiladas with mango enchilada sauce

Makes: 6 servings   Prep Time: 45 minutes   Cook Time: 55 minutes

Mangoes definitely have a place in Mexican food dishes. Just when you think your mouth has been overtaken by the heat and fire of a hot pepper, mango comes in and saves the day by cooling off your taste buds with its sweet flavor and sleek texture. That's why adding them to enchilada sauce, and even adding them to enchiladas themselves, is a great idea. These enchiladas happen to combine both the sweet and the spice in a most pleasant way.

SAUCE

2½ cups enchilada sauce, canned or homemade (page 249)
1 large mango, peeled, cored and chopped (about 1 cup)
2 teaspoons freshly squeezed lime juice

ENCHILADAS

1½ cups shredded cooked chicken
1 15-ounce can black beans, rinsed and drained
12 8-inch corn tortillas, warmed or fried (see Tips)
1 large mango, peeled, cored and finely chopped (about 1 cup)
2 cups shredded Monterey Jack cheese, divided

To prepare the enchilada sauce, add the sauce, mango and lime juice to a food processor or blender. Process until smooth.

Preheat the oven to 350°F. Spray a 9 x 13-inch pan with nonstick spray. Spread ¾ cup of the sauce in the bottom of the prepared pan to coat.

To assemble the enchiladas, in a medium bowl, mix the chicken and black beans. Place a tortilla on a flat work surface. Spoon ¼ cup of the chicken mixture down the middle of the tortilla. Top it with a spoonful of mango chunks, 2 tablespoons cheese and 1 tablespoon enchilada sauce. Wrap the tortilla tightly around the filling and place it seam side down in the pan. Repeat with the remaining tortillas and filling, placing the tortillas side by side in the pan. It's okay if they're snuggled in tightly. Pour the remaining sauce over the top of the stuffed enchiladas. Cover the pan with foil and bake for 30 minutes.

Remove the pan from the oven and take off the foil. Sprinkle the remaining cheese on top and return the pan to the oven. Bake for an additional 10 minutes, or until the cheese is melted and bubbly. Serve immediately.

GF GLUTEN-FREE ADAPTABLE Use brands of enchilada sauce, black beans and corn tortillas that are known to be gluten-free.

V VEGETARIAN ADAPTABLE Use 1½ cups cooked rice instead of chicken.

TIP To fry the tortillas: In a small pan, heat ⅓ cup vegetable oil to medium heat. Fry the tortillas one at a time, about 10 seconds on each side. Place them on a paper towel–lined plate to drain, adding a paper towel in between each tortilla. To warm the tortillas, wrap a stack of 3 at a time in damp paper towels and microwave them for 25 seconds, until they are warmed and softened. Alternatively, wrap them in foil with a few sprinkles of water and heat them in the oven at 350°F for 10 to 15 minutes, until they are warm and pliable.

CHANGE IT UP!

Serving idea: Place the enchiladas on a bed of chopped lettuce and top with sliced avocado, chopped tomatoes and sour cream.

Use ground or shredded beef in place of the chicken.

chicken with sweet apricot and balsamic vinegar glaze

Makes: 6 servings   Prep Time: 15 minutes   Cook Time: 40 minutes

On weeknights, we're usually rushing home from sports practices and trying to get homework done too. Easy, no-stress dinner ideas are "key" for times like these. This chicken recipe is great because you can throw rice on the stove and toss this in the oven. The sauce bakes up with the chicken, and your whole dinner is done in just 40 minutes.

12	boneless, skinless chicken thighs, trimmed of excess fat (see Tip)
¾	cup apricot jam
2	large garlic cloves, minced
1	teaspoon prepared horseradish
2	tablespoons balsamic vinegar
1	tablespoon cornstarch
1	teaspoon salt
½	teaspoon freshly ground black pepper

Preheat the oven to 375°F. Spray a 9-inch square pan with nonstick spray.

Place the chicken thighs side by side in the prepared baking pan.

In a small bowl, mix the jam, garlic and horseradish. In another small bowl, combine the vinegar and the cornstarch and stir to dissolve. Stir it into the jam mixture. Spread the sauce evenly over the tops of the chicken thighs. Sprinkle salt and pepper.

Bake, uncovered, for 40 to 50 minutes, or until the center of the chicken thighs registers 165°F. Serve immediately with juices drizzled over.

GF GLUTEN-FREE ADAPTABLE Use a brand of jam that is known to be gluten-free.

TIP I use chicken thighs with this recipe because they cook more tenderly than chicken breasts. The best chicken thighs can be found at markets that carry higher quality meats. Cheap chicken thighs tend to have a lot of fat attached and not enough meat. I like to spend a little more and find the better quality, meaty thighs for this dish.

SERVING TIP Serve over rice, orzo or potato—anything that would be good for scooping up the excess apricot sauce.

CHANGE IT UP!
Substitute orange marmalade for the apricot jam if you'd like, and add in 1 tablespoon brown sugar if you do so.

super-simple lemon and herb–marinated grilled chicken

Makes: 6 servings   Prep Time: 20 minutes + marinating time   Cook Time: 12 minutes

Lemon juice acts as the tenderizer in this no-oil marinade. Simply combined with fresh herbs, garlic and Dijon mustard, it turns out to be a surprisingly tender, moist and flavorful grilled chicken. It's a good recipe for summertime, when you're eating light and frantically struggling to squeeze into your swimsuit, and if you already look good in a swimsuit, it's probably because you eat good stuff like this.

½	cup freshly squeezed lemon juice
¼	cup Dijon mustard
¼	cup fresh herbs (any combination of thyme, oregano, and/or rosemary)
1	tablespoon Worcestershire sauce
2	large garlic cloves, minced
1	teaspoon onion powder
½	teaspoon salt
¼	teaspoon freshly ground black pepper
6	6- to 8-ounce skinless boneless chicken breast halves (see Tips)

In a medium bowl, whisk together the lemon juice, mustard, fresh herbs, Worcestershire sauce, garlic, onion powder, salt and pepper. Add the chicken and marinade to a large zip baggie. Marinate for 1 to 2 hours (see Tips).

Preheat the grill to medium. Drain and discard the marinade. Grill the chicken 6 to 8 minutes on each side, or until chicken is cooked through.

GF GLUTEN-FREE ADAPTABLE Use brands of Dijon and Worcestershire sauce that are known to be gluten-free.

TIPS In this recipe, you don't want to overmarinate the chicken. If left in the marinade for more than 2 hours, the lemon juice will begin to "cook" the chicken and give it a stronger-than-desired flavor.

Pound out the chicken breasts so they are all an even thickness. That will make them much easier to grill and they'll cook more evenly.

CHANGE IT UP!

Use this recipe for bone-in chicken too and bake it in the oven at 425°F for 25 to 35 minutes, or until the interior of the chicken measures 165°F.

This flavorful chicken makes a great addition to salad to make it a main dish.

tortilla-crusted chicken tenders with southwestern dipping sauce

Makes: 4 servings   Prep Time: 25 minutes   Cook Time: 10 minutes

My husband and I have encouraged our dear son to taste and enjoy all kinds of food. When he grows up, he can proudly declare that he was not raised on chicken tenders and boxed macaroni and cheese alone. Sure, we've always had a convenience food or two in our kitchen to get us through some busy nights, but we haven't allowed our child to become dependent on eating that kind of thing on a regular basis. Here's a homemade version of chicken tenders that uses corn tortillas for breading. The dipping sauce is wonderful, but picky kids can certainly opt for ketchup or Ranch dressing.

SAUCE

¼ cup mayonnaise
¼ cup buttermilk
2 tablespoons chopped fresh cilantro
2 teaspoons red taco sauce
1 teaspoon freshly squeezed lime juice
¼ teaspoon garlic powder
¼ teaspoon kosher salt
⅛ teaspoon dried oregano
⅛ teaspoon cumin powder

CHICKEN TENDERS

4 taco-size corn tortillas
4 tablespoons all-purpose flour
¾ teaspoon ground cumin
½ teaspoon salt
2 large egg whites, lightly beaten
1 tablespoon milk
1½ pounds chicken tenders
¼ cup vegetable or canola oil

To prepare the sauce, in a small bowl, whisk together the sauce ingredients. Cover and refrigerate the sauce until serving time.

To prepare the chicken, tear the tortillas into pieces and add them to a food processor. Process until the tortillas turn into fine crumbs. Transfer the tortilla crumbs to a bowl and mix them with the flour, cumin and salt. In a second bowl, whisk together the egg whites and milk.

Dip the chicken tenders into the egg white mixture and then into the crumb mixture to coat. In a large skillet, heat the oil over medium-high heat. Add the chicken strips to the skillet and cook until the chicken has a crispy golden exterior and is cooked through, 2 to 3 minutes on each side. Serve immediately with the sauce.

GF GLUTEN-FREE ADAPTABLE Use brands of mayonnaise, taco sauce and tortillas that are known to be gluten-free. Use a gluten-free flour blend in place of all-purpose flour.

TIP The sauce may be prepared up to 1 day ahead.

QUICK AND EASY TIP Place the crumb mixture into a large zip baggie. Coat the chicken strips all at once in the egg mixture, then drop the strips into the baggie, shaking off any excess egg as you go. Give the bag a few shakes and all of your chicken strips will be coated and ready for frying.

CHANGE IT UP!

Make a baked variety of chicken tenders instead. Place the coated chicken tenders on a greased baking sheet, spray them lightly with cooking spray and bake at 450°F for 15 to 20 minutes, or until they are golden and cooked through.

Try using turkey tenders for this recipe in place of chicken.

sweet lemon-glazed drumsticks

Makes: 4 to 6 servings   Prep Time: 15 minutes + marinating time   Cook Time: 50 minutes

There is something to be said about buying inexpensive meat once in a while. You'll spend less than half of what you might normally spend on dinner, which leaves more room for a nice side dish, a bottle of wine, or a tall vanilla latte. Chicken drumsticks fall into that category. Besides the fact that kids dig picking up a drumstick in their itty bitty fingers and nibbling the chicken right off the bone, they'll enjoy the sweet lemon flavor in this chicken, and not a soul will be the wiser that you've actually skimped on dinner.

12	chicken drumsticks (skin-on)
½	cup freshly squeezed lemon juice (about 4 medium lemons; see Tips)
¼	cup Dijon mustard
2	tablespoons extra-virgin olive oil
2	tablespoons chopped fresh herbs—oregano or thyme (or both)
2	tablespoons honey
2	tablespoons apple cider vinegar
1	tablespoon grated lemon zest
1	tablespoon packed light brown sugar
1	teaspoon minced garlic (1 medium clove)
1	teaspoon salt
½	teaspoon freshly ground black pepper

Rinse the chicken and pat it dry. Lay the drumsticks side by side in a 9 x 13-inch glass dish that has been sprayed with nonstick spray.

In a medium bowl, whisk together the remaining ingredients. Pour the marinade over the chicken and turn it to coat it completely. Cover the dish with plastic wrap and refrigerate for 1 hour (or up to 4 hours). Turn the chicken every once in a while to reincorporate the marinade ingredients.

Preheat the oven to 375°F. Drain the chicken from the marinade and transfer it to a roasting pan. Bake for 50 to 60 minutes, or until the chicken is tender and juices run clear when pierced with a fork.

GF GLUTEN-FREE ADAPTABLE Use a brand of Dijon mustard that is known to be gluten-free.

TIPS Zest your lemons before you juice them.

Why leave the skin on? The skin will crisp up nicely during the roasting process and provide the fat needed to keep the chicken from drying out. You can pull off the skin on your dinner plate if you don't wish to eat it, but I highly recommend that you try it first!

CHANGE IT UP!

Make this an orange-glazed chicken by substituting orange juice and zest for the lemon juice and zest.

This marinade works well with boneless chicken breasts too. Marinate using the same instructions and then throw them on the grill for quick and flavorful grilled chicken breasts.

mahimahi with creamy coconut-ginger sauce

Makes: 6 servings   Prep Time: 15 minutes   Cook Time: 20 minutes

I originally created this coconut-ginger sauce to use as a drizzle over fish for a dinner party. It was simple to make and so well received by my guests that I had to include it in the cookbook. Use the freshest mahimahi you can find. The sauce is delightfully creamy, and it delivers just a little punch of coconut and ginger flavor to this mild and flaky fish.

6	6-ounce portions skinless mahimahi fillets, rinsed and patted dry
2	tablespoons extra-virgin olive oil
1	tablespoon chilled salted butter, cut into 6 pieces
	Salt and freshly ground black pepper
1½	cups canned coconut milk (see Tips)
3	teaspoons freshly squeezed lime juice
3	teaspoons packed light brown sugar
1½	teaspoons chili paste
1½	teaspoons fish sauce
1½	teaspoons grated fresh ginger
	Chopped fresh chives, optional

Preheat the oven to 375°F. Spray a 9 x 13-inch pan with nonstick spray.

Place the fish in the prepared dish, leaving a small amount of space between each fillet. Drizzle the olive oil on top of the fillets. Top each fillet with a piece of butter. Sprinkle the fish generously with salt and pepper. Bake for 20 to 30 minutes, or until the fish is cooked through and flakes apart easily with a fork (time will vary depending on the thickness of your fillets).

Meanwhile, prepare the sauce. In a medium saucepan, bring the coconut milk, lime juice, sugar, chili paste, fish sauce and ginger to a boil over medium-high heat. Reduce the heat to low. Simmer, stirring often, until the sauce has thickened slightly, 2 to 3 minutes. Remove the sauce from heat.

Serve each mahimahi fillet with sauce drizzled on top. Garnish with chives, if desired.

GF GLUTEN-FREE ADAPTABLE Use brands of chili paste and fish sauce that are known to be gluten-free.

TIPS For best results, use regular coconut milk. If you opt for a low-fat coconut milk, you'll end up with a very thin sauce.

Both chili paste and fish sauce can be found in the Asian products section of your market. Ask your grocery manager if you are unable to locate them.

CHANGE IT UP!

Substitute salmon, halibut, or another flaky fish for the mahimahi.

epic shrimp tacos with chipotle cream

Makes: 8 tacos　Prep Time: 40 minutes　Cook Time: 10 minutes

I had my first fish taco in 1986. It was Spring Break, and I was down in San Felipe, Mexico, with a bunch of crazy college friends. We ate fish tacos daily during our stay, buying them from street carts for a buck and gobbling them up one after the other, washing them down with Mexican beer. Southern California is now pretty much a mecca for fish tacos. We eat them for lunch or we eat them for dinner. You can buy them in one of a zillion tiny Mexican fast-food places, or you can order them in fancy restaurants. Everyone seems to have their own unique twist on the fish taco. In this version, marinated, cooked shrimp are served up fajita-style with red bell pepper strips and onion. Then they're tucked into a warmed flour tortilla, topped with lettuce and cilantro and finished off with a simple, spiced-up sour cream sauce.

SHRIMP AND MARINADE

1½ pounds large, raw shrimp, peeled, deveined and tails removed
Grated zest of ½ medium orange
Grated zest of 1 large lime (see Tips)

CHIPOTLE CREAM SAUCE

1 8-ounce tub sour cream
2 tablespoons minced red onion
1 tablespoon chopped fresh cilantro
1 tablespoon freshly squeezed lime juice
1 medium garlic clove, minced
1 whole chipotle pepper in adobo sauce, seeded and chopped
1 teaspoon adobo sauce (from the can)
½ teaspoon ground cumin
⅛ teaspoon salt

REMAINING INGREDIENTS

1 tablespoon vegetable or canola oil
1 large red bell pepper, seeded, ribs removed and thinly sliced
½ medium red onion, thinly sliced
8 soft, taco-size flour tortillas, warmed (see Tips)
½ head iceberg lettuce, shredded
½ cup chopped fresh cilantro
8 lime wedges

Place the shrimp and zests in a large zip baggie. Move the bag around to coat the shrimp with the zest. Marinate the shrimp in the refrigerator for at least 30 minutes.

In a medium bowl, whisk together the sauce ingredients. Cover and refrigerate the sauce until ready to serve.

In a large skillet heat the oil over medium-high heat. Add the bell pepper and onion and cook, stirring, until softened, 3 to 4 minutes. Add the shrimp and cook, stirring often, until the shrimp turn pink and begin to curl up, 5 to 6 minutes. Remove the pan from heat.

continued on page 228

continued from page 227

Divide the shrimp, pepper and onion among the 8 tortillas. Add the lettuce, drizzle with the chipotle cream sauce and sprinkle with cilantro. Serve with a lime wedge for squeezing.

GF GLUTEN-FREE ADAPTABLE Be sure to use a brand of adobo sauce that is known to be gluten-free. Use gluten-free corn tortillas in place of flour tortillas.

TIPS Zest your lime before juicing it.

To warm the tortillas: Wrap a stack of 3 at a time in damp paper towels and microwave them for 25 seconds, until they are warmed and softened. Alternatively, wrap them in foil with a few sprinkles of water and heat them in the oven at 350°F for 10 to 15 minutes, until they are warm and pliable.

CHANGE IT UP!

Add ¼ cup Mexican beer or tequila to the zest in the shrimp marinade.

shrimp and cashew stir-fry with udon noodles

Makes: 4 servings   Prep Time: 25 minutes   Cook Time: 15 minutes

Stir-fry is just about the easiest meal you can make for your family. Everything can be prepped ahead—the sauce, the vegetables, chopping and preparing the protein. When the time comes to put it all together, throw some noodles or rice on the stove to cook, grab a skillet and mix all of your stir-fry ingredients together. It's so simple and healthy and delicious. The best part—it can be customized to add in the things that your family enjoys the most.

10   ounces udon noodles
½   cup sherry
3   tablespoons honey
2   tablespoons low-sodium soy sauce
1½ tablespoons chili-garlic sauce
1   tablespoon minced fresh ginger
1   tablespoon vegetable or canola oil
1   medium red bell pepper, seeded, ribs removed and thinly sliced
½   medium sweet onion, sliced
1½ pounds medium shrimp, peeled, deveined and tails removed
¾   cup raw cashews
¾   cup snow peas, sliced
1   8-ounce can sliced water chestnuts, drained

Cook the noodles according to package directions. While the noodles are cooking, prepare the rest of the ingredients.

In a medium bowl, whisk together the sherry, honey, soy sauce, chili-garlic sauce and ginger. Set aside.

In a large skillet, heat the oil over medium-high heat. Add the bell pepper and onion and cook, stirring, until they are slightly softened, 3 to 4 minutes. Add the shrimp and cashews and cook until the shrimp begin to turn pink and curl, 4 to 5 minutes. Decrease the heat to medium and add the snow peas, water chestnuts and reserved sauce. Bring the sauce to a boil and simmer until it is hot and slightly thickened. Divide the noodles among four bowls and top with the vegetable-shrimp mixture. Drizzle any pan juices on top and serve immediately.

GF GLUTEN-FREE ADAPTABLE Use brands of chili-garlic sauce and soy sauce that are known to be gluten-free. Serve over gluten-free noodles or rice in place of udon noodles.

TIPS Add in any of your favorite stir-fry vegetables.

Both udon noodles and chili-garlic sauce can be found in the Asian products section of your market. Ask your grocery manager if you are unable to locate them.

CHANGE IT UP!

Chicken may be substituted for the shrimp with similar results.

Serve this stir-fry over rice instead of noodles.

baked sole with lemon-panko crust

Makes: 4 servings   Prep Time: 20 minutes   Cook Time: 20 minutes

Every summer my family heads to the East Coast for a little R & R on Boston's South Shore. There is a wonderful little local fish market nearby where I can pick up fresh-off-the-boat fish any day of the week. That's where the inspiration for this dish comes from. There is really nothing like fresh fish combined with just a few ingredients to create a simple and delicious dinner. Nothing fancy here.

1¼ pounds sole fillets, rinsed and patted dry
2   tablespoons mayonnaise
1   tablespoon freshly squeezed lemon juice (see Tips)
½   teaspoon salt
¼   teaspoon freshly ground black pepper
1   cup panko bread crumbs
1   tablespoon freshly chopped flat-leaf parsley
2   teaspoons freshly grated lemon zest
½   teaspoon garlic powder
4   lemon wedges

Preheat the oven to 400°F. Line a large baking sheet with foil and place a rack on top. Spray the rack with nonstick spray.

Place the fillets on a piece of waxed paper in one layer. In a small bowl, mix the mayonnaise and lemon juice. Brush the mixture on the top of the fillets. Sprinkle the tops with the salt and pepper.

In a wide, shallow bowl, mix the bread crumbs, parsley, lemon zest and garlic powder. Dip the coated fillets into the crumb coating, covering both sides. Place the crumb-coated fillets onto the baking rack, mayonnaise side up.

Bake the fish, uncovered, for 15 minutes. Set the oven to broil and broil until the crumbs are browned and the fish is opaque, 3 to 4 minutes (see Tips). Serve with lemon wedges.

TIPS Zest your lemon before juicing it, since you'll need to use zest in the coating. Two lemons should be perfect for this recipe—one for zesting and juicing and one for slicing into wedges to serve with the fish.

Opaque, perfectly done fish will come apart easily when tested with a fork. Just stick your fork into one of the fillets and pull. If it comes apart without having to tug at it, your fish is done.

Meyer lemons are incredible and they give this dish a sweet bump in flavor. Look for Meyer lemons November through March in your market.

CHANGE IT UP!

Acceptable substitutes for sole are flounder, cod, orange roughy or haddock. Feel free to use any of those in place of the sole for a similar outcome. If the fish is thicker than thin-cut sole, you'll need to adjust the baking time accordingly.

W

oven-roasted
barbecued salmon

Makes: 4 servings   Prep Time: 15 minutes   Cook Time: 20 minutes

I have my sister Susie to thank for this recipe. Living in the Northwest, Susie has access to some pretty amazing varieties of fresh salmon. She has made this salmon recipe for as long as I can remember. I've always loved it because it's a fast, no-fuss way to prepare salmon, and its sweet flavor is one that is attractive to kids and totally family-friendly.

4   6-ounce salmon fillets
    (bones removed)
3   tablespoons Dijon mustard
2   tablespoons low-sodium soy
    sauce
1   tablespoon honey
1   tablespoon salted butter,
    melted
1   tablespoon packed light
    brown sugar
1   tablespoon olive oil
1   teaspoon minced garlic
    (1 medium clove)
4   lime wedges

Spray a 9-inch square glass dish (or similarly sized casserole dish) with nonstick spray. Place the salmon fillets in the prepared dish.

In a small bowl, whisk together the Dijon, soy sauce, honey, butter, sugar, olive oil and garlic. Spoon the marinade evenly over the salmon. Cover the dish with plastic wrap and refrigerate for 30 to 60 minutes.

Preheat the oven to 425°F.

Remove the plastic wrap and bake the salmon for 20 to 25 minutes, or until the fish is cooked through and flakes away easily with a fork. Serve the fillets with lime wedges for squeezing.

GF GLUTEN-FREE ADAPTABLE Use brands of soy sauce and Dijon that are known to be gluten-free.

DF DAIRY-FREE ADAPTABLE Leave out the butter.

TIP You can leave skin on the salmon (on one side), or you can ask your seafood department to remove it completely. If the skin is on, cook it skin side down and the fish will easily flake away from the skin when you dish it out to serve.

CHANGE IT UP!

Cook the salmon on a medium-heated grill instead. Drain the marinade from the salmon, place it on a grill pan and grill for 12 to 18 minutes, or until the salmon is cooked through and flakes away easily with a fork.

newlywed pasta

Makes: 2 servings   Prep Time: 20 minutes   Cook Time: 10 minutes

I knew how to cook when I got married some eighteen years ago. Or at least I could follow a recipe. As a young bride, I wasn't particularly great at creating things from scratch, or from my head or from looking at what I had in the refrigerator. But I knew what we liked best (pasta), and I fiddled with variations of it quite often. This is the combination that we liked best, and we ate it for dinner fifty-two times the first year we were married. Its simple list of ingredients is not overwhelming for someone who is new to cooking, and it packs a big flavor punch.

6	ounces angel hair pasta
2	tablespoons extra-virgin olive oil
1	teaspoon minced garlic
½	teaspoon red pepper flakes
¼	cup fresh basil, cut into thin strips
¼	cup sun-dried tomatoes (dried or packed in oil; see Tips)
¾	cup freshly grated Parmesan cheese, divided
¼	cup toasted pine nuts (see Tips)
	Salt and freshly ground black pepper, to taste

Cook the noodles according to the package directions.

While the noodles are cooking, in a large skillet, heat the olive oil over medium heat. Add the garlic and red pepper and cook, stirring, until fragrant, about 1 minute. Add the basil and sun-dried tomatoes and cook, stirring, for 1 additional minute. Scoop the cooked angel hair pasta into the skillet and toss gently until warmed through. Add ½ cup of the cheese and the pine nuts and toss again. Divide the pasta between 2 bowls and sprinkle each with an additional 2 tablespoons of cheese. Sprinkle with salt and pepper, to taste.

TIPS If you choose to use sun-dried tomatoes packed in oil, just make sure you drain them thoroughly. If you use the dried version, measure out ½ cup, then hydrate them in 1 cup of very hot water for about 5 minutes, just until they are softened. Drain and use.

For toasting the pine nuts, heat a small skillet over medium heat. Add the raw pine nuts to the dry skillet. Stir constantly until the pine nuts begin to turn brown on all sides. Remove the pine nuts to a bowl to cool.

CHANGE IT UP!

Use any kind of pasta for this dish—even ravioli or tortellini!

Add in a splash of white wine while cooking the sun-dried tomatoes and basil.

barbecue-sauced shrimp and bacon with orzo

Makes: 4 servings   Prep Time: 40 minutes   Cook Time: 15 minutes

If there are two things I'm utterly and completely obsessed with in this world of food, it's barbecue sauce and bacon. I can barbecue sauce anything to make it taste good, and a little bit of added bacon has never made anything taste bad. This dish is completely family-friendly. If your family does not care for zucchini, go ahead and leave it out (or serve it on the side). I like to tell my son that vegetables in dishes like this just taste like the rest of the food in the dish, so eat up!

1½ cups orzo
1 tablespoon olive oil
1 cup chopped red onion (about 1 medium)
1½ pounds medium, raw shrimp, peeled, deveined and tails removed
1 large garlic clove, minced
¼ teaspoon red pepper flakes
⅓ cup dry white wine
1½ cups thinly sliced zucchini (about 2 medium)
1½ cups diced Roma tomato (about 3 large)
½ cup bottled barbecue sauce
2 teaspoons chopped fresh oregano (or ¾ teaspoon dried)
5 slices bacon, cooked and crumbled (see Tips)
1 4-ounce package crumbled feta cheese
Salt and freshly ground black pepper, to taste

Cook the orzo according to the package directions.

While the orzo is cooking, in a large skillet, heat the olive oil over medium heat. Add the onion and cook, stirring, until softened and lightly browned, 4 to 5 minutes. Stir in the shrimp, garlic and red pepper and continue to cook, stirring occasionally, just until the shrimp turn pink and begin to curl up, 3 to 4 minutes. Add the wine and stir until it is almost evaporated, 1 to 2 minutes. Stir in the zucchini and cook until the zucchini is slightly softened, 3 to 4 minutes. Add the tomato, barbecue sauce and oregano. Cook just until heated through, 4 to 5 minutes. Stir in the bacon and cheese. Divide the pasta among 4 bowls, top with the shrimp mixture and season each with salt and pepper, to taste.

GF GLUTEN-FREE ADAPTABLE Use brands of barbecue sauce and bacon that are known to be gluten-free. Use a gluten-free pasta alternative.

DF DAIRY-FREE ADAPTABLE Leave out the feta cheese.

TIP For easy clean-up, cook your bacon in the oven. Preheat the oven to 400°F. Line a large, rimmed baking sheet with foil and place a rack on top. Spray the rack with nonstick spray. Lay the bacon slices on the rack. Bake for 15 to 20 minutes, or until the bacon is crisp. Timing will vary depending on the thickness of your bacon.

TIME-SAVING TIP Use cooked shrimp instead of peeling and deveining fresh shrimp yourself. Add it in with the tomato to heat through with the rest of the ingredients.

CHANGE IT UP!
Serve this dish over steamed rice or quinoa instead of orzo.

cheese ravioli with brown butter and fresh tomato sauce

Makes: 6 servings   Prep Time: 8 minutes   Cook Time: 12 minutes

My son has dubbed ravioli as his favorite dinner choice ever. It figures that he chose something that is usually purchased already made either frozen or fresh. That makes dinner easy for me, but I generally like to jazz things like that up a bit. This recipe drizzles brown butter and basil with lightly sautéed tomatoes over freshly cooked ravioli. It couldn't be simpler or more delicious.

2   9-ounce packages fresh ravioli

6   tablespoons (¾ stick) salted butter

2   cups cherry or pear tomatoes

½   cup finely chopped fresh basil

Salt and freshly ground black pepper, to taste

½   cup freshly grated Parmesan cheese

Cook the ravioli according to package directions.

While the ravioli is cooking, prepare the sauce. In a medium skillet, melt the butter over medium heat. Reduce the heat to low, add the tomatoes and cook until the tomatoes begin to soften and burst and the butter turns brown, about 7 minutes. Stir in the basil. Season the sauce with salt and pepper, to taste.

Serve the brown butter–tomato sauce over the freshly cooked ravioli. Sprinkle individual servings with cheese.

 GLUTEN-FREE ADAPTABLE Use gluten-free ravioli.

TIPS This recipe can easily be halved. Just purchase one package of ravioli and cut the rest of the ingredient amounts in half.

I love to use multicolored sweet cherry tomatoes for this recipe—it makes it pretty!

CHANGE IT UP!

Drizzle this sauce over any type of pasta, or use it as a topping for chicken too.

Add sautéed, sliced zucchini or mushrooms to the sauce.

creamy skillet-baked penne pasta

Makes: 4 to 6 servings   Prep Time: 20 minutes   Cook Time: 30 minutes

Is there anything more comforting than a baked pasta dish? I don't think so. It's comfort food all the way. This dish of pasta is simmered for a short time on the stove before you pop it into the oven to create a melted layer of cheese that clings to the noodles. And even more irresistible is the fact that you'll only dirty one pan in the preparation of dinner.

3	tablespoons salted butter
6	medium garlic cloves, minced
¼	teaspoon red pepper flakes
3	tablespoons all-purpose flour
1½	cups 2% low-fat milk, slightly warmed (see Tips)
1½	cups warm tap water
1	28-ounce can crushed tomatoes
12	ounces dry penne pasta
½	teaspoon salt
½	cup freshly grated Parmesan cheese
¼	cup finely chopped fresh basil
1	cup shredded mozzarella cheese

Preheat the oven to 475°F.

In a large, oven-safe skillet, melt the butter over medium heat. Add the garlic and red pepper and cook, stirring, for 1 minute. Whisk in the flour and cook until lightly browned, 1 to 2 minutes.

Increase the heat to medium-high. Slowly whisk in the milk and cook, stirring, until slightly thickened, about 3 minutes. Add the water, tomatoes, pasta and salt. Bring to a boil. Cover the skillet and reduce the heat to low. Simmer until the pasta is almost tender, 15 to 18 minutes. Remove the pan from heat and stir in the Parmesan and basil. Sprinkle the mozzarella cheese on top and place the skillet into the oven for 10 minutes, or until the cheese is hot and bubbly.

TIPS To warm the milk, just pour it into a glass measuring cup and heat it in the microwave or in a small saucepan on the stove. It should only take a short time, but watch it closely so it doesn't bubble up and over the cup.

If you only have a skillet with a plastic handle, you can still turn it into an oven-safe skillet. Simply wrap the plastic handle of the skillet tightly with foil. Or you may opt to transfer the pasta to a casserole dish before baking.

CHANGE IT UP!

Ziti and rigatoni work well for this dish, too.

Add more red pepper flakes if you like things spicy.

chicken spaghetti casserole

Makes: 6 servings   Prep Time: 40 minutes   Cook Time: 35 minutes

I live in San Diego, which isn't really the Casserole Capital of America. People here eat grilled chicken, tofu, egg white omelettes, and salad with no dressing. Casseroles are among the evils that aren't spoken here in SoCal. Whatever. . . . I eat casseroles. It must be because all of my distant Swedish relatives live in Minnesota, where comfort food is more welcomed. It's in my genes, and it's probably in my jeans too. This is a baked, cheesy spaghetti kind of casserole with chunks of chicken and a few vegetables tucked in there as well. It's a big-time family favorite of ours.

7   ounces thin spaghetti
6   tablespoons (¾ stick) salted butter
2   cups sliced mushrooms
1   medium onion, chopped
1   large garlic clove, minced
3   tablespoons all-purpose flour
1   cup low-sodium chicken broth
1   cup milk
2½ cups shredded cheddar cheese, divided
2   cups chopped cooked chicken
1   10-ounce can Ro-Tel original diced tomatoes and green chiles
    Salt and freshly ground black pepper, to taste
½   cup shredded Monterey Jack cheese

Preheat the oven to 350°F. Spray a 2-quart casserole dish with nonstick spray.

Cook the pasta according to the package directions, but only until it's al dente (you still want a little bit of a bite to it). Set aside.

In a large, deep skillet, melt the butter over medium heat. Add the mushrooms, onion and garlic and cook, stirring, until the vegetables are softened, 4 to 5 minutes. Whisk in the flour, and then slowly whisk in the chicken broth. Turn the heat to medium-high. Slowly whisk in the milk, and continue to whisk while bringing the mixture to a boil. Continue to whisk until the mixture becomes slightly thickened, 3 to 5 minutes. Remove the skillet from heat and stir in 2 cups of the cheddar cheese, the chicken and tomatoes. Add salt and pepper, to taste. Stir in the cooked noodles. Pour the noodles and sauce into the prepared casserole dish. Sprinkle the remaining ½ cup cheddar cheese and the Jack cheese on top.

Bake 35 minutes, or until the casserole is hot and bubbly and golden brown.

TIPS Use any pasta for this casserole. It doesn't necessarily have to be spaghetti.

If you're not into mushrooms, substitute something else. Zucchini or peas would work well in this recipe.

CHANGE IT UP!

Turn this casserole into a day-after-Thanksgiving meal by adding in leftover roasted turkey meat instead of chicken.

spinach and cheese-stuffed manicotti

Makes: 6 servings (2 manicotti per serving)   Prep Time: 45 minutes   Cook Time: 60 minutes

Manicotti is the ultimate family-friendly dish. It's completely filling and the leftovers are even better than a freshly made batch. We make this when we have a handful of friends or family around, and it's our go-to meal on Christmas night, when everyone is too exhausted to cook. It's a nice, no-fuss recipe that everyone seems to love. Make it ahead, keep it in the fridge and toss it in the oven when everyone is ready to eat.

1	10-ounce package frozen spinach, thawed and squeezed dry
15	ounces ricotta cheese
8	ounces shredded mozzarella cheese (2 cups)
4	ounces cream cheese, softened
1	cup shredded Parmesan or Romano cheese, divided
2	large eggs
½	teaspoon salt
½	teaspoon freshly ground black pepper
4	cups bottled tomato-basil marinara sauce
1	box manicotti noodles (12 to 14 shells)

Preheat the oven to 350°F.

In a large bowl, mix the spinach, ricotta, mozzarella, cream cheese, ½ cup of the Parmesan, the eggs, salt and pepper. Stir together until well blended.

Spread 1½ cups of the sauce in the bottom of a 9 x 13-inch pan to coat.

Use a very small spoon or fork to stuff the uncooked shells with the filling (see Tips), letting it generously peek out of each end of the shell. Place the filled shell into the pan. Repeat with the remaining manicotti until you run out of shells and filling. You should be able to fill 12 to 14 shells.

Pour the remaining sauce over the shells, making sure it covers the noodles. Sprinkle the remaining ½ cup of Parmesan on top. Cover the pan tightly with foil and bake for 50 minutes, then remove the foil and bake for an additional 10 minutes.

TIPS I prefer to use the bag method of filling the manicotti noodles. Fill a large plastic freezer zip baggie (or a piping bag) with the filling. Snip the corner, gather the top of the bag together and squeeze the filling into the corner. Hold an uncooked manicotti shell in your hand and squeeze the bag to allow the filling to squeeze inside of the shell.

If you run out of room in your 9 x 13-inch pan, use a separate, smaller pan to accommodate the extra manicotti.

MAKE-AHEAD TIP Cover the pan of stuffed manicotti with foil and refrigerate (up to 8 hours ahead). Remove it from the refrigerator and let it sit at room temperature for 30 minutes before baking.

CHANGE IT UP!

Make this recipe a little bit lighter by using part-skim ricotta and low-fat cream cheese.

If you're not a big fan of spinach, it's okay to leave it out and turn this into a cheese-stuffed manicotti.

bacon macaroni and cheese

Makes: 4 main-dish (or 6 side-dish) servings   Prep Time: 30 minutes   Cook Time: 50 minutes

Macaroni and cheese has always seemed like such an over-the-top sort of meal, one that I enjoy immensely but should avoid at all costs if I ever wish to maintain any sort of control over my body jiggle. We'll ignore the diet for now. With a good dose of cheddar cheese and a generous handful of crispy bacon, I can easily call this a dish worthy of breaking through your daily calorie limit. Guests in our home dubbed this macaroni and cheese as "ridiculous"—translation: "out of this world!" Leftovers are just as good, so double this recipe if you want more.

8   ounces pasta (elbows or shells)
6   ounces (6 slices) center-cut bacon, chopped into 1-inch pieces
2   tablespoons butter
¼   cup all-purpose flour
2¾   cups whole milk, warmed (see Tips)
1   tablespoon chopped fresh thyme
½   teaspoon mustard powder
½   teaspoon red pepper flakes
½   teaspoon kosher salt
¼   teaspoon freshly ground black pepper
⅛   teaspoon ground nutmeg
3   cups shredded sharp cheddar cheese
½   cup shredded Swiss or Parmesan cheese

Preheat the oven to 375°F. Butter a 2- to 3-quart casserole dish.

Bring a medium pot of water to boil on the stove. Add the pasta and cook until very al dente, 6 to 10 minutes (time will vary depending on the type of pasta that you use; see Tips).

In a large skillet, fry the bacon over medium to medium-high heat until crisp, 6 to 8 minutes. Remove the bacon to a paper towel–lined plate to drain. Discard all but 1 tablespoon bacon drippings. Add the butter to the bacon drippings and heat over medium heat. When the butter is melted, whisk in the flour and cook for 1 minute. Slowly whisk in the warmed milk. Continue cooking, whisking constantly, until the mixture bubbles up and becomes thick. Remove the pan from heat and stir in the thyme, mustard powder, red pepper, salt, black pepper and nutmeg. Stir in the cheddar cheese, then the cooked pasta and bacon.

Pour the mixture into the prepared casserole dish (it will be very soupy). Sprinkle with the Swiss. Bake for 30 minutes, or until browned on top. Transfer the dish to a wire rack to cool for 5 minutes before serving.

continued on page 242

continued from page 240

 VEGETARIAN ADAPTABLE Leave out the bacon.

TIPS To warm the milk, just pour it into a glass measuring cup and heat it in the microwave or in a small saucepan on the stove. It should only take a short time, but watch it closely so it doesn't bubble up and over the cup.

Cooking the pasta "al dente" means that the pasta will still have the slightest bit of bite to it (cook for 2 to 3 minutes less than the suggested cooking time on the box).

Serve a bottle of Tabasco on the side for those who like things spicy.

CHANGE IT UP!

Add a crumb topping to this dish. In the bowl of a food processor fitted with a steel blade, combine 1 medium garlic clove and 1½ tablespoons finely chopped parsley and pulse until they're minced. Add 3 slices of bread torn into pieces (crusts removed) and pulse until the bread turns into crumbs. Drizzle in 1 tablespoon melted salted butter and pulse until it is blended in. Sprinkle the herbed bread crumbs onto the macaroni and cheese before baking.

You can be creative with the cheese choices if you wish. Other good melting cheeses for macaroni and cheese are Monterey Jack, Swiss, Gouda, Havarti, fontina and Gruyère. Avoid using low-fat cheeses for melting—they don't melt well at all.

sausage-stuffed zucchini boats

Makes: 6 zucchini boats · Prep Time: 30 minutes · Cook Time: 30 minutes

My son Brooks took up the hobby of fishing one summer while we were on vacation. He hooked up with his East Coast cousins and their fishing neighbor Eric. Brooks spent a lot of time with Eric and his endless supply of fishing equipment that summer. Eric taught the kids how to catch fish off the docks and the jetty of Boston's South Shore. I think Brooks would have fished all day every day if we'd let him. One day he came home from fishing and told us he'd already eaten lunch, Stuffed Zucchini Boats, at Eric's house. Now, you have to understand that my boy would no sooner eat a small piece of zucchini floating in a bowl of soup, let alone an entire zucchini stuffed with stuff. Yet he came home and told me how much he loved Eric's Zucchini Boats. I moved Eric into "God" category and got to work re-creating his masterpiece. Brooks tells me that Eric's version is better, but then again . . . I don't fish.

3	medium 8-inch zucchini, ends trimmed, then cut in half lengthwise
1	tablespoon olive oil
½	cup finely chopped onion (about ½ medium)
3	medium garlic cloves, minced
¾	pound sweet Italian turkey sausage
½	cup freshly grated Parmesan cheese
½	cup shredded mozzarella cheese
½	cup bottled tomato-basil marinara sauce
3	tablespoons chopped fresh basil
	Salt and freshly ground black pepper, to taste

Preheat the oven to 350°F. Spray a 9 x 13-inch baking pan with nonstick spray.

Use a small spoon to scrape out the pulp of each zucchini half, saving the pulp. Don't scrape the zucchini all the way to the skin—just make a deep pocket where you'll be able to put the stuffing. Chop up the pulp.

In a large skillet, heat the olive oil over medium heat. Add the zucchini pulp, onion, garlic and sausage. Cook, stirring often, until the onion is softened and the sausage is cooked through, 4 to 6 minutes. Pour the mixture through a fine sieve to drain the excess moisture. Transfer the meat mixture to a medium bowl.

In a small bowl, mix the cheeses. Reserve 2 tablespoons of the cheese. Add the remaining cheese to the meat mixture along with the marinara sauce and basil. Add salt and pepper, to taste.

Divide the meat mixture among the hollowed out zucchini, filling and mounding the mixture into each one. Set the stuffed zucchini into the prepared pan and sprinkle the reserved cheese on top.

Bake 30 minutes, or until baked through and tender.

GF GLUTEN-FREE ADAPTABLE Use brands of sausage and marinara sauce that are known to be gluten-free

V VEGETARIAN ADAPTABLE Leave out the sausage and add in ¾ cup cooked rice instead.

TIP The zucchini boats are delicious on their own, or you can serve them over rice.

CHANGE IT UP!

Substitute ground beef or ground turkey for the Italian sausage.

baked eggplant parmesan rolatini

Makes: 4 servings   Prep Time: 45 minutes   Cook Time: 5

I've been accused of being a "sneaky Mommy" at times. I've tucked zucchini inside of enchiladas, well mixed with beef and sauce and virtually unrecognizable by my little one, and once I ground up mushrooms so tiny that they took on a ground beef texture, which was perfect for the mushroom burgers that I managed to pull off without revealing what they actually were. Yep, sometimes you need to trick kids into eating something before they'll admit that they like it. That's where this recipe comes in handy. Eggplant is treated just as chicken is in a chicken Parmesan recipe. It's lightly breaded and baked, and then it's rolled up with cheeses and sauce and baked some more. It's a sneaky way to get eggplant-weary people to try and enjoy this purple vegetable.

2   medium eggplants
      (3 to 4 pounds) or 1 very
      large eggplant
      Salt
¾   cup all-purpose flour
3   large eggs
1½   cups panko bread crumbs
1¼   cups freshly grated
      Parmesan cheese, divided
3   cups (12 ounces) finely
      shredded mozzarella
      cheese, divided
1¼   cups ricotta cheese
1   cup chopped fresh spinach
¾   cup chopped fresh basil
⅓   cup toasted pine nuts (see
      Tips)
½   teaspoon salt
¼   teaspoon freshly ground
      black pepper
3   cups bottled tomato-basil
      marinara sauce
16   ounces angel hair pasta,
      cooked according to
      package directions

Preheat the oven to 350°F. Spray 2 baking sheets with nonstick spray.

To prepare the eggplant, cut the ends off the eggplant. Cut the eggplant lengthwise into ¼- to ½-inch slices (about 8 slices). Lay the eggplant slices out on a double layer of paper towels and sprinkle them with salt. Let them sit for 15 minutes to draw out the moisture in the eggplant. Rinse the eggplant slices and pat dry.

Set out three low and wide bowls for the dipping mixtures. Place the flour in the first bowl. In the second bowl, whisk together the eggs. In the third bowl, mix the bread crumbs and 1 cup of the Parmesan. Dip an eggplant slice in flour, then in egg and then in bread crumb mixture, making sure to cover all sides of the eggplant slice with each dip. Place the eggplant slice on a prepared baking sheet and repeat with the remaining eggplant slices. Bake the breaded eggplant for 10 minutes, then turn the eggplant slices over and bake for an additional 10 minutes. Remove from the oven and let them cool (keep the oven heated at 350°F).

To prepare the filling, in a medium bowl, mix 2 cups of the mozzarella, the ricotta, spinach, basil, pine nuts, salt and pepper. Spread 1 cup of the marinara sauce in the bottom of a 9 x 13-inch baking dish. Lay an eggplant slice on a flat surface. Spread ⅓ cup of the cheese filling onto the slice, spreading it to the edges. Roll it up tightly from one short side to the other and then place it seam side down in the sauce-lined pan. Repeat with the remaining eggplant and filling. Drizzle the remaining 2 cups marinara sauce over the tops of the eggplant rolls. Bake, uncovered, for 20 minutes. Sprinkle with the remaining 1 cup mozzarella and ¼ cup Parmesan and bake for an additional 10 minutes, just until the cheese is melted and bubbly.

Serve the eggplant rolatini over the pasta.

GF GLUTEN-FREE ADAPTABLE Substitute a gluten-free all-purpose flour blend for the all-purpose flour and gluten-free bread crumbs or crushed gluten-free pretzels for the bread crumbs. Be sure to use a brand of marinara that is known to be gluten-free. Serve over gluten-free pasta or rice instead of the angel hair.

TIP For toasting the pine nuts: Heat a small skillet over medium heat. Add the raw pine nuts to the dry skillet. Stir constantly until the pine nuts begin to turn brown on all sides. Remove the pine nuts to a bowl to cool.

CHANGE IT UP!

To give the dish a slightly different flavor, substitute shredded provolone cheese for ½ of the mozzarella cheese.

sausage, sweet potato and caramelized red onion pizza with sage pesto

Makes: 1 pizza (6 servings)   Prep Time: 60 minutes   Cook Time: 60 minutes

Friday night is family pizza night at our house. I make the crust, a simple recipe in the food processor, with little work involved, and the family decides what should go on the pizza. Some nights are classics like pineapple and bacon, and others are fancier with things like arugula, goat cheese and prosciutto. I love that about pizza—pretty much anything you're craving works out okay. Here's a fun version of pizza with sage pesto as a delicious, alternative sauce, and topped with sausage, sweet potatoes and sweet, caramelized red onion. There are a few steps to this recipe, but everything can be prepped ahead and it's all worth it in the end.

CARAMELIZED ONION
- ½ tablespoon olive oil
- 1 large red onion, peeled and thinly sliced
- 1 teaspoon granulated white sugar
- ¼ teaspoon salt
- ⅛ teaspoon freshly ground black pepper

SWEET POTATOES
- 1 small sweet potato, peeled and sliced ¼ inch thick
- 1 tablespoon olive oil

PESTO
- ¾ cup (loosely packed) fresh sage leaves
- ⅓ cup extra-virgin olive oil
- ¼ cup chopped walnuts
- ¼ cup freshly grated Parmesan cheese
- 1 medium garlic clove
- ½ teaspoon salt
- ⅛ teaspoon freshly ground black pepper

PIZZA
- 1 pound ball of pizza dough, purchased or homemade (recipe follows)
  Cornmeal, for dusting
- 1½ cups shredded mozzarella cheese
- 12 ounces sweet Italian sausage, cooked, drained and crumbled

To prepare the caramelized onion, in a large skillet, heat the olive oil over medium heat. Add the onion and cook, stirring frequently, until the onion turns a deep, golden brown (see Tips), 25 to 30 minutes. Stir in the sugar, salt and pepper and remove the onion from heat. Let cool.

To prepare the potatoes, preheat the oven to 400°F. Spray a baking sheet with nonstick spray or line with parchment paper.

Pile the sliced potatoes onto the baking sheet, drizzle the olive oil on top and toss the potatoes to coat. Spread them out evenly on the baking sheet. Roast the potatoes for 20 minutes, turning them about halfway through. Let cool.

CHANGE IT UP!

Make this a quick and easy pizza by purchasing ready-made pizza dough, using store-bought basil pesto and tossing the red onions into the oven with the potatoes to roast. Use prosciutto instead of sausage.

To prepare the pesto, in a mini food processor or blender, combine all of the pesto ingredients and process until incorporated and the sauce is smooth.

To prepare the pizza, place a pizza stone or inverted baking sheet on the lowest oven rack. Preheat the oven to 500°F (or the oven's highest temperature setting).

Roll out the dough into a 12- to 14-inch circle on a lightly floured surface, then transfer the rolled out dough to a pizza peel or a second inverted baking sheet that has been generously dusted with cornmeal. Brush the dough with the sage pesto. Top the pesto with ¾ cup of the mozzarella, then the potato slices, onions and cooked sausage. Sprinkle the remaining ¾ cup mozzarella on top. Slide the pizza onto the hot stone or baking sheet that is in the oven. Bake for 10 to 15 minutes, or until the pizza crust is golden and the cheese is melted. Remove the pizza from the oven and let it cool for 5 minutes before slicing.

 VEGETARIAN ADAPTABLE Leave out the sausage or substitute a vegetarian sausage.

TIPS Caramelizing onions is a slow process of gradual browning. If your onions appear to be browning too quickly over medium heat, reduce the heat to medium-low.

All of the prep in this recipe can be done up to a day ahead. Just keep the ingredients wrapped and refrigerated until you are ready to assemble.

pizza dough

Makes: One 1-pound ball of dough   Prep Time: 15 minutes + resting time

I've never liked the dough that you purchase in the can all that much. It feels fake, like trying to eat pizza that has been created on top of breadstick dough. Here's a super-simple way to make homemade pizza dough in your food processor. It's pizza dough, for real.

2   cups all-purpose flour
1¼   teaspoons active dry yeast
1   teaspoon salt
1   teaspoon granulated white
        sugar
¾   cup warm water (110°F to
        115°F; see Tips)
1   tablespoon olive oil

In a food processor, combine the flour, yeast, salt and sugar. Pulse to mix. Combine the warm water and oil in a measuring cup. With the food processor motor running, gradually pour in the warm liquid until the mixture forms a sticky ball. The dough should be soft. If it's dry, add 1 to 2 tablespoons additional warm water. If it's too sticky, add 1 to 2 tablespoons additional flour. Continue to process the dough until it forms a ball, and then process it for 1 minute to knead. Transfer the dough to a lightly floured surface. Cover it loosely with a clean dish towel. Let the dough rest 10 to 20 minutes before rolling.

TIPS If you don't have an instant-read thermometer to test the water temperature, use water that is warm but not hot (similar to the temperature of milk in a baby bottle).

This pizza dough is great for all kinds of pizza. Prepare the dough and let it rest, and by the time you've gathered together all of your toppings, it's ready to roll!

enchilada sauce

Makes: 2½ cups   Prep Time: 15 minutes   Cook Time: 20 minutes

Why would you ever buy that canned stuff that tastes so reminiscent of metal when you can make it so easily homemade?

¼   cup vegetable or canola oil
2   tablespoons all-purpose flour
2   tablespoons chili powder
1½ cups low-sodium chicken broth
1   8-ounce can tomato sauce
½   teaspoon ground cumin
½   teaspoon garlic powder
½   teaspoon onion salt
¼   teaspoon salt

In a large skillet, heat the oil over medium-high heat. Whisk in the flour and chili powder. Reduce the heat to medium and continue to whisk until it is lightly browned. Gradually whisk in the chicken broth, tomato sauce, cumin, garlic powder, onion salt and salt. Stir until the mixture is smooth and continue simmering over medium heat until it is slightly thickened, about 10 minutes. Remove the sauce from heat and let cool.

GF GLUTEN-FREE ADAPTABLE Use an alternative thickener to the sauce instead of flour such as potato starch or cornstarch.

 VEGETARIAN ADAPTABLE Use vegetable broth instead of chicken broth.

Sweet Treats

Let's talk favorite things. I'll include cookies, cheesecake, bread pudding, red licorice, long walks on the beach and Chardonnay on that "favorite things" list. I totally blame my Dad for tempting me with sweet treats from a very young age, or it could be my mom's fault for not swatting my hand when I wanted to take nibbles of cookie dough. It's too late now. I just love dessert. If I could subsist solely on sweet treats, my world would be a happy place to be indeed. Someday there will be a Recipe Girl Dessert Cookbook in the works because my brain works constantly on overtime creating sweet treat recipes. Until then, I'll share just a sampling of my favorite dessert things.

Recipes

W WEB FAVORITE   V VEGETARIAN *(or adaptable)*   GF GLUTEN-FREE *(or adaptable)*   DF DAIRY-FREE *(or adaptable)*

butterfinger brownies

Makes: 25 brownies   Prep Time: 20 minutes   Cook Time: 25 minutes

Dear Butterfinger Candy Bar Fans, this is a brownie created just for you. I've featured enough Butterfinger dessert recipes on my website to know that there are a whole lot of fans of the Butterfinger out there. The great thing about this recipe is that these brownies can take on other favorite candy bars too. Just add your favorite chopped candy bar and mix it right on in there to create something new.

4   ounces unsweetened chocolate, chopped
8   tablespoons (1 stick) salted butter, melted
½   cup creamy peanut butter (see Tips)
2   cups packed light brown sugar
4   large eggs
2   teaspoons vanilla extract
1   cup all-purpose flour
16 .65-ounce Butterfinger candy bars, chopped (or 10.4 ounces total; see Tips)

Preheat the oven to 325°F. Line a 9 x 13-inch pan with parchment paper or foil and spray with nonstick spray.

In a glass bowl, melt the chocolate and butter in the microwave in short bursts of 30 seconds, stirring after each burst. Remove from the microwave when melted and smooth. (Alternatively, you can also melt the chocolate on the stove—see Tips.) Set it aside to cool slightly.

In a large mixing bowl, whisk together the peanut butter, sugar, eggs and vanilla. Whisk in the melted chocolate. Add the flour and stir. Reserve ½ cup of the Butterfingers. Gently stir the remaining Butterfingers into the batter.

Spread the batter into the prepared pan and top with the reserved Butterfingers. Bake 30 to 35 minutes, or until a toothpick inserted in the center comes out clean. Let the brownies cool completely (see Tips).

TIPS Don't use natural peanut butter for this recipe unless you're using a very creamy natural peanut butter.

continued on page 254

continued from page 253

When chopping the Butterfingers, don't try to chop them too finely as they tend to flake apart pretty easily. Opt for larger-cut chunks, but add everything into the batter, and if you really love Butterfingers, you may wish to add even more of them!

To melt the chocolate on the stove, place a heatproof bowl over a pan of simmering water (the bottom of the bowl should not touch the water). Add the chopped chocolate to the bowl and stir until melted and smooth.

Get a nice, clean cut on these brownies by chilling them in the refrigerator until they are firm. Use a large, sharp knife, wiping it clean with a paper towel after each cut, and you'll end up with neatly cut brownies.

CHANGE IT UP!

Instead of sprinkling the extra Butterfinger chunks on top, add a chocolate glaze first. Place 1 cup semisweet chocolate chips in a medium bowl. In a small saucepan, boil ½ cup heavy whipping cream and pour it over the chocolate. Let it stand for 5 minutes, then stir until melted and smooth. Spread the glaze evenly over the brownies and sprinkle Butterfinger chunks on top. Let it set at room temperature.

snickerdoodle blondies

Makes: 12 blondies   Prep Time: 15 minutes   Cook Time: 45 minutes

Blondies are such a versatile and unfussy little dessert that they can take just about anything that you'd like to throw in them. Since I'm utterly obsessed with snickerdoodles, I decided to throw my all-time favorite cookie into these blondies, and they took it well. Each bite delivers a cinnamon-sugar flavor with a hint of snickerdoodle cookie.

BLONDIES

1½	cups all-purpose flour
1	teaspoon baking powder
1	teaspoon ground cinnamon
½	teaspoon cream of tartar
¼	teaspoon salt
1⅔	cups packed light brown sugar
¾	cup (1½ sticks) salted butter, at room temperature
2	large eggs
1½	teaspoons vanilla extract
1	cup cinnamon chips (see Tips)

CINNAMON TOPPING

2	tablespoons granulated white sugar
1	teaspoon ground cinnamon

Preheat the oven to 350°F. Spray a 9-inch square baking pan with nonstick spray.

In a medium bowl, whisk together the flour, baking powder, cinnamon, cream of tartar and salt.

In a large bowl, use an electric mixer to combine the sugar and butter. Add the eggs and vanilla and mix until well combined. Gently stir in the dry ingredients until incorporated. Stir in the cinnamon chips. Spread the batter into the prepared pan. Combine the topping ingredients and sprinkle evenly onto the batter.

Bake for 45 to 50 minutes, or until golden brown and a toothpick inserted in the center comes out somewhat clean. The blondies will feel firm when done, but the inside will be moist and tender.

TIPS Cinnamon chips are packaged in the same manner as chocolate chips. If your market does not carry them, ask your grocery manager if they can be ordered. You can always leave them out of the blondies if you can't locate them.

Keep an eye on the blondies while baking. If they are browning more quickly than you'd like them to, loosely cover the top of the pan with a piece of foil.

CHANGE IT UP!

Chocolate lovers can change this recipe into something that suits their taste buds—use chocolate chips in place of the cinnamon chips to create Chocolate Chip Snickerdoodle Blondies.

chocolate chip cookie dough lover brownies

Makes: 16 brownies   Prep Time: 30 minutes + chill time   Cook Time: 25 minutes

Mom let us kids nibble the dough whenever she baked up a batch of chocolate chip cookies. It's safe to say that I now actually enjoy cookie dough over baked cookies any day of the week. I wouldn't say that I'd be happy sitting with a bowl of dough and a spoon and going to town with it, but a nibble now and then is good to me. These brownies are baked, but they're also topped with an "unbaked" layer of egg-free chocolate chip cookie dough. These are brownies for all of the cookie dough lovers out there.

BROWNIES

¾	cup (1½ sticks) unsalted butter
1½	cups bittersweet chocolate chips
1	cup granulated white sugar
½	cup packed light brown sugar
4	large eggs
1	teaspoon vanilla extract
½	teaspoon salt
1	cup all-purpose flour

EGG-FREE COOKIE DOUGH

¾	cup (1½ sticks) unsalted butter, room temperature or almost melted
¾	cup granulated white sugar
¾	cup packed light brown sugar
¼	teaspoon salt
2	tablespoons milk or cream
1½	teaspoons vanilla extract or vanilla bean paste
1	cup all-purpose flour
1	cup miniature chocolate chips
	Additional miniature chocolate chips for garnish, optional

Preheat the oven to 350°F. Line a 9-inch square pan with foil or parchment paper and spray with nonstick spray.

To prepare the brownies, in a glass bowl, melt the butter and chocolate in the microwave in short bursts of 30 seconds, stirring after each burst. Remove from the microwave when melted and smooth. (Alternatively, you can melt the butter and chocolate on the stove—see Tips.) Set it aside to cool slightly.

In a large bowl, whisk together the sugars, eggs, vanilla and salt. Add the chocolate mixture and whisk until smooth. Stir in the flour just until combined.

Spread the brownie batter into the prepared pan. Bake for 25 to 30 minutes, or until the brownie layer is cooked through (a toothpick inserted into the center comes out clean). Place the pan of brownies in the refrigerator to speed up the cooling process (or cool at room temperature and add the cookie dough layer later).

To prepare the cookie dough, in a medium bowl, use an electric mixer to combine the butter, sugars and salt for 1 to 2 minutes, or until the mixture is soft and creamy. Mix in the milk and vanilla. Mix in the flour, just until combined. Stir in the chocolate chips.

continued on page 258

continued from page 256

When the brownie layer is chilled and firm, spoon the cookie dough over the cooled brownies. Wet your hands or spray them with nonstick spray and pat the cookie dough into an even layer. Sprinkle additional chocolate chips on top, if desired. Refrigerate until the dough is quite firm (see Tips). Use a sharp knife to cut the brownies. You may need to wipe the knife off with a paper towel in between cuts since the fudgy brownies and cookie dough will tend to stick to the knife. Store the brownies in a covered container in the refrigerator until ready to serve.

TIPS To melt the butter and chocolate chips on the stove, place a heatproof bowl over a pan of simmering water (the bottom of the bowl should not touch the water). Add the butter and chocolate chips to the bowl and stir until melted and smooth.

It's okay to speed up the cooling process and place the cookie dough brownies in the freezer too. The firmer the dough, the easier it will be to cut into neat squares.

Leftovers may be wrapped individually and stored in the freezer for up to 1 month.

CHANGE IT UP!

If you'd like to add chocolate drizzle on top, melt ½ cup chocolate chips with 1 teaspoon of shortening in the microwave and stir until smooth. Scoop the melted chocolate into a zip baggie and snip off the corner. Squeeze the bag to drizzle the chocolate on top of each brownie. Sprinkle additional chocolate chips on top, if desired.

Quick and easy variation: Bake boxed brownies, as instructed and then add a layer of cookie dough on top.

irish cream brownies with brown butter icing

Makes: 16 brownies   Prep Time: 40 minutes   Cook Time: 45 minutes

Irish Cream liqueur reminds me of skiing. It's the perfect warm-you-up drink added to a steaming mug of hot chocolate or coffee on a quick break from the slopes, and for that reason, it has its place in brownies too. This recipe incorporates the delicious flavor of Irish cream into the brownies themselves, but it's also mixed into a brown butter icing spread on top of the brownies.

BROWNIES

2½ cups all-purpose flour
1   teaspoon salt
½   teaspoon baking powder
2   cups semisweet chocolate chips
1   cup (2 sticks) unsalted butter
1½ cups packed light brown sugar
2   large eggs
½   cup + 1 tablespoon Irish cream liqueur, divided

ICING

4   tablespoons (½ stick) salted butter
2   tablespoons Irish cream liqueur
1   tablespoon heavy whipping cream
1½ to 2 cups powdered sugar (measured, then sifted)

Preheat the oven to 350°F. Line a 9-inch square pan with foil or parchment paper and spray with nonstick spray.

To prepare the brownies, in a medium bowl, sift together the flour, salt and baking powder. Set aside.

In a glass bowl, melt the chocolate and butter in the microwave in short bursts of 30 seconds, stirring after each burst. Remove from the microwave when melted and smooth. (Alternatively, you can melt the chocolate and butter on the stove—see Tips.) Set it aside to cool slightly.

In a large bowl, whisk together the sugar, eggs and ½ cup of the Irish cream. Add the chocolate mixture and whisk until smooth. Stir in the dry ingredients, just until combined.

Spread the batter into the prepared pan. Bake for 40 to 45 minutes, or until the top of the brownies cracks slightly and a toothpick inserted into the center comes out mostly clean (see Tips). Remove the brownies from the oven and immediately brush them with the remaining 1 tablespoon Irish cream. Let the brownies cool completely.

To prepare the icing, in a medium saucepan melt the butter over medium-high heat, stirring often and watching closely, until it is lightly browned, 3 to 5 minutes. Remove the butter from heat as soon as it has browned and add the Irish cream and whipping cream. Whisk in 1 cup of the powdered sugar. Add more powdered sugar ¼ cup at a time until you achieve a thick,

continued on page 260

continued from page 259

smooth icing that is still pourable. Pour the icing on top of the cooled brownies and spread it to the edges to cover completely. Refrigerate the brownies until the icing is set (see Tips). Cut into squares. Store the brownies in a covered container. They're best if eaten within 2 to 3 days.

TIPS To melt the chocolate and butter on the stove, place a heatproof bowl over a pan of simmering water (the bottom of the bowl should not touch the water). Add the butter and chocolate chips and stir until melted and smooth.

If the tester toothpick comes out slightly gooey on the bottom, that's okay. You want your brownies to be tender and moist.

Chilled brownies are easiest to cut. Use a large, sharp knife, wiping it clean with a paper towel after each cut, and you'll end up with neatly cut brownies.

CHANGE IT UP!

Add a teaspoon of espresso powder to the egg mixture. Espresso has a tendency to intensify the flavor of the chocolate.

Try using Kahlúa in place of the Irish cream.

nutella-filled mexican wedding cookies

Makes: 2½ dozen cookies   Prep Time: 45 minutes   Cook Time: 14 minutes

Nutella is a treasured jar of goodness in our house. We spread it on graham crackers with a little Marshmallow Fluff for snacks, we swirl it into our banana bread, and we bake it into the occasional treat. Mixed with chopped hazelnuts, Nutella makes the perfect surprise filling for these very buttery Mexican Wedding Cookies.

FILLING

- ½ cup Nutella (or another chocolate hazelnut spread)
- ⅓ cup milk chocolate chips
- ½ cup sifted powdered sugar + extra for rolling
- ⅓ cup chopped hazelnuts, optional

COOKIE DOUGH

- 3 cups all-purpose flour
- 1½ cups (3 sticks) salted butter, at room temperature
- 1 tablespoon vanilla extract
- 2 tablespoons milk

Preheat the oven to 400°F. Line a baking sheet with parchment paper or a Silpat mat, or spray with nonstick spray.

To prepare the filling, in a medium bowl, microwave the Nutella and chocolate chips in short bursts of 30 seconds, stirring after each burst. Remove from the microwave when melted and smooth. (Alternatively, you can melt the Nutella and chocolate chips on the stove—see Tips.) Stir in the powdered sugar and hazelnuts and set aside to cool.

To prepare the cookie dough, in a large bowl, use an electric mixer to combine the flour, butter and vanilla. Mix until well blended (the mixture will be very dry). Add the milk and stir until the mixture comes together in clumps.

To assemble the cookies, scoop out about 1½ tablespoons of the dough into your hand. Squeeze the dough together and use your hands to flatten it out into a round pancake shape. Scoop 1 teaspoon of the Nutella mixture into the center of the flattened dough. Wrap the dough around the Nutella mixture and shape it into a round ball. Place the ball on the prepared baking sheet and repeat with the remaining dough and filling. The cookies won't spread, so you can place them fairly close together on the baking sheet.

Bake the cookies for 14 to 16 minutes, or until they are slightly golden and firm.

Place the extra powdered sugar in a bowl. Roll the warm cookies in the powdered sugar and set them on a wire rack to cool completely.

TIPS To heat the Nutella and chocolate on the stove, place a heatproof bowl over a pan of simmering water (the bottom of the bowl should not touch the water). Add the Nutella and chocolate chips and stir until melted and smooth.

These cookies will freeze well. Keep them in a covered container with waxed paper in between stacked layers.

CHANGE IT UP!

If you're making this cookie around the holidays, add colored sugar sprinkles to the powdered sugar before rolling your warm cookies.

lemon shortbread cookies with white chocolate drizzle

Makes: 3 to 4 dozen cookies   Prep Time: 35 m...   ...ne   Cook Time: 30 minutes

Sunny, yellow lemons remind me of summer. This lemon-scented shortbread is a cheerful cookie to serve in warm weather, and it'll brighten up anyone's day in the midst of a cold and dreary winter too. The light white chocolate drizzle on top is the perfect sweet complement to the tart flavor of lemon.

SHORTBREAD

- 1   cup (2 sticks) unsalted butter, at room temperature
- ¾   cup powdered sugar
- 2   tablespoons freshly grated lemon zest (about 2 medium lemons) (see Tips)
- 1   teaspoon vanilla extract
- 2¼ cups all-purpose flour
- 1   teaspoon sea salt

DRIZZLE

- 4   ounces white chocolate, chopped
- 1   teaspoon shortening
- 2   tablespoons freshly grated lemon zest (about 2 medium lemons)

To prepare the dough, in a large bowl, use an electric mixer to combine the butter and sugar at medium speed until fluffy, about 2 minutes. Mix in the zest and vanilla. Add the flour and salt and continue to mix until the flour is incorporated and the dough comes together.

Divide the dough in half and turn it out onto two sheets of waxed paper. Form two 8 x 2½-inch logs. Roll each log carefully until it is well shaped and rounded. Wrap each log in wax paper, twisting the ends to seal and refrigerate for at least 1 hour (see Make-Ahead Tip).

Preheat the oven to 300°F. Line cookie sheets with parchment paper or Silpat mats, or spray with nonstick spray.

Remove the cookie dough logs from the refrigerator and use a very sharp knife to cut ¼-inch-thick slices. Place the slices 1 inch apart on the cookie sheets. Bake 30 to 35 minutes, just until set and the edges begin to turn golden brown. Remove cookies to a wire rack and let them cool completely before adding the drizzle.

To prepare the drizzle, in a medium bowl microwave the white chocolate and shortening in short bursts of 30 seconds, stirring after each burst. Remove from the microwave when the chocolate is melted and smooth. (Alternatively, you can melt the chocolate and shortening on the stove—see Tips.) Scoop the chocolate mixture into a strong zip baggie. Snip a tiny piece off of the corner of the bag. Squeeze the chocolate onto the cookies in a back-and-forth drizzle pattern. Sprinkle a few pieces of lemon zest on top of the chocolate as you go along. If the melted chocolate begins to solidify during this process, just pop the bag back into the microwave and heat briefly to soften it again. Let the drizzle set at room temperature. These cookies may be stored in a covered container for up to 1 week or in the freezer for up to 3 months.

TIPS To heat the white chocolate and shortening on the stove, place a heatproof bowl over a pan of simmering water (the bottom of the bowl should not touch the water). Add the white chocolate and shortening and stir until melted and smooth.

Since you're not using any actual lemon "juice" in this recipe, go ahead and squeeze the lemons after you zest them. Collect the juice in a freezer zip baggie and store in the freezer until you have the need for freshly squeezed lemon juice. Better yet, measure the juice out by the tablespoon into ice cube trays, freeze it, then store the cubes in a baggie and defrost tablespoons of lemon juice as you need them.

MAKE-AHEAD TIP Prepare the cookie dough logs and keep them refrigerated for up to 2 days before proceeding with baking and drizzling.

CHANGE IT UP!

Try using Meyer lemons for this recipe. They're a little sweeter and they're easiest to find during the winter months.

Turn the cookies into Orange Shortbread Cookies, substituting oranges for lemons.

blackberry-cornmeal thumbprint cookies

Makes: 2 dozen cookies   Prep Time: 30 minutes   Cook Time: 12 minutes

A few years ago, I made a Christmas cookie that had a crunchy cornmeal texture to it with savory sage mixed into the dough and I topped the cookie with jam. I adored it, and I thought it was quite a clever twist for a Christmas cookie, but people either really loved it or they thought it strange that sage was added in. Here's my version of that cookie. I left out the sage, but if you're feeling adventurous . . .

¾ cup (1½ sticks) salted butter
½ cup granulated white sugar
1 large egg yolk
1 teaspoon vanilla extract
1¼ cups all-purpose flour
¼ cup cornmeal (see Tips)
⅓ cup seedless blackberry jam

Preheat the oven to 350°F. Line two baking sheets with parchment paper or Silpat mats, or spray with nonstick spray.

In a large bowl, use an electric mixer to combine the butter and sugar. Add the egg and vanilla and mix well. Add the flour and cornmeal and continue to mix until well combined.

Scoop out 1½ tablespoons of dough and use your hands to roll it into a ball. Place it on the cookie sheet and use your thumb to make an impression in the center of the cookie. Spoon about ¾ teaspoon of jam into the center of the cookie. Continue with the remaining cookie dough and jam, leaving about 2 inches between cookies.

Bake the cookies for 12 to 15 minutes, or until golden on the edges. Let cool on the cookie sheets for 10 minutes and then transfer them to a wire rack to cool completely.

TIPS If you'd like the cookies to have a more crunchy texture, use whole grain cornmeal.

The dough may be made up to 2 hours ahead, then covered and refrigerated until firm, if desired.

CHANGE IT UP!

Change the flavor of the jam—strawberry, apricot and raspberry are equally good in these cookies.

Add in 1 teaspoon of crushed, dried sage along with the flour to create a savory twist to this cookie recipe.

caramel–apple pie crust cookies

Makes: 2 dozen cookies   Prep Time: 45 minutes + chill times   Cook Time: 25 minutes

It might seem a little odd that I remember pie crust "cookies" when I was growing up in my Mom's house, but I don't remember any actual "pies." Mom rolled out pie crust scraps, then buttered and topped them with generous doses of sugar and cinnamon. Then she rolled them up and baked them into logs of pie crust cookies, sliceable after baking. It was like eating little bits of sugary pie. My modern-day version of Mom's pie crust cookies have fresh apple mixed in, and they are topped with a drizzle of caramel glaze too.

CRUST

1½ cups all-purpose flour
1   teaspoon granulated white
     sugar
     Pinch of salt
8   tablespoons (1 stick) cold,
     unsalted butter, cut into
     ½-inch pieces
1   8-ounce package cold cream
     cheese, roughly cut into
     tablespoons

FILLING

1   large egg white
1   tablespoon water
⅓   cup granulated white sugar
1   tablespoon ground cinnamon
1½   cups very finely diced,
     peeled apple (1 large; see
     Tips)

CARAMEL GLAZE

2   tablespoons salted butter
¼   cup packed light brown
     sugar
1   to 2 tablespoons milk
⅛   teaspoon vanilla extract
¼   to ½ cup powdered sugar

To prepare the crust, in a food processor, combine the flour, sugar and salt. Process for 10 seconds to blend. Add the butter and process for just a few seconds, until the mixture looks like crumbs. Add the cream cheese and pulse quickly about 25 times, or until a clump of pie dough has formed. Turn the clump of dough onto waxed paper and knead gently 2 to 3 times to bring the dough together. Flatten it into a 7-inch square. Wrap the dough in plastic wrap and chill for at least 30 minutes. (The crust can be prepared up to 2 days ahead. Wrap in plastic wrap as directed and refrigerate).

Place the chilled dough on a lightly floured surface. Roll it into a rectangle that is roughly 9 x 12 inches (don't worry about trying to make it a perfect rectangle—see Tips), with the long side facing you. In a small bowl, whisk together the egg white and water until foamy. Brush the dough with the egg wash. In another small bowl, whisk together the sugar and cinnamon. Sprinkle it evenly over the dough. Sprinkle the apples on top. Starting with the long edge facing you, carefully roll the dough into a log, sealing the edge by giving it a brush of the egg wash and gently pressing down on the dough with your fingers. Roll the log onto plastic wrap or parchment paper, wrap it and freeze it until slightly firm (about 1 hour).

Preheat the oven to 325°F. Line two baking sheets with parchment paper or Silpat mats, or spray them with nonstick spray.

continued on page 266

continued from page 265

Remove the pie crust cookie log from the freezer and unwrap it. Use a sharp knife to cut it gently into ½-inch slices. The filling will want to slide out of the slices; just push it back into place with your fingers. Transfer the slices to the prepared baking sheets. Bake the cookies for 25 to 28 minutes, or until the crusts are golden. Let the cookies cool on the baking sheets for a few minutes and then transfer them to a wire rack to let cool slightly before glazing.

To glaze the cookies, in a small saucepan, melt the butter over medium-low heat. Stir in the sugar and 1 tablespoon of the milk. Cook for 1 minute. Transfer to a small mixing bowl and cool the mixture slightly. Stir in the vanilla and ¼ cup of the powdered sugar. Beat with an electric mixer until well blended. If necessary, add more powdered sugar or milk for desired drizzling consistency (it should be thick, but pourable). Drizzle or spoon the glaze over warm cookies. The glaze will harden when left at room temperature for a while.

TIPS Apple varieties best for baking are Granny Smith, Braeburn, Jonathon or Golden Russet.

If the crust sticks to your rolling surface, gently use a metal spatula to guide it up and off the surface.

QUICK AND EASY TIP Use store-bought pie crust instead of homemade and proceed with the instructions as written.

CHANGE IT UP!

Top the cookies with a cream cheese glaze instead: In a large bowl, use an electric mixer to combine 4 ounces softened cream cheese with 2 tablespoons softened butter until soft and creamy. Beat in ½ cup powdered sugar and vanilla until well blended. Add a little milk or whipping cream if you need to thin it out. Place the frosting in a piping bag with a small tip (or a plastic baggie with the corner cut off) and drizzle the icing onto the cookies.

kahlúa-espresso chocolate chip cookies

Makes: 4 dozen cookies   Prep Time: 25 minutes   Cook Time: 10 minutes

I hope that you can imagine just how wonderful these cookies must be when they're fresh out of the oven. Pull them apart and bite into those melty chocolate chips. The Kahlúa is a nice touch too.

2⅔ cups all-purpose flour
1 teaspoon baking soda
1 teaspoon ground cinnamon
½ teaspoon salt
1 tablespoon Kahlúa (or another coffee liqueur)
½ tablespoon espresso powder (see Tips)
1 cup (2 sticks) salted butter, at room temperature
1 cup packed light brown sugar
½ cup granulated white sugar
2 large eggs
1 teaspoon vanilla extract
⅓ cup semisweet chocolate chips, melted and cooled slightly
1 12-ounce package semisweet chocolate chips

Preheat the oven to 375°F. Line cookie sheets with parchment paper or Silpat mats.

In a medium bowl, whisk together the flour, baking soda, cinnamon and salt. Set aside.

In a small bowl, combine the Kahlúa and the espresso powder. Stir until the espresso powder is dissolved.

In a large bowl, use an electric mixer to combine the butter and sugars, mixing until creamy. Add the Kahlúa mixture, eggs and vanilla and beat until thoroughly combined. Add the melted chocolate and continue to beat until it is mixed in. Add the flour mixture and beat at low speed until all of the flour is incorporated into the dough, scraping down the sides of the bowl as needed. Stir in the chocolate chips.

Drop the cookie dough by tablespoonfuls (see Tips) 2 inches apart onto the prepared cookie sheets. Bake 8 to 10 minutes, or until they are golden brown and no longer look gooey in the middle. Let the cookies cool for a few minutes on the cookie sheet and then transfer them to a wire rack to cool completely.

TIPS You can locate espresso powder near the instant coffee in most supermarkets or in specialty markets.

I highly recommend investing in a cookie dough scoop for baking even and rounded cookies. Just scoop up the dough and press the spring to release the dough onto the cookie sheet. So easy!

If you prefer not to add Kahlúa, just leave it out. Increase the vanilla extract to 1 tablespoon and dissolve the espresso powder in the vanilla instead.

CHANGE IT UP!

Try using another flavor of liqueur in these cookies, such as chocolate or hazelnut.

chocolate–peanut butter swirl cookies

Makes: 5 dozen cookies   Prep Time: 40 minutes + chill time   Cook Time: 12 minutes

These cookies bake up perfectly—not too soft and not too crisp, and the peanut butter cookie is a nice complement to that wonderful chocolate swirl. It's the perfect cookie for those who enjoy having their peanut butter and chocolate in every bite, since those two flavors are so uniformly swirled together.

PEANUT BUTTER COOKIE

1   cup (2 sticks) salted butter, at room temperature
1   cup creamy peanut butter (see Tips)
1   cup granulated white sugar
1   cup packed light brown sugar
2   large eggs
2½ cups all-purpose flour
1½ teaspoons baking soda
1   teaspoon baking powder
½   teaspoon salt

CHOCOLATE SWIRL

1   12-ounce bag semisweet chocolate chips
1   14-ounce can sweetened condensed milk
1   tablespoon shortening

In a large bowl, use an electric mixer to combine the butter, peanut butter, sugars and eggs.

In a separate bowl, whisk together the flour, baking soda, baking powder and salt. Add the dry ingredients to the wet ingredients and beat together until combined.

Divide the dough in half. Pat each half into a ball and wrap with plastic wrap. Refrigerate until the dough is firm (about 1 hour should be perfect).

On a thin, floured towel, flexible mat or well-floured surface, roll out 1 ball of dough into a large rectangle (about 11 x 15 inches—not too thin). The dough will be soft, so roll gently.

To prepare the chocolate swirl, in a medium bowl, microwave the chocolate chips, sweetened condensed milk and shortening for 1 minute, then stir. Continue melting in short bursts of 30 seconds, stirring after each burst. Remove from the microwave when the chocolate is melted and smooth. (Alternatively, you can melt the chocolate, sweetened condensed milk and shortening on the stove—see Tips.)

Spoon half of the chocolate mixture onto the rolled-out dough, then spread it carefully to cover most of the rectangle. Using the towel as a guide, carefully lift the towel to help roll the rectangle into a log, or just gently roll the dough with your fingers into a log. Wrap the log in plastic wrap and place it on a flat surface in the freezer for about 20 minutes, or until the dough has had a chance to firm up slightly. It's okay to leave it in the freezer longer than 20 minutes. It's easiest to cut when firm.

While the first batch is in the freezer, repeat making a log with the second ball of dough and the remaining melted chocolate. If the chocolate mixture has firmed up a bit, just stick it back into the microwave to melt again and stir until smooth.

When ready to bake, preheat the oven to 350°F. Line cookie sheets with parchment paper, or spray with nonstick spray.

Remove the cookie dough logs from the freezer and place them on a cutting board. Carefully slice into ¼-inch slices and place them on the cookie sheets, leaving 2 inches of space between cookies.

Bake for 12 to 15 minutes, or until the cookies no longer look or feel gooey.

TIPS Don't use natural peanut butter for this recipe unless you're using a very creamy natural peanut butter.

To heat the chocolate chips, sweetened condensed milk and shortening on the stove, place a heatproof bowl over a pan of simmering water (the bottom of the bowl should not touch the water). Add the chocolate chips, sweetened condensed milk and shortening and stir until melted and smooth.

CHANGE IT UP!

Use a smooth, creamy almond butter for this recipe in place of the peanut butter.

brown butter–chocolate chip cookies

Makes: 2½ dozen cookies   Prep Time: 30 minutes + chill time   Cook Time: 10 minutes

Brown butter imparts a slightly nutty flavor to these cookies, without actually adding any nuts at all. The browning of the butter is very easy to do—you just need a watchful eye and a little bit of patience to allow the butter to brown slowly. Oh, brown butter, and chocolate chip cookies, how I love them both. They sure make a delightful coupling in my favorite chocolate chip cookie recipe of all time.

2	cups all-purpose flour
½	cup oats, old-fashioned or quick-cooking (measure and then grind in the blender; see Tips)
1½	teaspoons baking soda
1	teaspoon kosher salt
1	cup (2 sticks) unsalted butter
1	cup packed dark brown sugar
½	cup granulated white sugar
2	tablespoons whipping cream
1	tablespoon freshly squeezed lemon juice
2	teaspoons vanilla extract
1	large egg
1	large egg yolk
2	cups bittersweet chocolate chips

In a large bowl, whisk together the flour, ground oats, baking soda and salt. Set aside.

In a medium saucepan, melt the butter over medium-high heat. Watch it closely, stirring every 30 seconds or so, and continue to cook the butter until it begins to turn brown, 3 to 5 minutes. Remove the butter from heat and pour it into a large mixing bowl. Add the sugars and use an electric mixer to combine. Beat in the whipping cream, lemon juice and vanilla. Add the egg and egg yolk and beat to combine. Mix in the dry ingredients a little at a time until incorporated. Stir in the chocolate chips. Cover the bowl with plastic wrap and refrigerate the dough for at least 1 hour and up to 24 hours before baking.

Preheat the oven to 375°F. Line two cookie sheets with parchment paper or Silpat mats, or spray with nonstick spray.

Scoop a heaping tablespoonful of dough and use your hands to roll it into a ball. Place it on the cookie sheet. Continue with the remaining dough, leaving 2 inches between cookies. Bake for 10 to 12 minutes, or until cookies are set in the middle and lightly browned on the edges. Cool for 10 minutes on the baking sheets and then remove the cookies to a wire rack to cool completely.

TIP Use a blender to grind the oats into powder. If you don't have a blender, it's okay to add the oats as they are.

CHANGE IT UP!

Change up the flavors of chips. I prefer bittersweet chocolate, but try using milk chocolate, semisweet or even butterscotch.

peanut butter cup cookie cupcakes

Makes: 16 cupcakes   Prep Time: 35 minutes   Cook Time: 14 minutes

Another one for the chocolate–peanut butter lovers, these cookies . . . er, cupcakes . . . are for people who can't decide whether they'd like a cookie or a cupcake. It's also a sneaky way to bake a cookie into a more substantial size and still call it one serving, and it's a brilliant ploy to get permission to eat a cookie and a candy bar at the same time.

1¼ cups all-purpose flour
¾   teaspoon baking soda
½   teaspoon baking powder
¼   teaspoon salt
½   cup crunchy peanut butter
      (see Tips)
8   tablespoons (1 stick) salted
      butter, at room temperature
½   cup granulated white sugar
½   cup packed brown sugar
1   large egg
16 whole, full-size peanut
      butter cups, unwrapped

Preheat the oven to 350°F. Spray two 12-cup muffin tins with nonstick spray.

In a medium bowl, whisk together the flour, baking soda, baking powder and salt. Set aside.

In a large bowl, use an electric mixer to combine the peanut butter and butter. Add the sugars and mix until combined. Beat in the egg. Add in the dry ingredients a little at a time and mix just until they are incorporated.

Fill 16 muffin cups about half full with cookie dough. Bake for 14 to 16 minutes, or until the cookie cupcakes are golden on the edges. Expect them to sink slightly in the centers. When they come out of the oven, place a peanut butter cup in the center of each warm cookie cupcake and press down lightly. Place the cupcake pans into the refrigerator or freezer to expedite the cooling process. Once the peanut butter cups have hardened, remove the cookie cupcakes from chilling and bring them to room temperature before serving.

TIPS Don't use natural peanut butter for this recipe unless you're using a very creamy brand of natural peanut butter.

Look for peanut butter cups sold in bulk in your market's candy aisle for a more affordable option.

You can substitute the smaller, snack-size peanut butter cups for the larger ones if you'd like.

These cookie cupcakes freeze well. Keep them in a covered container, or zip them into individual baggies for easy school lunch desserts.

CHANGE IT UP!

If you'd like these to be extra decadent, stir 1 cup chopped peanut butter cups into the cookie dough (about 8 whole peanut butter cups).

This peanut butter cookie dough also makes excellent peanut butter cookies, made the traditional way and baked for 12 minutes.

chocolate-stuffed gingerbread cookies

Makes: 3 dozen cookies   Prep Time: 45 minutes + chill time   Cook Time: 20 minutes

For centuries, a Christmas treat in England and Ireland has been Chocolate-Covered Ginger. They view the pairing of these two flavors as naturally delicious, and I wholeheartedly agree. With this recipe, I took a classically soft ginger cookie and wrapped it around a gooey chocolate center. It's a wonderful cookie to bake up for the holidays.

COOKIES

3½   cups all-purpose flour
2½   teaspoons ground ginger
2   teaspoons ground cinnamon
½   teaspoon ground cloves
½   teaspoon ground nutmeg
2   teaspoons baking soda
3   teaspoons hot water
1   cup (2 sticks) unsalted
     butter, at room temperature
1   cup packed dark brown
     sugar
½   cup molasses
1   large egg

FILLING

1   cup semisweet chocolate
     chips
½   cup sweetened condensed
     milk
1   tablespoon shortening
     Granulated sugar, for
     dipping

To prepare the cookie dough, sift together the flour, ginger, cinnamon, cloves and nutmeg. Set aside. In a small bowl, dissolve the baking soda in the hot water. Set aside.

In a large mixing bowl, use an electric mixer to beat the butter until creamy, about 1 minute. Beat in the sugar, molasses and egg and mix until well combined, about 1 minute. Add half of the dry ingredients and mix until they are incorporated. Add the baking soda mixture and mix in. Add the remaining dry ingredients and mix until well combined. Cover the bowl with plastic wrap and refrigerate the dough until slightly firm, at least 1 hour and up to 4 hours.

Preheat the oven to 325°F. Line baking sheets with parchment paper or Silpat mats, or spray with nonstick spray.

To prepare the filling, in a medium bowl, microwave the chocolate chips, sweetened condensed milk and shortening for 1 minute and stir. Continue melting in short bursts of 30 seconds, stirring after each burst. Remove from the microwave when the chocolate is melted and smooth. Alternatively, you can melt the chocolate chips, sweetened condensed milk and shortening on the stove—see Tips.) Set aside to cool.

continued on page 274

continued from page 273

Once it has cooled, roll the chocolate into thirty-six ¾-inch balls. Place them on a waxed paper–lined surface.

Scoop up about 1½ tablespoons of the dough and use your hands to flatten it into a pancake. Place one of the chocolate balls into the center of your cookie dough pancake. Bring the dough up and around the filling, enclosing the chocolate ball all the way around. Roll the cookie in the palms of your hands to smooth it out. Repeat with the remaining dough and filling. Dip the tops of the cookies in sugar and set them on the prepared baking sheets, 2 inches apart. Bake the cookies for 20 minutes, or until set.

TIP To heat the chocolate chips, sweetened condensed milk and shortening on the stove, place a heatproof bowl over a pan of simmering water (the bottom of the bowl should not touch the water). Add the chocolate chips, sweetened condensed milk and shortening and stir until melted and smooth.

CHANGE IT UP!

If you're making this as a holiday cookie, roll the tops of the cookies in red or green colored sugar.

Substitute 1 cup of chopped white chocolate for the regular chocolate to create a white chocolate filling instead.

cadillac margarita cupcakes

Makes: 12 cupcakes   Prep Time: 45 minutes   Cook Time: 18 minutes

These cupcakes are perfect for a Cinco de Mayo party, but they surely can be made for any festive, adult occasion. They are wildly fun to serve on a large platter with shots of tequila scattered throughout. Watch your party get really crazy if you bake them into larger-size cupcakes, add the frosting and place a shot glass of tequila smack dab in the middle of each cupcake.

CUPCAKES

- 1⅔ cups all-purpose flour
- ½ teaspoon baking soda
- ⅛ teaspoon salt
- 1⅓ cups granulated white sugar
- 6 tablespoons (¾ stick) unsalted butter, at room temperature
- 2 large eggs
- ½ cup lime-flavored nonfat yogurt
- 2 tablespoons good quality tequila (see Tips)
- 1 tablespoon Grand Marnier
  Grated zest and juice of 1 large lime

FROSTING

- 8 tablespoons (1 stick) unsalted butter, at room temperature
- 2½ to 3 cups powdered sugar
- 2 teaspoons good quality tequila
- 2 teaspoons freshly squeezed lime juice
- 1 teaspoon Grand Marnier
- ½ teaspoon finely grated lime zest
  Pinch of salt
  Green food coloring, optional
  Small lime slices for garnish, optional

Preheat the oven to 350°F. Line a 12-cup muffin tin with paper liners. Spray the liners lightly with nonstick spray.

To prepare the cupcakes, in a medium bowl, whisk together the flour, baking soda and salt.

In a large bowl, use an electric mixer to combine the sugar and butter. Beat in the eggs, one at a time. Add the yogurt, tequila, Grand Marnier and lime zest and juice and mix until well combined. Add the dry ingredients and mix until almost smooth, about 2 minutes.

Spoon the batter into the cupcake liners and bake for 18 to 22 minutes, or until a toothpick inserted in the center of a cupcake comes out clean. Let the cupcakes cool for 10 minutes in the pan and then remove them to a wire rack to cool completely.

To prepare the frosting, in a large bowl, use an electric mixer to beat the butter until it is fluffy, 1 to 2 minutes. Add 2½ cups of the powdered sugar and mix until it is smooth. Add the tequila, lime juice, Grand Marnier, lime zest, salt and food coloring, if desired, and mix to combine. Add additional powdered sugar 1 tablespoon at a time, as needed, to achieve a smooth texture for frosting or piping.

Frost the cooled cupcakes and store them in a covered container. Garnish the cupcakes with lime slices just before serving, if desired.

TIP A regular Cadillac Margarita cocktail is made with good-quality tequila and Grand Marnier. Substitute another orange-flavored liqueur in place of the Grand Marnier, if needed. If you don't wish to purchase large-size bottles of liquor, both tequila and Grand Marnier can be purchased in small, sampler bottles.

CHANGE IT UP!

Sprinkle a little bit of grated lime zest and/or a pinch of flaked sea salt onto the frosting too.

banana–carrot cake cupcakes with cinnamon–cream cheese frosting

Makes: 24 cupcakes   Prep Time: 40 minutes   Cook Time: 20 minutes

Banana is a welcome addition to cakes and breads because it brings with it a whole lot of natural ability to keep them moist and tender. Added carrots turn this one into carrot cake, and a cinnamon–cream cheese frosting allows these cupcakes to shine in a world full of sweet treats. Serve these up on Easter Sunday or on any day where the craving for carrot cake is impossible to resist.

CUPCAKES

2	cups all-purpose flour
2	teaspoons baking soda
1	teaspoon ground cinnamon
½	teaspoon salt
1½	cups granulated white sugar
3	large eggs
½	cup buttermilk
1	teaspoon vanilla extract
1½	cups finely grated carrots (about ¾ pound)
1	cup mashed ripe banana (2 large or 3 medium bananas)
8	tablespoons (1 stick) unsalted butter, melted and cooled slightly

FROSTING

12	ounces cream cheese, at room temperature
8	tablespoons (1 stick) unsalted butter, at room temperature
1	pound powdered sugar, sifted
2	tablespoons packed light brown sugar
2	teaspoons vanilla extract
1	teaspoon ground cinnamon
½	cup pecans, chopped, optional

Preheat the oven to 350°F. Line two 12-cup cupcake pans with paper liners.

To prepare the cupcakes, sift together the flour, baking soda, cinnamon and salt. Set aside.

In a large bowl, use an electric mixer to combine the sugar and eggs. Mix until it looks like the mixture has about tripled in volume, 3 to 4 minutes. Mix in the buttermilk and vanilla. Stir in the carrots and banana. Add the dry ingredients and stir just until they are incorporated into the batter. Add the butter and stir until it is mixed into the batter. Scoop the batter into the cupcake liners, filling each liner three-fourths full.

Bake for 20 to 25 minutes, or until a toothpick inserted in the center of a cupcake comes out clean. Let the cupcakes cool completely before frosting.

To prepare the frosting, in a medium bowl, use an electric mixer to combine the cream cheese and butter. Add the sugars, vanilla and cinnamon. Spread a thick layer of frosting onto the cooled cupcakes (see Tips). Sprinkle with pecans, if desired.

TIP This frosting recipe is perfect for piping if you'd like to scoop it into a piping bag and frost the cupcakes with a decorative swirl.

> **CHANGE IT UP!**
>
> Top these cupcakes with a classic cream cheese frosting instead by leaving out the brown sugar and cinnamon.
>
> Bake this batter into a cake instead. Spray a 9 x 13-inch pan with nonstick spray and increase the baking time to 35 to 40 minutes.

cherry limeade pound cake

Makes: 10 to 12 servings   Prep Time: 30 minutes   Cook Time: 1 hour and 15 minutes

My family took a summertime cross-country road trip a couple of years ago, passing through small towns and stopping at a Sonic Drive-In every chance we got to cool off with their infamous Cherry Limeade. Once we reached our East coast destination, we found ourselves obsessed with eating baskets upon baskets of sweet cherries. Inspired by Sonic and those endless baskets of fresh cherries, I developed a pound cake recipe that summer that was reminiscent of those cherry limeade flavors. It won't cool you off, but it'll give you a little taste of what cherry limeade is all about.

CAKE
3	cups all-purpose flour
½	teaspoon salt
3	cups granulated white sugar
1½	cups (3 sticks) unsalted butter, at room temperature
1½	teaspoons finely grated fresh lime zest
5	large eggs
¾	cup Cherry 7-Up (see Tips)
2	cups pitted and quartered fresh, sweet cherries

GLAZE
1¼	cups powdered sugar, sifted
2	tablespoons Cherry 7-Up
1½	teaspoons finely grated fresh lime zest

Preheat the oven to 325°F. Grease and flour a 12-cup Bundt cake or tube pan.

To prepare the cake, in a medium bowl, whisk together the flour and salt. Set aside.

In a large bowl, use an electric mixer to combine the sugar and butter. Add the lime zest. Beat in the eggs, one at a time, until each is well incorporated. Mix in one-third of the flour mixture at a time, alternating with the 7-Up. Stir in the cherries.

Scoop the batter into the prepared pan. Tap the pan on the counter several times to rid the batter of any air bubbles. Bake 1 hour and 15 minutes, or until a thin, sharp knife inserted into the center of the cake comes out clean. Place the pan on a wire rack and let the cake cool for 20 minutes. Place a serving platter over the top of the pan and carefully flip it over. Give the bottom of the pan a few taps with a knife if you need to loosen the cake from the pan. Let the cake cool completely on the serving platter before topping with the glaze.

To prepare the glaze, in a medium bowl, whisk together the glaze ingredients until smooth. Drizzle the glaze over the cooled cake.

TIP If you only have regular 7-Up, Sprite or even generic lemon-lime soda on hand, go ahead and utilize that. Add in a splash of maraschino cherry juice to turn it into a cherry-flavored soda and make sure it still measures out to ¾ cup. For the glaze, use 1½ tablespoons soda + ½ tablespoon maraschino cherry juice.

CHANGE IT UP!

Turn this into a Cherry Lemonade Cake by substituting lemon zest for the lime zest in both the cake and the glaze.

pineapple upside-down cake

Makes: 8 to 10 servings   Prep Time: 30 minutes   Cook Time: 40 minutes

It might seem like kind of an odd choice to add to a cookbook nowadays since its origin dates back to the 1920s, but I've always been kind of obsessed with pineapple upside-down cake. It reminds me of the 1970s, when housewives were looking for easy recipes to bring to potlucks. The upside-down cake was popular because the fruit created instant decoration when flipped upside down, and it was all done with minimal effort put forth. It still serves that same purpose, so I'm going to bring the Pineapple Upside-Down Cake back into style with my simple version.

⅔   cup packed light brown
       sugar
⅓   cup unsalted butter, cut into
       pieces
1   20-ounce can pineapple
       slices, drained (you'll have
       3 slices left over)
1½   cups all-purpose flour
1½   teaspoons baking powder
½   teaspoon salt
¾   cup granulated white sugar
4   tablespoons (½ stick)
       unsalted butter, at room
       temperature
2   large eggs
¾   cup buttermilk
1   tablespoon vanilla extract

Preheat the oven to 350°F. Spray a 9-inch round pan with nonstick spray.

Sprinkle the brown sugar and butter pieces into the prepared pan. Place the pan in the oven, about 5 minutes or just until the butter is melted. Remove the pan from the oven and stir the brown sugar into the melted butter until the sugar is dissolved and the mixture is smooth.

Arrange the pineapple slices in a decorative fashion on top of the brown sugar mixture in the pan. Cut some slices in half if you need to.

In a medium bowl, whisk together the flour, baking powder and salt. Set aside.

In a large bowl, use an electric mixer to combine the sugar and butter. Add the eggs, one at a time, until they are incorporated. Mix in half of the buttermilk at a time, alternating with the dry ingredients, ending with the flour. Stir in the vanilla. Scrape the batter over the pineapple in an even layer in the pan.

Bake for 40 to 45 minutes, or until a toothpick inserted into the center comes out clean. Let the cake sit for about 5 minutes in the pan.

Run a sharp knife along the outside edge of the cake. Place a serving plate over the top of the pan and carefully flip it over. Give the bottom of the pan a few taps with a knife if you need to loosen the cake from the pan. Serve warm, or let cool and serve at room temperature.

TIP Make your own buttermilk: Add ¾ tablespoon vinegar or lemon juice to ¾ cup milk. Let it sit for about 10 minutes. You have buttermilk!

CHANGE IT UP!

Sprinkle walnuts or maraschino cherries into the center of each pineapple slice to create an even more decorative outcome when the cake is turned upside down.

red velvet–cheesecake cake

*Makes: 12 to 14 servings   Prep Time: 1 hour + cooling and chill times
Cook Time: 1 hour and 15 minutes*

If you've ever been to The Cheesecake Factory, and if you're a red velvet cake fan, you've probably ordered up their Red Velvet Cheesecake Cake. I went to town with that idea and included my version of that recipe here. It's kind of the most amazing thing ever—a red velvet layer cake with a layer of cheesecake smack dab in the middle and surrounded by cream cheese frosting. The cheesecake layer is perfect and velvety in the center. It's almost like a giant, interior layer of frosting, except that when you bite into it, you realize that it's cheesecake instead!

CHEESECAKE

2   8-ounce packages
     cream cheese, at room
     temperature
⅔   cup granulated white sugar
     Pinch of salt
2   large eggs
⅓   cup sour cream
⅓   cup heavy whipping cream
1   teaspoon vanilla extract

RED VELVET CAKE

2½ cups all-purpose flour
2   tablespoons cocoa powder
½   teaspoon salt
1½ cups canola or vegetable oil
1½ cups granulated white sugar
2   large eggs
1   teaspoon vanilla extract
1   teaspoon white vinegar
1   teaspoon baking soda
1   cup buttermilk
2   1-ounce bottles (¼ cup) red
     food coloring

FROSTING

2   8-ounce packages
     cream cheese, at room
     temperature
½   cup (1 stick) unsalted
     butter, at room temperature
2½ cups powdered sugar
1   tablespoon vanilla extract
     White chocolate shavings,
     optional

To prepare the cheesecake layer, preheat the oven to 325°F. Place a large roasting pan on the lower rack of the oven. Place a kettle full (or 8 to 10 cups) of water on the stove to boil. Spray a 9-inch springform pan with nonstick spray and line the bottom with a round of parchment paper. Wrap a double layer of heavy-duty foil around the bottom and up the sides of the pan (you want to seal it so the water from the water bath doesn't seep into the pan; see Tips).

In a large bowl, use an electric mixer to beat the cream cheese until it is smooth and creamy, 1 to 2 minutes. Beat in the sugar and salt and blend for 2 minutes, scraping down the sides of the bowl as needed. Add the eggs, one at a time, mixing after each addition. Mix in the sour cream, whipping cream and vanilla until smooth.

continued on page 282

continued from page 281

Pour the batter into the prepared pan. Place the cheesecake into the roasting pan in the preheated oven. Carefully pour the boiling water into the roasting pan. Pour enough water so that there is about 1 inch of water coming up the foil along the sides of the springform pan. Bake the cheesecake for 45 minutes. It should be set to the touch and not jiggly. Remove the cheesecake from the roasting pan and let it cool on a wire rack for at least 1 hour. When it has cooled, place the pan into the freezer and let the cheesecake freeze completely (4 to 5 hours or overnight).

To prepare the cake layers, preheat the oven to 350°F. Spray two 9-inch round pans with nonstick spray and line each pan with a round of parchment paper.

In a medium bowl, sift together the flour, cocoa powder and salt. Set aside.

In a large bowl, use an electric mixer to combine the oil and sugar and beat for 2 minutes. Add the eggs, one at a time, and then the vanilla and beat for an additional 2 minutes.

In a small bowl, combine the vinegar and baking soda and stir to dissolve the baking soda. Add the vinegar mixture to the sugar mixture, along with the buttermilk and food coloring. Beat on medium-low speed for 1 minute, until blended. Add the dry ingredients and increase the speed to medium-high, scraping down the sides of the bowl while mixing, for 2 additional minutes.

Divide the batter evenly between the prepared pans. Bake for 30 to 35 minutes, or until a toothpick inserted into the center comes out with a few moist crumbs attached. Let the cakes cool in the pans on a wire rack for 20 minutes. Run a sharp knife along the edge of the pans, then invert the cakes onto the wire rack to cool completely.

To prepare the frosting, in a large bowl, use an electric mixer on medium-high speed to combine the cream cheese and butter and beat until creamy and smooth. Add the powdered sugar and vanilla and continue to beat, scraping down the sides of the bowl as needed, until the frosting is smooth and spreadable.

Place one cake layer in the center of a cake plate or platter. Remove the cheesecake from the freezer, take off the sides of the pan and slide a knife under the parchment to remove the cheesecake from the pan. Peel off the parchment. Trim the cheesecake, as needed to match the size of your cake layers (see Tips). Place the cheesecake layer on top of the first cake layer. Place the second cake layer on top of the cheesecake.

Apply a crumb coat layer of frosting to the cake (see Tips) and refrigerate the cake for 30 minutes, or until the frosting is set. Add a large scoop of frosting onto the top of the cake. Use a long, thin spatula or knife to spread the frosting evenly across the top and then spread it down the sides of the cake too. Decorate, as desired. I recommend topping the cake with white chocolate shavings, if desired (see Tips).

TIPS To wrap the pan properly with foil, it's easiest to use the larger size box of heavy-duty foil. You need a good seal to protect any water from seeping into the bottom of the pan. Place two large (18 x 18-inch) pieces of foil on top of each other and then place the springform pan in the center. Wrap the foil gently around the pan and up the sides.

You can certainly bake this cheesecake in the oven without a water bath, but you run the risk of cracking the top of the cheesecake. The water bath is a safeguard against cracking.

Measure your cheesecake layer against the cake layers. If the cheesecake layer turns out to be a slightly larger size round than your cake layers, move it to a cutting board and use a knife to gently shave off some of the exterior of the cheesecake.

To apply a crumb coat layer of frosting: Use a long, thin spatula or knife to cover the cake completely with a thin and even layer of frosting. Wipe off the spatula each time you're about to dip it back into the bowl to get more frosting (this way you won't be transferring any red crumbs into the bowl of frosting). Don't worry at this point about the crumbs being visible in the frosting on the cake. When your cake has a thin layer of frosting all over it, place it into the refrigerator for 30 minutes to "set" the frosting. Once the first layer of frosting is set, apply the second layer.

To make white chocolate shavings, you'll need a block or bar of white chocolate, something you can hold in your hand. Microwave the chocolate to soften it up slightly (10 to 30 seconds, depending on the thickness). Use a potato peeler to run down the side of the chocolate to create shards, shaves and curls of white chocolate. Shave them onto a paper plate and then just slide the chocolate onto the top of the cake.

If you are serving this cake at a party, it's perfectly okay to leave the cake at room temperature for a couple of hours—the cheesecake thaws quickly. Otherwise, keep it stored in the refrigerator. It also freezes perfectly. Freeze it as is, then wrap it in plastic wrap and store it in the freezer until it is needed. Leftover slices may also be wrapped and frozen.

CHANGE IT UP!

Use this same "cheesecake cake" concept with some of your other favorite layer cake recipes too. It will even work fine with a boxed cake mix.

chocolate chip–butter cake

Makes: 12 servings   Prep Time: 15 minutes   Cook Time: 35 minutes

Sometimes the simplest of cakes can be exactly what you're looking for in a dessert. Chocolate chips are always on everyone's radar as a favorite, and this cake will have you shaking your head and asking, "Why, oh why did I ever consider making a boxed mix?" This one is a great little snack cake, perfect for eating straight from your hand.

2¾ cups all-purpose flour
1   cup granulated white sugar
1   tablespoon baking powder
½   teaspoon baking soda
½   teaspoon salt
2   cups chocolate chips, divided
3   large eggs
1   cup buttermilk
1   cup (2 sticks) salted butter, melted
1   tablespoon vanilla extract

Preheat the oven to 350°F. Spray a 9 x 13-inch baking pan with nonstick spray.

In a medium bowl, whisk together the flour, sugar, baking powder, baking soda and salt. Stir in 1½ cups of the chocolate chips. Set aside.

In a large bowl, whisk together the eggs, buttermilk, melted butter and vanilla. Add the dry ingredients, stirring just until combined.

Spread the batter evenly into the prepared pan and sprinkle the remaining ½ cup chocolate chips on top. Bake for 35 to 40 minutes, or until a toothpick inserted into the center of the cake comes out clean. Let the cake cool completely before slicing.

TIPS Use whatever flavor of chocolate chips you'd like for this recipe. (I like to use semisweet.) And if you're not into chocolate, use cinnamon chips or blueberries instead!

To make your own buttermilk, mix 1 tablespoon vinegar or lemon juice with 1 cup of milk. Let it sit for 10 minutes. You have buttermilk!

CHANGE IT UP!

Chocolate lovers can add a chocolate ganache to the top of this cake. Place 8 ounces of chopped chocolate (or chips) in a stainless-steel or glass bowl and set aside. Bring ¾ cup heavy whipping cream and 2 tablespoons granulated white sugar just to a boil in a small saucepan (or microwave), then pour over the chocolate. Whisk together until smooth and then stir in 2 tablespoons salted butter until melted. Drizzle over the top of your cooled cake.

meyer lemon loaf cake

Makes: 12 servings   Prep Time: 20 minutes   Cook Time: 50 minutes

Have you jumped on the Meyer lemon bandwagon yet? I happily discovered these little lemon beauties several years ago after hearing so much raving about them from my other food blog friends. I loved them so much that I promptly went out and bought myself a Meyer lemon tree to plant in the backyard. If you've not yet tried them, you need to know that they aren't like other lemons. They have a yellow-orange hue and a much sweeter flavor and scent than the sour variety, making them a perfect addition to baked goods like this loaf cake. I wish I could tell you that my backyard is now overflowing with Meyer lemons, but it appears that I'm a much better baker than gardener.

CAKE

2   cups all-purpose flour
1½ teaspoons baking powder
¼   teaspoon salt
1   cup granulated white sugar
    Grated zest from 2 Meyer
    lemons (see Tips)
8   tablespoons (1 stick) butter,
    at room temperature
2   large eggs
⅓   cup milk
1   tablespoon lemon extract

GLAZE

⅓   cup granulated white sugar
¼   cup freshly squeezed Meyer
    lemon juice
    Fresh whipped cream for
    serving, optional (see Tips)

CHANGE IT UP!

Turn this into a blood orange loaf cake. Follow the same instructions, substituting blood oranges for the lemons.

Add 1 tablespoon of rum to the glaze.

Preheat the oven to 350°F. Spray a 5 x 8-inch loaf pan with nonstick spray.

To prepare the cake, sift together the flour, baking powder and salt. Set aside.

In a large bowl, mix the sugar and the zest with a wooden spoon until the sugar is lemon scented. Use an electric mixer to beat in the butter, mixing until fluffy, about 2 minutes. Beat in the eggs, one at a time, and then add the milk and lemon extract. Add the dry ingredients and stir just until combined.

Scrape the batter into the prepared pan and bake 50 to 55 minutes, or until a toothpick inserted in the center comes out clean. Check at 30 minutes and cover the cake lightly with foil if the cake appears to be browning too quickly. Let the cake cool in the pan for 10 minutes and then turn it out onto a cooling rack set over a rimmed pan.

While the cake is cooling, prepare the glaze. In a small saucepan, combine the sugar and lemon juice over low heat and stir until the sugar has dissolved.

Poke holes all over the top of the cake with a skewer or toothpick. Brush the cake generously with the warm glaze until it's all used up. Serve warm or at room temperature with whipped cream, if desired.

TIPS Zest the lemons before you juice them.

Meyer lemons are easiest to find in the winter. Substitute regular lemons if you're unable to find the Meyer variety.

To make your own whipped cream, place your mixing bowl and beaters into the freezer for 10 minutes. Use an electric mixer to whip 1 cup heavy whipping cream just until stiff peaks begin to form (when you scrape the cream up with the beaters, the cream will keep its shape), then mix in 1 teaspoon vanilla extract and 1 tablespoon powdered sugar. Don't overbeat.

flourless chocolate cake with chocolate ganache drizzle

Makes: 12 servings   Prep Time: 20 minutes   Cook Time: 30 minutes

A chocolate cake with only four ingredients is a breath-of-fresh-air recipe for any home cook. A version of this recipe was given to me by a friend a long time ago. This very fudgy and dense flourless cake is a good one for those who must remain gluten-free. It's incredibly rich, so unless you are a chocolate purist, you'll want to serve up a small wedge with a generous scoop of vanilla ice cream.

CAKE

8   ounces bittersweet chocolate chips (I prefer Ghirardelli brand)
1   cup (2 sticks) unsalted butter
1   cup granulated white sugar
4   large eggs, beaten

GANACHE

⅓   cup heavy whipping cream
⅓   cup bittersweet chocolate chips
    Vanilla ice cream for serving, optional

Preheat the oven to 350°F. Spray an 8-inch round cake pan with nonstick spray and line the bottom of the pan with a round of parchment paper.

In a medium bowl, microwave the chocolate chips and butter for 1 minute, then stir. Continue melting in short bursts of 30 seconds, stirring after each burst. Remove from the microwave when the mixture is melted and smooth. (Alternatively, you can melt the chocolate chips and butter on the stove—see Tips.) Whisk in the sugar and then the eggs and continue to whisk until the ingredients are combined and the batter is smooth.

Scrape the batter into the prepared pan. Bake for 30 to 35 minutes, or until a dry crust forms on top of the cake. Let the cake cool in the pan on a wire rack for 20 minutes. Run a sharp knife along the edge of the pan and turn the cake onto the wire rack to cool completely.

Place the cake on a serving platter and prepare the ganache. Heat the whipping cream in a small bowl in the microwave for about 30 seconds until it is hot and bubbly (see Tips). Add the chocolate chips to the bowl and let them sit for 2 minutes, then whisk the mixture until the ganache turns into a dark chocolate color and is smooth and pourable. Drizzle the ganache over the cake in a decorative manner and let it fall down the sides of the cake. Serve immediately with vanilla ice cream, if desired, or refrigerate until ready to serve.

GF GLUTEN-FREE ADAPTABLE Use a brand of chocolate that is known to be gluten-free.

TIPS To heat the chocolate chips and butter on the stove, place a heatproof bowl over a pan of simmering water (the bottom of the bowl should not touch the water). Add the chocolate chips and butter and stir until melted and smooth.

The whipping cream for the ganache may also be heated on the stove.

CHANGE IT UP!

Create a white chocolate ganache to drizzle onto the cake instead. Use ⅓ cup chopped white chocolate and proceed with the ganache instructions as directed.

maple-pumpkin cheesecake with graham cracker–pecan crust

Makes: 12 to 14 servings   Prep Time: 45 minutes   Cook Time: 1 hour and 35 minutes

I'm not one to live with a lot of regrets, but I do feel a little sad that I didn't insist on having an unorthodox, multilayer wedding cake made entirely of cheesecake. I love cheesecake. But I don't usually like a bunch of fancy stuff mixed in and drizzled over my cheesecake. It's so good and creamy on its own, that there really is no need to overadorn it. This cheesecake is simply flavored with pumpkin and a tiny hint of maple. If you're a cheesecake purist, you may not even need any whipped cream with this one.

CRUST

9   whole graham crackers (or 1½ cups graham cracker crumbs)
½   cup chopped pecans
4   tablespoons (½ stick) salted butter, melted
2   tablespoons granulated white sugar

FILLING

3   8-ounce packages cream cheese, at room temperature
2   tablespoons all-purpose flour
1   cup unsweetened pumpkin puree
⅔   cup granulated white sugar
¼   cup maple syrup
1½ teaspoons vanilla extract
3   large eggs

TOPPING

1   cup sour cream
¼   cup granulated white sugar
1   tablespoon maple syrup

Preheat the oven to 325°F. Place a large roasting pan (one in which your 9-inch springform pan can fit inside) on the lower rack of the oven. Place a kettle full (or 8 to 10 cups) of water on the stove to boil. Spray a 9-inch springform pan with nonstick spray. Wrap the bottom and sides of the pan with a double layer of heavy-duty foil (you want to seal it so the water from the water bath doesn't seep into the pan; see Tips).

To prepare the crust, in the bowl of a food processor, combine the graham crackers and pecans (see Tips if you don't have a food processor). Process until the graham crackers turn into crumbs and the pecans are ground. Scrape the mixture into a bowl and add the butter and sugar. Stir to combine. Use clean hands to press the crust evenly and firmly onto the bottom and about 1 inch up the sides of the prepared pan. Set the pan aside while you prepare the filling.

To prepare the filling, in a large bowl, use an electric mixer to mix the cream cheese until it is smooth and creamy, about 1 minute. Beat in the flour. Add the pumpkin, sugar, syrup and vanilla and mix to combine. Add the eggs one at a time, scraping down the sides of the bowl and mixing after each addition until the filling is smooth and all of the ingredients are incorporated. Pour the filling into the crust-lined pan, smoothing out the top.

Place the cheesecake into the roasting pan in the oven. Carefully pour the boiling water into the roasting pan. Pour enough water so that there is about 1 inch of water coming up the foil along the sides of the springform pan. Bake for 1¾ hours, or until almost set. Do not open the oven while baking. The cheesecake is done when the center barely jiggles when the pan is

continued on page 288

continued from page 287

touched.

In a small bowl, combine the topping ingredients and mix until smooth. Spoon the topping onto the surface of the cheesecake and use the bottom of the spoon to spread it to the edges. Bake for an additional 5 minutes and then remove the cheesecake from the oven. Carefully remove the cheesecake from the water bath and place it on a wire rack. Run a thin, sharp knife around the outer edge of the cheesecake. Cool on the rack for 2 hours, or until the cheesecake becomes close to room temperature. Cover and chill for at least 8 hours (or overnight). Remove the sides of the springform pan, slide a long, sharp knife under the crust and gently slide it onto a serving plate.

GF GLUTEN-FREE ADAPTABLE Use gluten-free gingersnap cookies in place of the graham crackers, use a gluten-free flour blend in place of the all-purpose flour, and be sure to use brands of maple syrup and vanilla that are known to be gluten-free.

TIPS To wrap the pan properly with foil, it's easiest to use the larger size box of heavy-duty foil. You need a good seal to protect any water from seeping into the bottom of the pan. Place two large (18 x 18-inch) pieces of foil on top of each other and then place the springform pan in the center. Wrap the foil gently around the pan and up the sides.

If you don't have a food processor, purchase graham cracker crumbs and finely chop the pecans. Proceed with the crust preparation as directed.

You can certainly bake this cheesecake in the oven without a water bath, but you run the risk of cracking the top of the cheesecake. The water bath is a safeguard against cracking.

CHANGE IT UP!

Use gingersnap or shortbread cookie crumbs in place of the graham cracker crumbs to create a crust with a slightly different flavor.

snickers bar cheesecake pie

Makes: 10 servings   Prep Time: 30 minutes   Cook Time: 35 minutes

My son Brooks, who has a food blog of his own at RecipeBoy.com, has won pie contests in our local community with both a Snicker's Bar Pie and a Twix Bar Cheesecake Pie. He feels strongly that baking a pie with candy bars is what influences those judges to sway positively in the direction of his pies. I'm pretty sure he's right! I've taken his pie recipes and combined them to create what I feel is the ultimate candy bar pie creation.

CRUST

22 Oreo cookies (or other chocolate sandwich cookies)
3   tablespoons salted butter, melted

FILLING

2   8-ounce packages cream cheese, at room temperature
½   cup granulated white sugar
2   large eggs
16 Snickers "fun size" candy bars, chopped (2 cups total)

TOPPING

2   tablespoons chocolate syrup
2   tablespoons caramel syrup
¼   cup chopped peanuts
6   Snickers "fun size" candy bars, chopped (¾ cup total)

To prepare the crust, crush the Oreo cookies or process them to fine crumbs in a food processor (see Tips). In a medium bowl, mix the cookie crumbs with the butter. Use clean hands to press the crust into the bottom and up the sides of a 9-inch pie plate. Place the crust into the freezer for 30 minutes while you prepare the filling.

Preheat the oven to 325°F.

To prepare the filling, in a large bowl, use an electric mixer to beat together the cream cheese, sugar and eggs until smooth. Stir in the chopped candy bars. Pour the filling into the frozen crust and bake until set, 35 to 40 minutes. Set the pie on a wire rack and let it cool completely.

To prepare the topping, when the pie is cool, drizzle the chocolate and caramel syrups on top of the pie in a decorative fashion and garnish with peanuts and chopped candy bars.

Keep the pie refrigerated until ready to serve. Keep the leftovers covered with plastic wrap and enjoy for 4 to 5 days.

TIP The easiest way to crush Oreo cookies if you do not have a food processor is to place them in a large freezer zip baggie and use a rolling pin to crush them.

CHANGE IT UP!

Change this into a Milky Way pie. Substitute Milky Way candy bars for the Snickers bars and leave out the peanuts.

dulce de leche pear pie with oatmeal cookie crust

Makes: 10 servings   Prep Time: 35 minutes   Cook Time: 45 minutes

I'm actually quite surprised that this is the only recipe I included in the cookbook that utilizes dulce de leche, the most heavenly of all dessert ingredients. It truly is one of my favorite indulgences. Dulce de leche is made by slowly heating sweetened milk until it reaches a consistency and flavor similar to caramel. It may also be found canned in the Latin American products section of your market. In this pie, the dulce de leche is lightly tossed with fresh pears and baked into a crust made from oatmeal cookie dough.

CRUST
- 3 cups old-fashioned oats
- 1 cup (2 sticks) salted butter, melted
- 1 cup all-purpose flour
- 1/3 cup packed light brown sugar
- 1 1/2 teaspoons ground cinnamon
- 1 teaspoon vanilla extract
- 1/2 teaspoon salt

FILLING
- 6 cups peeled and sliced fresh, ripe Bartlett pears (see Tips)
- 2 tablespoons freshly squeezed lemon juice
- 1/2 teaspoon vanilla extract
- 1/3 cup packed light brown sugar
- 1/3 cup granulated white sugar
- 1/3 cup cornstarch
- 1/4 teaspoon ground cinnamon
- 1/4 teaspoon ground nutmeg
- Pinch of salt
- 1/2 cup dulce de leche (see Tips)

Preheat the oven to 375°F.

To prepare the crust, in a medium bowl, combine the crust ingredients and mix well. Remove 1 cup of the crust crumbles and set aside. Press the remaining crust crumbles into the bottom and up the sides of a 9-inch pie plate, forming a thick crust and pinching the edges to form a rim.

To prepare the filling, in a large bowl, toss the pears with the lemon juice and vanilla. In a medium bowl, combine the sugars, cornstarch, cinnamon, nutmeg and salt. Add the sugar mixture to the pears and toss. Add the dulce de leche in spoonfuls and gently toss again. Scrape the filling into the prepared crust. Sprinkle the reserved crust crumbles on top.

Bake for 30 minutes and then check on the pie to make sure the top is not browning too quickly (if it already appears brown, lightly place a piece of foil on top of the pie). Bake for an additional 15 to 20 minutes until the crust is crisp and the filling is bubbling. Let the pie cool on a wire rack for at least 1 hour before serving.

TIPS How to tell if a pear is ripe: Since you'll rarely find ripe pears at the store, it's best to bring pears home from the market and let them ripen on your counter for a few days. Hold a pear in your hand and press your thumb gently into the flesh near the stem. If it yields without too much pressure, the pear is ripe and ready for eating or baking.

Sometimes the consistency of dulce de leche can be rather thick. If yours is thick, soften it slightly by placing it in a glass bowl and heating it for 10 to 15 seconds in the microwave. Alternatively, it can be heated briefly in a small pan on the stove.

CHANGE IT UP!
Substitute apples for the pears to make a dulce de leche apple pie instead.

puff pastry peach pie

Makes: 8 servings   Prep Time: 25 minutes   Cook Time: 45 minutes

I'm the first one to admit that I'm not always very good at making pie crust. I do like to bake pies, but more often than not, I pick up one of those ready-made crusts. Most people cannot tell the difference between homemade and store-bought, and to me they're just plain headache-free. Fresh peach pie is my favorite, and when it's tucked into a store-bought puff pastry crust, it bakes up as a wonderful summer pie with flaky crust that you don't have to fret over.

8	cups peeled and sliced fresh peaches (about 3 pounds; see Tips)
¾	cup granulated white sugar
⅓	cup all-purpose flour + extra for dusting
½	teaspoon ground cinnamon
1	17.3-ounce box of puff pastry (2 sheets), thawed according to package instructions
1	large egg white whisked with 1 tablespoon water
	Coarse sugar, for topping

Add the peaches to a large bowl. In a small bowl, whisk together the sugar, the ⅓ cup flour and the cinnamon. Sprinkle over the peaches and toss lightly to combine.

On a lightly floured surface, roll out one sheet of puff pastry into a large square (roughly 14 x 14 inches—it does not have to be perfect). Place the rolled out pastry in a deep-dish 9-inch pie plate, letting the excess hang over the sides. Scoop the peaches and their juices onto the pastry. Roll out the second piece of puff pastry (roughly 12 x 12 inches) and place it on top. Trim and crimp the edges of the puff pastry crust to seal. Cut several slits into the top of the pie with a sharp knife. Brush the top of the pie with the egg wash and sprinkle sugar on top. Place the pie in the freezer for 30 minutes.

Preheat the oven to 375°F.

Bake the pie for 45 minutes to 1 hour, or until the crust is golden and the peaches are bubbling up through the slits. Check on the pie after 30 minutes to make sure the crust is not browning too quickly (if it's already a nice golden brown color, cover the crust lightly with foil until it is finished baking). Let the pie cool for at least 1 hour before serving. It may be stored at room temperature and leftovers may be enjoyed for 3 to 4 days.

TIP How to peel a peach: Bring a large pot of water to boil. Using a slotted spoon, fully submerge the peach in the boiling water for 45 seconds. Transfer to a large bowl filled with ice water. Remove the peach from the ice water and the skin should be easy to slide off with your hands or with a small knife.

CHANGE IT UP!

Substitute 2 pounds of frozen peaches for the fresh peaches.

Try using the puff pastry crust with berries or apples too.

apple-cranberry hand pies

Makes: 12 hand pies   Prep Time: 45 minutes + chill time   Cook Time: 30 minutes

We rarely visited fast-food places when I was a kid. On the occasion that we did, I'd beg Mom to buy me a hot apple hand pie for dessert. Once in a great while, Mom succumbed to my begging, and it felt like a real treat when she did. I loved how I could just hold it in my hand and nibble around the edges, saving the filling (the best part) for last. These hand pies are reminiscent of the fast-food variety, but they're infinitely more delicious and satisfying to make at home.

CRUST

2½ cups all-purpose flour
½ teaspoon salt
1 cup (2 sticks) cold unsalted butter, cut into pieces
5 to 6 tablespoons ice water

FILLING

2 cups diced peeled Gala apples (2 large)
¾ cup halved frozen cranberries (see Tips)
1 tablespoon freshly squeezed lemon juice
¼ cup packed light brown sugar
1½ teaspoons all-purpose flour
¼ teaspoon ground cinnamon
⅛ teaspoon salt

FOR THE TOP CRUST

1 large egg white, beaten and mixed with 1 tablespoon water
Sparkling or granulated white sugar

To prepare the crust, in a large bowl, whisk together the flour and salt. Cut in the cold butter until a crumb mixture forms (see Tips). Drizzle in 5 tablespoons of the water and mix until the dough comes together. Add an additional tablespoon of water, if needed. Gather the dough into a ball and wrap it with plastic wrap. Chill the dough for 1 hour before rolling.

To prepare the filling, in a large bowl, toss the apples and cranberries with the lemon juice. In a small bowl, mix the sugar, flour, cinnamon and salt. Add the sugar mixture to the fruit mixture and toss to combine.

To assemble the hand pies, line a large baking sheet with parchment or Silpat mats, or spray with nonstick spray.

Remove the dough from the refrigerator. On a floured surface, roll it out to ¼ inch thick. Cut the dough using a 5-inch round cutter (see Tips), gently rerolling dough scraps as needed. Scoop 2 to 3 tablespoons of the filling mixture onto one side of each round. Rub a little bit of water around the edge of each round, then fold the rounds over so the edges meet and use a fork to seal the edges. Transfer the hand pies to the baking sheet, leaving 1½ inches between each pie. Use a knife to cut three slits into the top of each pie, brush with the egg wash and sprinkle with sugar. Chill for 30 minutes.

Preheat the oven to 375°F.

Bake the pies for 30 to 35 minutes, or until they are golden brown throughout. Let the pies cool for 10 minutes on the baking sheet and then transfer them to a wire rack to cool completely. The pies may be made up to 1 day ahead.

continued on page 294

continued from page 292

TIPS How to cut the butter into the flour: the easiest way to do this is in a food processor. Add the flour and salt and butter to the food processor and process a few times until a crumb-like mixture forms. Alternatively, use either two knives or a pastry blender to cut the butter into the flour until you create a crumb-like mixture.

Frozen cranberries are much easier to cut in half than fresh cranberries.

No need to scour the Internet to find a 5-inch round cutter. Check out your plastic bowls and find one with a 5-inch diameter. Use the top of the bowl to "cut" your hand pies.

CHANGE IT UP!

Substitute dried cranberries or raisins for the fresh cranberries.

Use the same crust and filling ingredients to create cherry or peach hand pies too.

neapolitan ice cream squares

Makes: 8 servings   Prep Time: 35 minutes + freezing time

When our family vacations on the beach in Massachusetts in the dead of summer, we need cold treats to cool us off. This simple, layered ice cream recipe was created during one of our annual summer stays, amidst a sweltering heat with no air-conditioning in sight. Kids really love the Oreo crust and the pop of color that the pink strawberry ice cream brings.

CRUST

12 Oreo cookies (or another chocolate cookie with cream filling), crushed into crumbs
2   tablespoons butter, melted

LAYERS

2   cups strawberry ice cream, softened
½   cup toffee bits (see Tips)
2   cups mint chocolate chip ice cream, softened
1   cup hot fudge sauce
2   cups chocolate ice cream, softened
9   Oreo cookies (or another chocolate cookie with cream filling), crumbled

Mix the crust ingredients in a medium bowl and use clean hands to pat into the bottom of a 9-inch square pan. Place the pan into the freezer for 20 minutes to set.

Scoop the strawberry layer onto the frozen crust, spreading it evenly, and sprinkle it with toffee bits. Freeze again for 20 minutes.

Scoop the mint chocolate chip ice cream on top of the toffee bits, spreading it evenly, and spoon the hot fudge sauce on top. Freeze again for 20 minutes.

Spoon the chocolate ice cream on top of the fudge sauce, spreading it evenly over the top. Sprinkle with cookie crumbs and freeze until firm, 2 to 3 hours. Cut and serve.

GF GLUTEN-FREE ADAPTABLE Substitute gluten-free chocolate sandwich cookies for the Oreo cookies and use brands of ice cream, toffee bits and fudge/chocolate sauce that are known to be gluten-free.

TIPS If you don't wish to buy a bag of toffee bits, chop up three chocolate-toffee candy bars (Heath or Skor bars) and use those instead.

To soften ice cream in the refrigerator, place the ice cream in the refrigerator 20 to 30 minutes before it is needed. Alternatively, let it stand at room temperature for 10 to 15 minutes.

CHANGE IT UP!

Play around with other flavors of ice cream and sundae toppings in this frozen dessert.

chocolate cookie–mint chip ice cream sandwiches

Makes: 14 ice cream sandwiches (and some leftover ice cream)
Prep Time: 1 hour + freezing and processing times   Cook Time: 12 minutes

My dear husband needed a recipe created in his honor, so this is it. In the 20-plus years I've known him, he has always chosen mint chip ice cream as his scoop of choice. This version is just like that you'd find in an ice cream shop. Make the ice cream and eat it on its own, or scoop it onto chocolate cookies for a special summertime treat. My husband gave this ice cream the big double thumbs-up (and that's an endorsement worth listening to).

ICE CREAM
- 2 cups whole milk
- 2 cups heavy whipping cream
- 1 cup granulated white sugar
- ¼ teaspoon salt
- 1 teaspoon mint extract (see Tips)
- ½ teaspoon vanilla extract
  Green food coloring, optional
- 1 cup shaved or very finely chopped milk chocolate (see Tips)

COOKIES
- 6 ounces semisweet chocolate chips
- 2 cups all-purpose flour
- 2 teaspoons baking soda
- ¼ teaspoon salt
- ⅔ cup salted butter, at room temperature
- ½ cup granulated white sugar
- ¼ cup light corn syrup
- 1 large egg
  Additional sugar, for rolling

GARNISH
- 1½ cups miniature chocolate chips

To prepare the ice cream, in a medium saucepan, heat the milk, cream, sugar and salt over medium heat until the sugar has dissolved completely, 2 to 3 minutes. Remove the pan from heat and stir in the mint and vanilla extracts. Add enough food coloring to tint the mixture green, if desired. Remove the pan from heat and let it cool to room temperature. Transfer the ice cream base to a covered plastic container and chill for 24 hours.

Remove the ice cream base from the refrigerator and give it a few whisks to reincorporate the ingredients. Follow your ice cream machine manufacturer's instructions for processing the ice cream. It usually takes 25 to 35 minutes for the ice cream to become creamy and frozen. Add in the chopped chocolate just before you're about to turn off the machine and let the machine mix it in for 30 seconds. Scrape the ice cream into a freezer-safe container and freeze for several hours, or until the ice cream is firm enough to scoop (overnight is best). The ice cream will keep in the freezer for up to 2 weeks.

To prepare the cookies, in a medium glass bowl, melt the chocolate chips in the microwave in short bursts of 30 seconds, stirring after each burst. Remove from the microwave when the chocolate is melted and smooth. (Alternatively, you can melt the chocolate on the stove—see Tips). Set the chocolate aside to cool slightly.

In a medium bowl, whisk together the flour, baking soda and salt. In a larger bowl, use an electric mixer to combine the butter and sugar. Mix in the corn syrup and egg. Then mix in the melted chocolate. Add the dry ingredients and mix until combined. Wrap the bowl with plastic wrap and refrigerate the dough for 2 hours, or until the dough is firm.

Preheat the oven to 350°F. Line two baking sheets with parchment paper or Silpat mats, or spray with nonstick spray.

CHANGE IT UP!

Eat the ice cream on its own and/or substitute chopped Oreo cookies for the chocolate.

Make your own ice cream sandwiches with these cookies using your favorite flavor of purchased ice cream.

Scoop 1½ tablespoons of the chilled dough into your hands and roll into balls. Roll the balls in sugar and place them on the prepared baking sheet 2 inches apart. Bake for 12 to 15 minutes, or until the cookies are set. Let the cookies cool on the baking sheet for 10 minutes and then transfer them to a wire rack to cool completely.

To assemble the ice cream sandwiches, place a large scoop of ice cream between 2 chocolate cookies and press down gently to squish the ice cream to the edges. Roll the ice cream edges in chocolate chips, wrap the sandwich with plastic wrap and place it in the coldest part of your freezer. Repeat with the remaining cookies and ice cream. Serve when your ice cream sandwiches feel frozen enough for hands to hold and eat.

GF GLUTEN-FREE ADAPTABLE The ice cream can easily be made gluten-free; use a brand of chocolate that is known to be gluten-free. The cookies are not gluten-free adaptable, but you could always purchase your favorite gluten-free chocolate cookies and turn them into ice cream sandwiches.

TIPS Be sure to use mint extract, not peppermint. Peppermint extract will make your mint ice cream taste more like mint chewing gum.

For the chocolate (chip) shavings, I recommend using a king-size (4.4-ounce) Hershey's milk chocolate bar.

Most ice cream machines ask that you freeze the insert for 24 hours prior to processing your ice cream. This is what I recommend too.

To melt the chocolate on the stove, place a heatproof bowl over a pan of simmering water (the bottom of the pan should not touch the water). Add the chocolate chips to the bowl and stir until melted and smooth.

Homemade ice cream doesn't tend to become quite as frozen-solid as its store-bought counterpart, so it should be soft enough to work with. If your ice cream is too firm to work with, leave it at room temperature for 20 minutes to soften it up a bit.

marshmallow-malt ice cream

Makes: 8 servings   Prep Time: 25 minutes + chill and processing times   Cook Time: 10 minutes

As a young teenager, I worked at a mom and pop fast-food joint in Carson City, Nevada. This place was known for its fantastic burgers, but it was also the place to go to get the best soft-serve ice cream in town. They had dips and sprinkles, ice cream sodas, and every shake and malt flavor you could imagine. As an employee there, I had my pick of whatever I wanted to eat while working. More often than not, I filled a cup with ice cream and milk, added a generous scoop of malt powder and topped it off with marshmallow sundae syrup. With a few whirls of the shake mixer, I had created the best malt known to mankind. Here's the ice cream version of that malt, with added malt balls too.

2   cups whipping cream
2   cups half-and-half
4   cups mini marshmallows (or 32 large marshmallows; see Tips)
¾   cup malt powder
½   teaspoon vanilla extract
     Pinch of salt
2   cups chopped malted milk balls

In a large saucepan, heat the whipping cream and half-and-half over medium heat. Once the mixture is warm, add the marshmallows and stir until the marshmallows are melted. Whisk in the malt powder, vanilla and salt and stir until the malt is dissolved. Remove the pan from heat and let it cool to room temperature. Transfer the ice cream base to a covered plastic container and chill for 24 hours.

Remove the ice cream base from the refrigerator and give it a few whisks to reincorporate the ingredients. Follow your ice cream machine manufacturer's instructions for processing the ice cream. It usually takes 25 to 35 minutes for the ice cream to become creamy and frozen. Add in the malt balls just before you're about to turn off the machine and let the machine mix them in for 30 seconds. Scrape the ice cream into a freezer-safe container and freeze for several hours, or until the ice cream is firm enough to eat. The ice cream will keep in the freezer for up to 2 weeks.

GF GLUTEN-FREE ADAPTABLE Leave out the malt powder and the malt balls and use a brand of marshmallows that is known to be gluten-free.

TIPS Miniature marshmallows will melt more quickly and evenly than the large marshmallows.

Most ice cream machines ask that you freeze the insert for 24 hours prior to processing your ice cream. This is what I recommend too.

CHANGE IT UP!

You may wish to leave the malt balls out of the ice cream and top individual servings with them instead. This also gives you the freedom to drop a couple of scoops of ice cream into a blender with some milk and create instant marshmallow malts.

Use malted milk eggs around Easter time to create a fun and colorful Spring ice cream.

shirley temple ice cream sodas

Makes: 8 ice cream sodas (and some leftover ice cream)   Prep Time: 20 minutes + chill time

My husband and I gave our son RecipeBoy.com (his own food blog) for his 10-year-old birthday. It may seem an odd gift to most, but he had been asking for such a long time, wanting to experience what his Mommy does day in and day out. His very first post remains a very popular one on his site: "How to Make a Shirley Temple." Like most kids, he loves his Shirley Temples and he wanted to share them with the world. I did my best to re-create his favorite drink in ice cream soda form. He thought I was crazy, but it all worked out in the end.

ICE CREAM

1	cup whole milk
1	cup heavy whipping cream
¾	cup flat lemon-lime soda (see Tips)
½	cup granulated white sugar
2	tablespoons grenadine
1	tablespoon maraschino cherry juice (from the jar)
	Pinch of salt

SODA

8	cans of lemon-lime soda
8	maraschino cherries, for garnish

To prepare the ice cream, in a medium saucepan, heat the milk, cream, soda and sugar over medium heat, stirring until the sugar has dissolved completely, 2 to 3 minutes. Stir in the grenadine and cherry juice. Remove the pan from heat and let it cool to room temperature. Transfer the ice cream base to a covered plastic container and chill for 24 hours.

Remove the ice cream base from the refrigerator and give it a few whisks to reincorporate the ingredients. Follow your ice cream machine manufacturer's instructions for processing the ice cream. It usually takes 25 to 35 minutes for the ice cream to become creamy and frozen. Scrape the ice cream into a freezer-safe container and freeze for several hours, or until the ice cream is firm enough to scoop (overnight is best). The ice cream will keep in the freezer for up to 2 weeks.

To assemble the ice cream sodas, fill a tall glass three-fourths full with lemon-lime soda. Add two scoops of ice cream and garnish with a maraschino cherry. Serve with a tall spoon and a straw.

GF GLUTEN-FREE ADAPTABLE Use brands of grenadine, maraschino cherries and lemon-lime soda that are known to be gluten-free.

TIP For flat soda, just pour the soda into a measuring cup and leave it at room temperature for a couple of hours, or until the bubbles disappear. For testing purposes, I used 7-Up.

CHANGE IT UP!

If you'd like to accentuate the flavor of maraschino cherries in the ice cream, mix ½ cup of maraschino cherries in a blender with ½ cup of the milk and add it to the pan to heat up with the rest of the ingredients.

---

three-berry crisp

Makes: 8 servings   Prep Time: 20 minutes   Cook Time: 45 minutes

My son Brooks adores raspberries so completely that he just might have a tough time choosing between raspberries and chocolate. I keep a good supply of blueberries in the house all year long since he happily chows down on those too. It's clear that someday I need to own land on which I can grow endless amounts of berries. My family enjoys them all, and they're delightfully sweet in this simple summer berry crisp.

BERRIES

2   cups blueberries, washed and patted dry
1½ cups raspberries, washed and patted dry
1½ cups blackberries, washed and patted dry
1   teaspoon finely grated lemon zest (see Tips)
1   tablespoon freshly squeezed lemon juice
¼   cup all-purpose flour
¼   cup granulated white sugar
¼   teaspoon ground cinnamon

TOPPING

1   cup oats
½   cup all-purpose flour
½   cup packed light brown sugar
½   cup finely chopped walnuts
¾   teaspoon ground cinnamon
⅛   teaspoon salt
6   tablespoons (¾ stick) salted butter, melted
    Ice cream or whipped cream for serving, optional

Preheat the oven to 350°F. Spray a 9-inch pie plate with nonstick spray.

To prepare the berries, place the berries in a large bowl and toss them with the lemon zest and juice. In a small bowl, stir together the flour, sugar and cinnamon. Add to the berries and gently toss to combine. Scrape the berries into the prepared pie plate.

To prepare the topping, in a medium bowl, stir together the oats, flour, sugar, walnuts, cinnamon and salt. Stir in the butter and then sprinkle the mixture on top of the berries.

Bake for 45 minutes, or until the topping is browned and the juices from the berries are bubbling up through the cracks. Let cool for at least 30 minutes before serving. Serve warm or at room temperature with a scoop of ice cream or whipped cream (see Tips), if desired.

GF GLUTEN-FREE ADAPTABLE Use a brand of oats that is known to be gluten-free and substitute 2 tablespoons of cornstarch for the all-purpose flour. Serve with gluten-free ice cream or whipped cream, if desired.

TIPS Zest your lemon before you squeeze the juice out of it.

To make your own whipped cream, place your mixing bowl and beaters into the freezer for 10 minutes. Use an electric mixer to whip 1 cup heavy whipping cream just until stiff peaks begin to form (when you scrape the cream up with the beaters, the cream will keep its shape), then mix in 1 teaspoon vanilla extract and 1 tablespoon powdered sugar. Don't overbeat.

CHANGE IT UP!

Use whatever combination of berries suits your needs. You'll need a total of 5 cups of berries.

peanut butter s'mores turnovers

Makes: 12 turnovers   Prep Time: 25 minutes   Cook Time: 15 minutes

I'm not much of a camper. When my husband takes our son on father-son camping trips, I happily stay behind and thank the gods for our bug-free house, cozy bed and well-stocked kitchen. When they return from their camping weekends, I hear mostly about the evenings sitting around the campfire. Storytelling, snuggling in blankets, singing songs and roasting marshmallows for s'mores seem to be recurring favorites. It all "sounds" great and everything, but it's just not for me. I'll happily tell a story, snuggle in a blanket and sing a song next to a roaring fire inside a mountain cabin instead. Here's my version of a jazzed-up stay-at-home camping treat.

1   17.3-ounce box of puff pastry (2 sheets), thawed according to package instructions
3   whole graham crackers, broken or gently cut into fourths
9   mini milk chocolate bars (see Tips)
½   cup creamy peanut butter
1   large egg, whisked with 1 tablespoon water
½   cup marshmallow crème (see Tips)

Preheat the oven to 400°F. Line a baking sheet with parchment paper or a Silpat mat, or spray with nonstick spray.

Lay the puff pastry on a cutting board. Working with one sheet of puff pastry at a time, cut three rectangles (about 10 x 3 inches). Then cut each rectangle in half horizontally to create a total of 6 pieces for each sheet of puff pastry.

To assemble the turnovers, lay 1 graham cracker piece on one side of each piece of puff pastry, top with 1 chocolate bar and scoop 1 tablespoon of peanut butter on top of each chocolate bar. Wet the edges of the puff pastry and fold it over the filling to meet the opposite edges. Gently push the edges together to seal. Use a fork to press down and seal the edges more firmly. Repeat with each turnover. Gently move the turnovers to the prepared baking sheet (at this point, you may refrigerate the turnovers for up to 1 hour before baking).

Brush the turnovers with the egg wash and then use a sharp knife to cut two small slits into the top of each turnover. Bake 15 minutes, or until the turnovers are puffed and golden. Remove from the oven and let cool for 5 minutes. Scoop marshmallow crème into a bowl and microwave for 8 seconds to soften. Transfer it to a sandwich-size zip baggie. Snip a small piece off of the corner of the bag and squeeze the bag to drizzle marshmallow onto the top of each turnover. Serve immediately.

TIPS For testing purposes, I used Hershey's .49-ounce mini chocolate bars. Use any sort of chocolate that sounds good to you—just break it into pieces that will fit on top of a graham cracker.

Marshmallow crème (such as the brand sold as Marshmallow Fluff) comes in a jar and is usually found in the baking aisle near the marshmallows.

CHANGE IT UP!

Substitute peanut butter cups for the chocolate bars and leave out the peanut butter.

brownie-butterscotch whipped cream trifle

Makes: 12 servings   Prep Time: 40 minutes   Cook Time: 35 minutes

I brought this dessert to a dinner party once, along with a host of other sweet treats for people to sample. For some reason, the men at the party were all really drawn to this trifle. They raved about the brownies and wanted to know what exactly I had added to the whipped cream to make it taste so incredible. It's a tasty dessert, but I still was a bit surprised at its lofty success. The draw could be the fancy, layered-look of a trifle, or it could be that this dessert is just that good.

BROWNIES

- ¾ cup all-purpose flour
- ¾ cup unsweetened cocoa powder
- ½ teaspoon baking powder
- ¼ teaspoon salt
- 1¾ cups granulated white sugar
- ¾ cup (1½ sticks) salted butter, melted
- 3 large eggs
- 1½ teaspoons vanilla extract

WHIPPED CREAM

- 1½ cups heavy whipping cream
- ½ cup whipped cream cheese
- 3 tablespoons butterscotch syrup (see Tips)

REMAINING INGREDIENTS

- 1 cup chopped walnuts, toasted (see Tips)
- 6 tablespoons butterscotch syrup
- Mint leaves for garnish, optional

To prepare the brownies, preheat the oven to 350°F. Spray the bottom of a 9-inch square pan with nonstick spray.

In a medium bowl, whisk together the flour, cocoa, baking powder and salt. In a large bowl, whisk together the sugar, butter, eggs and vanilla. Whisk in the dry ingredients and stir until combined. Scrape the batter into the prepared pan.

Bake for 35 to 40 minutes, or until the brownies are baked through and a toothpick inserted into the center comes out clean. Let the brownies cool completely in the pan, then cut into 1-inch pieces.

To prepare the whipped cream, in a large bowl, use an electric mixer to whip the cream to very soft peaks—when you draw the beaters through the cream, it will begin to take shape. Add the cream cheese and syrup and continue to mix just until combined, maintaining soft peaks. Don't overbeat.

To assemble the trifle, in a glass trifle dish or tall glass bowl, place a third of the brownie pieces on the bottom of the dish. Spoon a third of the whipped cream on top of the brownies, spreading it to the edges of the bowl. Sprinkle a third of the walnuts onto the whipped cream and drizzle with 2 tablespoons of the butterscotch syrup. Repeat with two more layers of brownie pieces, whipped cream, walnuts and syrup. Garnish with mint leaves, if desired, and refrigerate until ready to serve.

GF GLUTEN-FREE ADAPTABLE Prepare your favorite gluten-free brownies recipe (or use a boxed gluten-free brownie mix) and use a brand of butterscotch syrup that is known to be gluten-free.

TIPS Butterscotch syrup can be found near the ice cream with the hot fudge and other ice cream toppings in your grocery store.

To toast walnuts, preheat the oven to 400°F. Spread the walnuts on a baking sheet and bake for 3 to 4 minutes, just until the walnuts are scented and slightly browned. Watch them closely since they can transition from toasted to "burned" in a matter of seconds.

CHANGE IT UP!

Use your favorite boxed brownie mix and layer that into the trifle instead of using my homemade version.

Prepare this recipe with your favorite recipe for blondies instead.

cinnamon bun bread pudding

Makes: 9 servings   Prep Time: 20 minutes   Cook Time: 45 minutes

There is not a person in my family who doesn't love bread pudding with a passion. My husband and son might very well be pleasantly plump if I prepared bread pudding for them as much as they craved it, and my mother would probably fork out a fortune to anyone who could create a gluten-free bread pudding that is like the ones she loved so much when she able to eat gluten. My bread pudding recipe is reminiscent of cinnamon buns. It's traditionally baked in custard, but there's a lot of brown sugar–cinnamon bun stuff swirled in there too.

PUDDING

7	to 8 cups cubed day-old French bread (see Tips)
3	cups whole milk
4	large eggs
½	cup granulated white sugar
½	cup packed light brown sugar
1	tablespoon vanilla extract
½	teaspoon ground cinnamon

TOPPING

¼	cup granulated white sugar
¼	cup packed light brown sugar
2	tablespoons salted butter, melted
½	teaspoon ground cinnamon

Preheat the oven to 325°F. Spray an 8-inch square pan with nonstick spray.

To prepare the pudding, place the bread cubes in the prepared pan. In a medium bowl, whisk together the milk, eggs, sugars, vanilla and cinnamon. Pour over the bread cubes in the pan.

To prepare the topping, in a medium bowl, combine the topping ingredients. Crumble the topping over the top of the pudding.

Bake for 45 to 55 minutes, or until the custard is set, a knife inserted into the center of the pudding should come out fairly clean and the top is beginning to brown. Let the pudding cool for 15 minutes. Slice and serve warm.

TIP It's best not to use a very soft French bread. Let it sit for a day or two if it's soft. You can also use brioche or challah with success.

CHANGE IT UP!

Classic cinnamon buns often contain nuts and/or raisins. Sprinkle nuts or raisins into the bread pudding if you'd like.

strawberry-nutella galette

Makes: 6 servings   Prep Time: 25 minutes   Cook Time: 35 minutes

Hooray for easy desserts! You'll find this recipe to be just that. It uses a store-bought pie crust, but you're certainly welcome to use your own special pie crust recipe if you prefer. Here we're combining Nutella and strawberries, and you'll likely find yourself eating a whole lot more of this than you expected.

1   store-bought pie crust (see Tips)
¾   cup Nutella (or another chocolate hazelnut spread)
⅓   cup graham cracker crumbs (2 whole crackers)
2   cups sliced fresh strawberries
1   tablespoon granulated white sugar, divided
1   large egg white, beaten and mixed with 1 tablespoon milk

Preheat the oven to 375°F. Line a baking sheet with parchment paper or spray with nonstick spray.

Place the pie crust on the baking sheet and spoon the Nutella into the center. Spread the Nutella out to the edges of the pie, leaving a 1-inch border all the way around. Sprinkle the Nutella with the graham cracker crumbs. Layer the strawberry slices over the crumbs, overlapping as needed to use all of the slices. Sprinkle the strawberries with ½ tablespoon of the sugar. Fold the edges of the pie crust (about 1 inch from the edge) in toward the center of the crust and over the strawberries. The crust will overlap slightly as you fold in the edges. Brush the crust with egg wash and sprinkle with the remaining ½ tablespoon sugar.

Bake for 35 to 40 minutes, or until the crust is lightly browned and the strawberries are softened. Let cool for 20 minutes. Serve warm or at room temperature.

TIP Store-bought pie crust usually comes in a package of 2 crusts. You'll only need one for this recipe, that is, unless you'd like to double the recipe.

CHANGE IT UP!

Not in the mood for Nutella? Substitute apricot jam for the Nutella to make it an all-fruit galette.

---

bananas foster

Makes: 2 servings Prep Time: 15 minutes Cook Time: 5 minutes

Back in my college days, I held various jobs to keep the money rolling in for books and housing. I worked at a swimming pool company by day and sold ice cream sandwiches at concert venues by night. I soon transitioned to working the front desk of a drug rehabilitation center, and toward the end of college, I ran an after-school day care during the week and catered parties on the weekends. The catering job became a full-time, hard-working, good money gig. I prepped and cooked all of the food and then served it up to guests at the parties. How to make Bananas Foster will be forever cemented in my brain, since I prepared it in front of guests about a million times and took in all of their ooohs and ahhhs at this fun, flamed dessert.

2 tablespoons salted butter
3 heaping tablespoons light
   brown sugar
1 large banana, sliced
3 tablespoons dark rum
   Vanilla ice cream, for serving

In a medium skillet, melt the butter over medium-high heat. Add the sugar and stir until dissolved, 1 to 2 minutes. Add the banana and stir to coat and caramelize with the sugar mixture. Move the pan off the heat and pour the rum over the bananas. Return the pan to the burner and carefully tilt the pan slightly to let the rum catch fire from the flame, or light the pan with a long lighter. Stand back and let the alcohol burn off and the flame die down. Serve the warm bananas over vanilla ice cream with the sugar syrup drizzled over.

GF GLUTEN-FREE ADAPTABLE Use a brand of ice cream that is known to be gluten-free.

TIP Traditional Bananas Foster recipes cut the bananas vertically into wedges. I prefer to slice them since it makes them bite-size and easier to eat. Cut them how you see fit for your dessert.

> **CHANGE IT UP!**
>
> Add brandy to this dessert too (1½ tablespoons dark rum + 1½ tablespoons brandy).
>
> Use this recipe for breakfast as a topping for French toast.

Let's Party

When I'm surrounded by a boatload of good friends or (my favorite) relatives and they're eating and enjoying the food that I've prepared, and sipping and laughing too, this is where I'm happiest. Entertaining is what I do best. Do I stress out about preparing for a party? Yes, of course I do! But there are plenty of tricks and tips to get organized enough for a gathering in your home to alleviate a little bit of that freaking out before your guests arrive.

top 10 tips for easy and successful entertaining

1 INVEST IN THE BASICS If you plan to entertain often, purchase a set or two of plain white dishes and extra glassware. With plain dishes, you can choose any theme for your dinner—always focusing on the décor of your table to jazz things up. Look for a restaurant supply store where you can find things in bulk at much cheaper prices. Invest in card tables or 3-foot tables for displaying food. Consider sharing the cost of tables and chairs with a friend who also likes to entertain.

2 PLAN AHEAD There is nothing worse than the doorbell ringing and realizing that you're not ready for your guests. Write everything down on paper. What kind of menu do you want to have? Choose the recipes and make sure you are not creating a menu that is too overwhelming for you to accomplish. Write down the timing of those recipes, planning to make some of them a day or two ahead, if possible. Do all of the time-consuming chopping and slicing and dicing ahead of schedule so when the time comes to put everything together it will be a cinch. Set your table and arrange décor a day or two before your party. With a little bit of planning, you'll be relaxed and ready when that doorbell rings.

3 FIND OUT IF ANY OF YOUR GUESTS HAVE DIETARY RESTRICTIONS OR ALLERGIES There is nothing worse than having a guest arrive the night of your party and realizing that the guest is unable to eat what you've prepared.

4 UTILIZE WHAT YOU HAVE AVAILABLE TO YOU When you're hosting a party, you don't need to clean out your wallet to buy all new things. Utilize what you already have, and don't be afraid to borrow things that you might need. It's okay to mix and match dishes, just look for a color scheme that works. Mason jars and tall glasses can be used to make beautiful centerpieces. Use greenery and flowers from your yard to create them. Shop thrift stores for good deals on unique things that you can use for your party.

5 IT'S OKAY TO ADD IN SOME STORE-BOUGHT FOOD TO YOUR MENU Cut vegetables and fruit, fresh salsa, breads and rolls, cheeses, hummus. . . these are the kinds of things that you can get away with adding to your menu. Grocery store baked goods are tougher to pull off as they aren't always that good. Consider purchasing dessert from a specialty bakery if you're not a baker.

6 DON'T BE AFRAID TO ASK FOR HELP WITH THE MENU Your guests can make and bring dishes, and if you have a family, let them help with the cleaning before and after the party. Learn to delegate!

7 WRITE UP A MENU FOR DISPLAY Rather than repeat yourself all night long, write up a menu on a chalkboard or print out a menu and set it up for display. Guests enjoy knowing what they can look forward to for dinner.

8 ALWAYS INCLUDE PLENTY OF WATER AND NON-ALCOHOLIC BEVERAGES and always include water glasses on the table (with a pitcher for refills nearby). If guests don't have water readily available, they may consume too much alcohol.

9 CONSIDER A BEVERAGE NAME LABELING SYSTEM There is nothing more frustrating both for you and your guests if you can't keep track of whose drink is whose. If you don't have wine charms, set out tiny decorative stickers (themed for your party!), and let guests place the sticker of their choice on the stem of their glass or on the label of their bottle. Alternatively, use reusable acrylic themed or blank write-on labels (www.drinkinks.com) or bottle pens (www.oenohilia.com) that guests can use to write their own names on the glass, cup or stem. Having a system in place will save you and your guests a lot of grief and will prevent beverages from being wasted.

10 CONSIDER ENTERTAINMENT FOR YOUR PARTY Music is first. Decide what kind of music will set the mood for the theme of your party. Will you have any planned activities at your party—such as karaoke, a trivia game, conversation cards, etc.? Sometimes just casual conversation isn't enough. Assess the personalities of the people you're inviting, and plan accordingly.

20 themed menus for entertaining

Simple Anytime Brunch
Fall Breakfast with Friends
Holiday Morning Gathering
Serve Yourself Breakfast and Pastry Bar
Ladies Luncheon
Super Bowl Party
Easter Feast
Mexican Fiesta
Festive Fourth of July Celebration
Summer Barbecue
New England Feast
Labor Day Grilling Party
Souper Salad Party
Seafood Extravaganza
Tailgate Party
It's Italian!
Comfort Food Fix
Elegant Dinner Party
Gluten-Free Dinner Party
Romantic Dinner for Two

simple anytime brunch

Pictured on page 310–311. Serves 6

Here's a simple menu for brunch that can be served any time. Prepare the applesauce a day ahead, and prepare the quiche and coffee cake the day of your gathering. If you only have one oven, bake the coffee cake first and then the quiche.

Ham and Swiss Quiche (page 43)
Upside-Down Brown Butter–Banana Coffee Cake (page 38)
Maple-Cinnamon Applesauce (page 64)
Assorted juices and coffee

DÉCOR TIP Keep the décor for a small party like this simple. A lovely cloth tablecloth, colorful cloth napkins and a vase full of flowers will be perfect. Optional, but if you want to purchase six, small colorful bowls for the applesauce, that adds color to the table as well.

BEVERAGE TIP Have your coffeemaker all prepped with coffee grounds and ready to go so you'll just need to press the start button before the guests arrive. Set up a coffee station with creamer and sweeteners so guests can help themselves. Pour the juices into pitchers and have glasses ready for pouring. If you really want to impress your guests, buy a large bag of oranges and squeeze your own juice!

fall breakfast with friends

Serves 4

It's easiest to make pancakes when you don't have to make a lot of them. Here's a breakfast menu that is perfect when there are just four of you and you're all craving pumpkin. Pop the bacon into the oven while you make the pancakes, and quadruple the Pumpkin Spice Latte recipe.

Pumpkin Spice Pancakes (page 53)
Oven-Baked Maple Bacon (page 61)
Pumpkin Spice Latte (page 21)

DÉCOR TIP Fall is such an easy time to come up with ideas for décor for your table. Utilize brown, orange and gold in your table display and purchase small pumpkins and gourds to place around your table settings.

STRESS-REDUCER TIP Put somebody on Pumpkin Spice Latte duty. Have all of the ingredients out and ready for preparation, but give the instructions to a willing volunteer and let them get the drinks for everyone.

holiday morning gathering

Serves 12

My family always, always has a Christmas brunch gathering. We're usually exhausted from Christmas Eve festivities the night before and because the kids want to get up at the break of dawn to see what Santa left for them. So creating a meal that can be prepared mostly in advance is a big bonus. Both the breakfast casserole and the cinnamon rolls can be prepped entirely the night before, and you can let the cinnamon rolls rise in your cold oven overnight. If you only have one oven, bake the casserole first and then cover it tightly with foil while you bake the cinnamon rolls.

> Make-Ahead Overnight Breakfast Casserole (page 40)
> Grandma Billie's Cinnamon Rolls (page 30)
> Fruit salad
> Pomegranate Mimosas (page 25) or Brunch Punch (page 24)

BEVERAGE TIP Make the pomegranate mimosas with or without champagne (double the recipe) or serve the kid-friendly brunch punch, punch-bowl style so relatives can help themselves.

QUICK AND EASY TIP If you're short on time, purchase an already-cut fruit tray, cut some pieces into smaller bites if you need to, put it in a bowl and call it fruit salad.

TABLE SETTING TIP For a busy holiday family gathering, you can choose how fancy you'd like things to be. Some may wish to go elegant and break out their best china with a complete table setting. Others might want to seat the kids in one room and the adults in another, and still others may opt for using strong paper plates and a buffet-style gathering for easy clean-up on a busy holiday morning.

serve yourself breakfast and pastry bar

Serves 12

The best thing about this sort of menu is that it can be prepared entirely ahead of time. It's no-fuss, no formal table seating or grand décor is necessary, and you can enjoy stress-free time with your guests. Use this menu for a family or friend get-together, holiday morning, teacher appreciation, or work meeting.

> Apple Cider Bread (page 35)
> Peanut Butter and Jelly Muffins (page 33)
> Banana Scones with Cinnamon Glaze (page 29)
> Cranberry-Almond Granola (page 63)
> Vanilla yogurt (purchased)
> Assorted juices, coffee and water

TABLE DISPLAY TIP Fill multiple platters each with a little bit of each pastry. It will appear more abundant, and it won't be as obvious if some pastries disappear more quickly than others! Purchase large tubs of vanilla yogurt and place it all in a large bowl with a serving spoon. People can dish out what they'd like and add a sprinkle of granola.

MENU TIP With so many pastries, people will want to know what is being offered. Consider printing up a simple menu and displaying it in an 8½ x 11-inch acrylic stand-up sign holder.

BEVERAGE TIP Borrow an extra coffeemaker from a friend for gatherings of 12 or more. You won't have people waiting around for the coffee to finish brewing, and you can set the two coffeemakers up ahead of time so they're ready to go when needed.

ladies luncheon

Serves 8

Since ladies like to lunch, why not host something for your lady friends in your home? This is lighter fare, which is what many women prefer, but it's very filling too. Prepare the tea a day ahead. Assemble your salad ahead of time too and wait to add the dressing until just before serving. The soup and croutons may be prepared ahead, rewarming the soup when needed. Double all of the recipes here except for the cookies, of which you'll have plenty of extras.

Chopped Chicken and Couscous Salad with Sweet Basil Dressing (page 89)
Tomato-Basil Soup with Garlic-Cheese Croutons (page 69)
Lemon Shortbread Cookies with White Chocolate Drizzle (page 262)
Sweet Southern California Sun Tea (page 112)

BEVERAGE TIP You may have ladies attending who don't wish to have a sweetened tea. Consider leaving the sugar out of the tea and allowing guests to sweeten their own tea, if desired. Include alternative beverage choices too.

DÉCOR TIP Depending on the time of year, consider hosting this luncheon outside with white tablecloths and simple sunflower-filled vases.

PARTY FAVOR TIP The recipe for shortbread cookies makes quite a lot of cookies. Consider packaging sets of 3 to 4 extra cookies in small plastic bags (check craft stores) and then tying them with a pretty ribbon. Send a baggie of cookies home with each guest as they leave.

super bowl party

Serves 8 to 10

It's definitely a day to eat and enjoy food and football, and it's never been a day to worry about calorie consumption. My motto is "Relax, enjoy and exercise tomorrow!" This menu is full of comfort food for the football-watching crowd. They're usually a hungry bunch, so feel free to double or triple the recipes as needed depending on how many people are attending your Super Bowl Party.

Manly Man Chili (page 82)
Brown Butter and Smoked Gouda Skillet Cornbread (page 183)
Buffalo Chicken Dip (page 124)
Bacon-Wrapped Tater Tots (page 149)
Chips and salsa (purchased)
Peanut Butter Cup Cookie Cupcakes (page 272)
Assorted beverages: beer, wine, sodas, water

BEVERAGE TIPS Set up a help-yourself beverage station. Purchase decorative metal tubs in which you can pile in ice and beverages, and let your guests help themselves. Always include water and other nonalcoholic beverages as an option for drinking.

TIME-SAVING TIP Skip the dip and the tater tots and ask guests to bring a favorite appetizer to share. Find out what they're bringing so you don't have any overlap, and so you don't have five bowls of chips and salsa.

ENTERTAINMENT TIP Purchase a few fun gifts and create a trivia game with football, regional and team questions. Look for trivia questions on www.nfl.com. Have guests fill out the trivia questionnaire as they arrive, or play a live trivia game at halftime.

easter feast

Serves 6

As with all holiday meals, it's easiest if you do as much prep as possible before the day of the event. The dip and the cupcakes can be made one day ahead. Prep everything for the green beans, potatoes and lamb the night before to make cooking on Easter Sunday an easy task. If you only have one oven, do the first roasting of the potatoes early in the day, then put your lamb in the oven. When the lamb is finished cooking, pop the potatoes into the oven for their second roast. Double all recipes except the dip and the cupcakes if you plan to serve 12.

Rosemary and Garlic Leg of Lamb Roast (page 215)
Twice-Baked Crispy Greek Fingerling Potatoes (page 173)
Green Beans with Bacon and Thyme (page 188)
Curry-Dill Vegetable Dip (page 132)
Banana–Carrot Cake Cupcakes with Cinnamon–Cream Cheese Frosting (page 276)
Fizzy Lemonade Coolers (recipe follows)

QUICK & EASY BEVERAGE RECIPE To make the Fizzy Lemonade Coolers, mix 7 cups lemonade with a handful of mint leaves and two 12-ounce cans of club soda. Add sliced lemons and serve it in a pitcher.

DÉCOR TIP Fill vases with jelly beans, Easter grass and dyed eggs to add easy color to your decorated Easter table. Utilize shorter vases with simple stemmed daisies so your guests can easily visit with each other across the table.

SERVING TIP Serve the dip surrounded by carrots and celery. Purchase some carrots with greens attached, trim them and include them on the platter for a more decorative look.

ENTERTAINMENT TIP Organize an Easter Egg Hunt. Fill plastic eggs with treats, trinkets, coins and/or stickers and hide them around the yard before guests arrive. To manage the hunt, assign each child a color to hunt for, or let them know that they're looking for two pink, two yellow, etc.

mexican fiesta

Serves 6

Where I live in Southern California, we don't need an excuse to have a party with Mexican food. It's safe to say that we eat it at least once a week. But sometimes we go all out and do things up big, on Cinco de Mayo or whenever. This menu is another one that is easy to plan ahead. The cupcakes may be baked and frosted one day ahead. Assemble the salad entirely the morning of the party, and add in the avocado and dressing right before serving. Prepare the chimichurri sauce and the other taco fillings in the afternoon, and the guacamole about an hour before guests arrive. The cilantro rice can simmer on the stove while the meat is grilling. Assign someone to make the margaritas, so you don't have to. Double all recipes except the cupcakes if you are serving 12.

Flank Steak Tacos with Avocado-Chimichurri Sauce (page 140)
Cilantro Rice (page 178)
Mexican Salad with Sweet Honey-Lime Vinaigrette (page 163)
Mango-Chipotle Guacamole (page 134)
Tortilla chips and salsa (purchased)
Cadillac Margarita Cupcakes (page 275)
Mango Margaritas (page 122)
Mexican beer and nonalcoholic beverages

APPETIZER TIP Purchase fresh salsa instead of jarred salsa. You can usually find it in your market's deli section, and it's infinitely better than the processed variety.

DÉCOR TIP Do you have access to a Mexican hat? You can usually find them at party supply stores. Place your bowls of guacamole and salsa in the brim of the hat and scatter the tortilla chips around the rest of the brim. Party stores will also have accessories for decoration. If you're doing formal seating at a table for this party, use a Mexican serape (a long, thin blanket) as a runner down the middle of your table.

MUSIC TIP A Mexican-themed party isn't complete without a little bit of mariachi music. Look for a themed CD or download some festive Mexican music from iTunes.

festive fourth of july celebration

Serves 8

Here's a holiday that is right smack-dab in the middle of the summer, when everyone is happy and relaxed. You'll be happy and relaxed too while you throw this party. Assemble the salad the morning of your event, and add in the avocado and the dressing right before serving. The beans are baked in the slow cooker, so plan the timing for those. Surely there will be a grill master at your party, right? Assign grilling to someone who claims to know how to grill perfect burgers, unless you're willing to take the reigns. Double the burger recipe to serve eight.

Nostalgic Burgers (page 106)
Bacon and Brown Sugar Slow Cooker Baked Beans (page 182)
Triple Berry Salad with Sugared Almonds (page 161)
Pound Cake and Strawberry Skewers (recipe follows)
Blueberry-Pineapple Tequila Punch (page 118)
Assorted nonalcoholic beverages

BEVERAGE TIP To make the punch red, white and blue, add halved strawberries, and then take the time to cut out some stars from slices of fresh pineapple to float in the punch.

DESSERT TIP For a super-easy red, white and blue dessert, string cubes of pound cake and strawberries on mid-size skewers. Assemble the skewers the morning of your event. Display them on a platter, provide a bowl of whipped cream for dipping, and scatter blueberries around the platter.

DÉCOR TIP It's all about red, white and blue and stars and stripes—ribbons, balloons, confetti, tablecloths, napkins, and whatever you can get your hands on.

SUNTAN TIP If you're hosting outdoors, have a couple of bottles of sunscreen available for those guests who didn't plan ahead.

summer barbecue

Serves 8

Whether it's in the middle of the day or on a warm evening, people enjoy getting together during the long days of summer. This menu is simple, impressive and perfect for the middle of summer when fruits are fresh and corn is abundant. Vegetables and fruit may be cut one day ahead. Keep a damp paper towel stored along with them to keep them fresh and moist. The potato salad may also be prepared one day ahead. Bake your berry crisp and prepare the corn salsa the morning of your party. The bruschetta may be prepped in the afternoon. Sangria and Limeade are both much better when prepared 24 hours in advance (don't add the club soda until just before serving). Double the skirt steak recipe to serve eight.

Grilled Balsamic Skirt Steak with Grilled Corn Salsa (page 209)
Perfect Potato Salad (page 170)
Mixed fruit salad (purchased, or mix your own)
Sweet Nectarine Bruschetta (page 141)
Fresh vegetables with (purchased) hummus or ranch dressing
Three-Berry Crisp (page 301)
Cherry Limeade (page 113) or Raspberry and Peach Lemonade Sangria (page 116)

SEATING TIP Whenever there is potato salad and grilling involved, it calls for a more "casual" atmosphere. For this party, I think it's fine to let guests mingle and eat and find a place to sit on their own. Just make sure that everyone has a place to sit where they can actually set their plate down and cut their steak.

DÉCOR TIP If you prefer to do formal seating for this party, round up some brightly colored tablecloths to drape over your tables. Purchase clay flower pots and fill them with sand or pebbles and candles, wrapping a pretty ribbon around them to finish them off.

MUSIC TIP Search iTunes for summer-themed music, or break out the old Beach Boys CD.

new england feast

Serves 6

We spend so much time in New England visiting relatives, so we've had plenty of New England feasts! Ideally, this is a party hosted at the beach, but you can certainly re-create the mood of the party in your own backyard. Of course you can opt to steam lobster live and serve it with lobster crackers and melted butter, but lobster rolls are good for a make-ahead party plan. Triple the lobster roll recipe to serve six. The clam chowder and pies can be made a day ahead.

Lemon-Scented Lobster Rolls (page 94)
Clam Chowder (page 73)
Potato Chips
Grilled Clams (recipe follows)
Apple-Cranberry Hand Pies (page 292)
Samuel Adams beer
Assorted nonalcoholic beverages

APPETIZER TIP For the grilled clams, place a large disposable foil pan on a medium-high heated grill. Add 6 tablespoons butter, ½ cup white wine, 3 large cloves of minced garlic, 1 large minced shallot, and a couple of pinches of red pepper flakes. Add forty-eight 2-inch clams to serve 6 people. Close the lid on the grill and cook the clams for 8 to 10 minutes, or until they've all popped open. Move them to a serving tray and drizzle the butter mixture over the top. Sprinkle with parsley and display for serving with a bottle of Tabasco sauce.

DÉCOR TIP Cover the tables with red and white checked tablecloths. Look for nautical décor, such as shells and nets. Fill tall vases with white daisies and ornamental grasses. Wrap the utensils with blue cloth napkins and tie each with a piece of rope.

TABLE DISPLAY TIP If you have a specialty candy shop near you, look for Boston Baked Beans and gummy lobsters and display those along with snack packages of dried cranberries and whoopie pies.

labor day grilling party

Serves 8

Labor Day weekend is typically viewed as the last weekend of the summer, so it's indeed a good time to celebrate. The weather is still plenty warm on Labor Day, so plan to host this party entirely outdoors. The pie may be baked up to one day ahead. The corn salad and macaroni salad can both be prepared the morning of the event. Plan for the timing of the marinating chicken, and assemble the baked Brie just before your guests arrive. Add two chicken breasts to the chicken recipe to serve eight.

Super-Simple Lemon and Herb–Marinated Grilled Chicken (page 221)
Not-Your-Mama's Macaroni Salad (page 166)
Grilled Corn Salad (page 168)
Grilled Garlic Bread (recipe follows)
Baked Brie with Gingered Peach Sauce (page 123)
Fruit skewers
Snickers Bar Cheesecake Pie (page 289)
Wine, beer and assorted nonalcoholic beverages

APPETIZER TIP For the fruit skewers, choose fruit that is in season and easy to string onto a skewer (melon, strawberries and pineapple). Look for mid-size skewers in a party supply store. This appetizer may be prepared the morning of the party. Place the skewers on a serving platter, cover with damp paper towels and then with plastic wrap.

BREAD TIP To make the grilled garlic bread, cut 1 loaf of French bread in half lengthwise. In a medium bowl, mix 8 tablespoons (1 stick) softened salted butter, ⅓ cup finely grated Parmesan cheese, 2 large minced garlic cloves, 2 tablespoons fresh minced parsley, ½ teaspoon salt and ½ teaspoon pepper. Butter each cut half of bread and grill butter side down for 1 to 3 minutes (watch it closely since it can burn easily). Remove the bread from the grill, slice and serve.

DÉCOR TIP A grilling party is typically a casual one. If you'd like to seat your guests more formally, use white tablecloths with lots of candles. String white lights in the bushes and trees too. Utilize your garden and greens to put together simple arrangements for the tables. Add citronella torches if mosquitos are an issue.

souper salad party

Serves 8

Here's a fabulous dinner to host any time of year. Include these recipes, or mix and match and add in your own favorite soup or salad recipes. Your guests will get a sampling of soups and salads, and it will all be filling enough to call dinner. All of the soups and the cake can be prepared up to one day ahead (leave out the pancetta and sage until serving time). Prepare the salads the morning of the party, waiting to add the dressing until just before serving time. Endive may be stuffed in the afternoon and refrigerated. Double all recipes except the turkey salad and the cake to serve eight.

- Butternut Squash Soup with Pancetta and Crispy Sage (page 76)
- Slow Cooker Beef and Lentil Soup (page 71)
- Kale and Bacon Salad with Strawberry Jam Vinaigrette (page 158)
- Turkey and Cranberry Salad with Toasted Pecans and Smoked Gouda (page 87)
- Assorted sliced breads and/or rolls (purchased)
- Chilled Strawberry and Coconut Milk Soup Shooters (page 145)
- Stuffed Endive with Fig, Blue Cheese and Honeyed Walnuts (page 143)
- Meyer Lemon Loaf Cake (page 285)

APPETIZER TIP Serve the soup shooters in tall shot glasses or small plastic cups. Shot glasses can be found at beverage shops or restaurant supply stores. Small plastic cups will be available at a party store.

SERVING TIP If you have access to 2 soup tureens, use those to display your soups. For the soup, use cups and mugs instead of bowls, and use small plates for the salads. Be sure to display plenty of spoons and forks.

DÉCOR TIP Use a different colored round placemat under each of your dishes to set off each selection. Create standing signs for each soup and salad so your guests will know what they're sampling.

PARTY FAVOR TIP Search online for DIY instruction on how to make a soup mix in a jar to give as a gift. Make one jar for each couple to take home, complete with an attached recipe. There are many websites that have free printable labels and instructions.

CHANGE-IT-UP TIP This party can be organized in an entirely different way if you'd like your guests to be involved in the preparation of the dishes. Have each couple bring their favorite soup or salad to contribute to the party instead of making everything yourself. Be sure to find out what everyone is planning to bring so you don't have three kinds of tomato soup and two Caesar salads.

seafood extravaganza

Serves 8

Here's a party for the seafood lovers in your life. When you're deciding who to invite to this party, just make sure that you're not including anyone who is allergic to fish or shellfish. You can get really fun with an ocean-themed décor for this party (see the Tips). Double the salmon recipe and add 2 cups of greens to the salad recipe to serve eight.

- Oven-Roasted Barbecued Salmon (page 232)
- Coconut-Ginger Rice (page 175)
- Grilled Shrimp and Vegetable Salad with Lemon-Basil Vinaigrette (page 83)
- Hot Seafood Dip in a Bread Bowl (page 125)
- Smoked Salmon–Topped Cucumber Rounds (page 140)
- Pineapple Upside-Down Cake (page 279)
- Wine, beer and assorted nonalcoholic beverages

DÉCOR TIP Hang fishing nets with shells and/or plastic fish. Look for seashells and starfish to decorate your tables. Scatter salt water taffy on the table.

CENTERPIECE TIP Consider filling vases with rocks and water and a couple of live fish swimming around. Let your guests decide who would like to take the fish home.

MUSIC TIP Play a soundtrack of ocean waves crashing and seagulls squawking to set the mood.

tailgate party

Serves 12

Tailgate parties are popular in cities where there are stadiums that host large professional sports teams, or for college teams too. The purpose is to gather a small crowd of friends together in the venue's parking lot prior to the start of a game to share food and drink and get excited about the game. Some folks really get into their tailgating and bring their own grills, tables, décor, etc. This menu is meant to make ahead, with no preparation in the parking lot needed. Double the recipe for the muffins and triple the recipe for the wraps to serve 12.

> Buffalo Chicken Wraps (page 100)
> Corn Dog Mini Muffins (page 150)
> So-Cal 7-Layer Mexican Dip (page 131)
> Snickerdoodle Blondies (page 255)
> Brown Butter–Chocolate Chip Cookies (page 271)
> Assorted beverages

BEVERAGE TIP Be sure to find out if alcohol is permitted in the parking lot where you'll be tailgating, and if it is, then you'll need to find out if glass bottles are or are not allowed. Bring plastic cups, and be sure to pack bottle openers and corkscrews if needed. Bring plenty of nonalcoholic drinks too since people tend to get rowdy when they're excited about their team.

PACKING TIP Bring folding tables, folding chairs and throw-away paper tablecloths. Pack extra napkins, paper towels, plates, wipes, trash bags and toilet paper (in case the portable potties run out!).

ENTERTAINMENT TIP Sitting around and talking with friends can be enjoyable and relaxing, but you may wish to bring playing cards and a football for tossing around too.

it's italian!

Serves 12

I've never served our family's manicotti recipe to anyone who hasn't absolutely loved it. It's a safe bet for this party. The sangria can and should be prepared one day ahead. The manicotti may be prepared the morning of the party and then refrigerated until it's time to bake. Assemble the polenta squares and the salad in the afternoon, waiting until serving time to add the balsamic drizzle. The galette may also be assembled in the afternoon, and then covered with plastic wrap and refrigerated. The galette can be placed into the oven while you're eating your main dish. Triple the salad recipe and double the manicotti, the galette and the sangria to serve 12.

> Spinach and Cheese–Stuffed Manicotti (page 239)
> Crusty French Bread (purchased)
> Caprese Salad with Burrata Cheese (page 162)
> BLT Polenta Squares (page 136)
> Antipasto platter (purchased)
> Strawberry-Nutella Galette (page 308)
> Red Wine Sangria (page 115)
> Sparkling Italian soda and/or water

APPETIZER TIP Assemble your own antipasto platter. Purchase things like marinated vegetables, olives, Italian meats and cheeses, roasted nuts and baguette.

TABLE DÉCOR TIP Use red tablecloths, white napkins and lots of candles, and display glasses filled with tall and crispy, thin breadsticks and bowls of multi-colored grapes.

HOME DÉCOR TIP Place bunches of green, red and white balloons at the entry to your home and around the house. Display your menu written on a black chalkboard (which is what you often see at an Italian restaurant).

MUSIC TIP Italian-themed music is easily accessible in a music store.

PARTY FAVOR TIP Purchase mini bottles of olive oil and balsamic vinegar for your guests to take home.

EASY CLEAN-UP TIP Use disposable metal pans for the manicotti. Bake, serve and then throw the pans away!

comfort-food fix

Serves 8

This dinner party is all about warm and comforting food. I suggest hosting this themed party in the middle of a cold winter. Swap out the soup for a tossed green salad if you'd like to lighten it up a bit. This is a menu that you might like to have help with. Consider handling the meatloaf, mashed potatoes and vegetables yourself and then let your guests bring the other three dishes. Double recipes for the soup and potatoes to serve eight.

- Bacon-Wrapped Meatloaf with Brown Sugar Glaze (page 210)
- Dijon Mashed Potatoes (page 171)
- Steamed Vegetables (your choice)
- Macaroni and Cheese Soup with Roasted Cherry Tomatoes (page 81)
- Warm Artichoke and Bacon Dip (page 128)
- Cinnamon Bun Bread Pudding (page 306)
- Assorted chocolates (purchased)
- Wine, beer and assorted nonalcoholic beverages

DÉCOR TIP No need for fancy table settings at a comfort-food party. Create a warm and comforting ambience using brown and muted orange colors and low lighting.

ENTERTAINING TIP To add to the idea of "comfort," host a movie-watching marathon after dinner, complete with fuzzy comfortable blankets.

DESSERT TIP You may decide to go another route with the dessert and make chocolate chip cookies and hot chocolate. Or purchase comfort-food desserts at the market such as Hostess cupcakes, frosted animal cookies, Oreo cookies, M&Ms and caramel corn, and create a basket of goodies from which to nibble.

elegant dinner party

Serves 6

When you'd just like to have a few people over for dinner and enjoy a nice meal together, this is a menu that will work for you. You'll likely have leftover rolls, and you'll definitely have leftover dessert (which you can plan to send home with your guests). The cake can be made up to 2 days ahead. The squash may be prepared the morning of your event and then heated up again when it's time to serve. Assemble your mushrooms in the afternoon, cover with plastic wrap and refrigerate until ready to bake. Rolls may be started in the morning. Hold off on baking the rolls until the roast comes out of the oven to rest.

- Pork Loin Roast with Rosemary-Mustard Mushroom Sauce (page 204)
- Steamed white or brown rice
- Roasted Butternut Squash with Garlic, Sage and Pine Nuts (page 192)
- Buttery Asiago and Rosemary Cloverleaf Rolls (page 186), or bakery purchased
- Balsamic-Marinated Zucchini and Cheese-Stuffed Mushrooms (page 139)
- Red Velvet–Cheesecake Cake (page 281)
- Good quality wines and/or beverages of choice

BEVERAGE TIP If you're looking for a nice wine to go with the pork roast, consult a wine shop or specialty beverage store. Experts there are more than willing to give their opinion on what wine will pair best with your meal.

DÉCOR TIP Pull out your fine china and use a beautiful tablecloth. Create a grand centerpiece that will be the focal point of the table, using flowers and candles. Make individual place cards written in your fanciest writing or printed out using a fancy font.

CLASSY TIP Plan to deliver a formal toast at the beginning of dinner, thanking your guests for joining you.

MUSIC TIP Light classical or smooth jazz are both calm and appealing genres of music for an elegant dinner party.

gluten-free dinner party

Serves 8

It's hard enough to live a life without eating any gluten, and then you have to weave your way through dinner parties wondering if gluten is lurking among the dishes. Here's a menu that can be made completely free of gluten, following the adaptations included in the recipes. So if you need a menu for yourself, or if you'd like to be able to include someone in your dinner party who is gluten-free, this is the menu to use. The dip and the cake may be made the morning of your party. The salad may also be assembled in the morning, adding the avocado and dressing right before serving. Prepare the rolatini in the late afternoon, then cover with plastic wrap and refrigerate until ready to bake (no more than 2 hours ahead). The risotto should be prepared while the rolatini is baking (it will take a little longer to bake if it's chilled). Double the eggplant recipe to serve eight.

Baked Eggplant Parmesan Rolatini (page 244)
Tomato-Mascarpone Risotto (page 180)
Avocado–Pine Nut Salad (page 157)
Layered Mediterranean Spinach Dip (page 129)
Flourless Chocolate Cake with Chocolate Ganache Drizzle (page 286)
Assorted beverages

GLUTEN-FREE TIP If you're not familiar with being gluten-free, don't worry. Just follow all of the tips for mild adaptations in my recipes and you will successfully make the recipes free of gluten. If you're not sure if an ingredient or brand is gluten-free, look it up online and you will usually be able to find an answer.

PARTY FAVOR TIP Prepare and package a gluten-free treat to send home with each guest. Suggested: Cranberry-Almond Granola (page 63)

romantic dinner for two

Serves 2

When it's just you and a partner, it's kind of nice to be able to prepare a complete dinner that will only serve two people. There will be no leftovers to worry about, and chances of overeating are pretty slim. These recipes are all designed specifically to serve only two people. Since all of these recipes are pretty simplistic, impress your partner with the scallops, and then prepare the rest of the meal together. That's where the romance comes in (especially with the dessert).

Scallops with Bacon-Balsamic Cream Sauce (page 144)
Insalata Romantica (page 165)
French bread (purchased)
Newlywed Pasta (page 233)
Chocolate Ganache with Dippers (recipe follows)
Assorted beverages

ROMANTIC TIP Set your table just as a five-star restaurant would set a table for two. Use a luxurious tablecloth, add chargers under your dinner plates and include salad and bread plates too. Don't forget the candles! And use a small vase of flowers so you don't create a wall that is difficult to talk over between you and your partner.

DESSERT TIP To prepare the ganache, place 4 ounces chopped bittersweet chocolate in a bowl. Bring ½ cup heavy whipping cream and 1 tablespoon granulated white sugar just to a boil in a small saucepan on the stove (or in the microwave). Pour the hot cream over the chocolate. Let it sit for 1 minute and then stir until smooth. Pour the chocolate into a serving dish and use fresh strawberries, chunks of pound cake and marshmallows for dipping.

index

Page numbers in *italics* indicate illustrations

M

Macaroni
and Cheese, Bacon, 240, *241*, 242
and Cheese Soup with Roasted Cherry Tomatoes, 81
Salad, Not-Your-Mama's, 166
Mahimahi with Creamy Coconut-Ginger Sauce, 225

Mango
Enchilada Sauce, Chicken and Black Bean Enchiladas with, 218–219
Guacamole, -Chipotle, Sweet Smokin' Hot, 134–135
Margaritas, 122
and Peach Smoothies, Breakfast, 23
Manicotti, Spinach and Cheese-Stuffed, *238*, 239

Maple
Almonds, Roasted Spicy, 153
Bacon, Oven-Baked, *60*, 61
-Cinnamon Applesauce, 64
-Pumpkin Cheesecake with Graham Cracker-Pecan Crust, 287–288
Margarita Cupcakes, Cadillac, 275
Margaritas, Mango, 122

Marshmallow
-Malt Ice Cream, *298*, 299
S'mores Turnovers, Peanut Butter, 302–303
Mascarpone-Tomato Risotto, 180, *181*
Meatballs, Swedish, over Egg Noodles, 205
Meatloaf, Bacon-Wrapped, with Brown Sugar Glaze, 210–211
Mediterranean Spinach Dip, Layered, 129

Menus for entertaining
barbecue, summer, 317
breakfast, fall, 313
breakfast and pastry bar, serve yourself, 314
brunch, 313
comfort food dinner, 322
Easter feast, 316
elegant dinner, 322
Fourth of July, 317

gluten-free dinner, 323
holiday morning, 314
Italian-themed, 321
Labor Day grilling party, 318
ladies luncheon, 315
Mexican fiesta, 316
New England feast, 318
romantic dinner for two, 323
seafood extravaganza, 319
souper salad party, 319
Super Bowl party, 315
tailgate party, 321

Mexican
Dip, So-Cal 7-Layer, *130*, 131
menu, fiesta, 316
Salad with Sweet Honey-Lime Vinaigrette, 163
Wedding Cookies, Nutella-Filled, 261
Meyer Lemon Loaf Cake, 285
Mimosas, Pomegranate, 25
Mint Chip-Chocolate Cookie Ice Cream Sandwiches, 296–297
Mojito
Orange-Basil, *120*, 121
Strawberry-Basil, 121
Monte Cristo Sandwiches, Prosciutto and Brie, *96*, 97

Mozzarella
Eggplant Parmesan Rolatini, Baked, 244–245
Manicotti, Spinach and Cheese-Stuffed, *238*, 239
Penne Pasta, Creamy Skillet-Baked, 236
Pizza, Sausage, Sweet Potato, and Caramelized Red Onion, with Sage Pesto, 246–247
Pizza Pull-Apart Bread, Cheesy Pepperoni, 152

Muffins
Corn Dog Mini, 150, *151*
Eggnog-Cranberry, Steuseled, 32
Peanut Butter and Jelly, 33

Mushroom(s)
Balsamic-Marinated, Zucchini and Cheese-Stuffed, 139
Sauce, Rosemary-Mustard, Pork Loin Roast with, 204

Mustard
Dijon Mashed Potatoes, Creamy, 171
-Rosemary Mushroom Sauce, Pork Loin Roast with, 204
Whole Grain, Grilled Gruyère with Arugula, White Wine and, 91

N–O

Neapolitan Ice Cream Squares, 295
Nectarine Bruschetta, Sweet, 141
New England Clam Chowdah, 73–74
New England feast menu, 318
Newlywed Pasta, 233

Noodles. *See also* Pasta
Egg, Swedish Meatballs over, 205
Udon, Shrimp and Cashew Stir-Fry with, 229

Nutella
Mexican Wedding Cookies, -Filled, 261
Pumpkin Bread, -Swirled, 34
-Strawberry Galette, 308

Oatmeal
Berry Crisp, Three-, 301
-Blueberry Breakfast Bars, 65
Cookie Crust, Dulce de Leche Pear Pie with, 290
in Granola, Cranberry-Almond, 63
O'Brien Egg Frittata for Two, 49

Onion(s)
Caramelized, French Dip Sandwiches with Peppers and, Slow Cooker, 102
Dip, Caramelized, 126, *127*
Red, Caramelized, Sausage and Sweet Potato Pizza with Sage Pesto, 246–247
Rings, Baked Barbecued, 195

Orange
Mimosas, Pomegranate, 25
Mojito, -Basil, *120*, 121
Smoothies, Peach and Mango Breakfast, 23
Orzo, Shrimp and Bacon with, Barbecue-Sauced, 234

V

W

Z